VOLUME ONE

Occult THEOCRASY

The 1933 Classic

Lady Queenborough

EDITH STARR MILLER

DEFENDER
CRANE, MO

Occult Theocrasy: VOLUME I
By Lady Queenborough

Defender Publishing
Crane, MO 65633

Printed in the United States of America.

ISBN: 9781948014076

A CIP catalog record of this book is available from the Library of Congress.

Cover design by Jeffrey Mardis.

Occult Theocrasy: Part II
Chronological Series
Associations of the 16th Century

CONTENTS

Occult Theocrasy: Part I
The Mysteries of Freemasonry

Associations of the 17th Century

Associations of the 18th Century

FOREWORD

THIS BOOK MAKES no claim to literary merit. It is simply a work of research and documentation, giving evidence and facts which I trust will help the reader in drawing his own conclusions.

In the course of my researches as an international political investigator into the causes of social unrest, I have probed the depths of infamy which now surrounds , not ours only, but also the next generation, whose right to lead a decent life should be as good as was ours. As a woman of the world I have witnessed things the existence of which I did not suspect and I have realised that, due to my "protected" position in life, they should never have been expected to have come to my knowledge. Let me tell every woman, however much "protected", whether Dairymaid or Duchess, that the safeguards which she imagines to be thrown around herself are but a mirage of the past. Her own and her children's future are at the mercy of those "forces" the activities of which it has been my business, for the last ten years, to follow as one of a group of investigators.

Today, most of the good people are afraid to be good. They strive to be broadminded and tolerant! It is fashionable to be tolerant—but mostly tolerant of evil—and this new code has reached the proportions of demanding intolerance of good. The wall of resistance to evil has thus been broken down and no longer affords protection to those who, persecuted by evil doers, stand in need of it.

Worse still, there are cases wherein virtuous people's good name is relentlessly "filched from them", but no effort will be made by the presumed good people to rally to their defence. Happy are they if they themselves can discover the cause of their ruin, materiel or moral, either partial or total.

In offering this book to the public, I have endeavoured to expose some of the mean s and methods used by a secret world, one might almost say an underworld, to penetrate, dominate and destroy not only the so-called upper classes, but also the better portion of all classes. There are those who feel confident that if they refrain from joining any society or group and avoid entanglements, no harm can befall them. To such, let me say that situations can be, and are, created for innocent dupes every day and wrecked homes are the direct result. Neither fortune nor a blameless life led, as it were, in an island of strict virtue in the midst of a tumultuous sea of evil, spells security.

Irrefutable evidence of a particular example of underworld tyranny has come into my possession. The victim's guilt was her reluctance to step from virtue into the mire of evil which surrounded her. Moreover she was intolerant of evil and sought to oppose and destroy it. The case of her persecution at the hands of her foes is complete. She belonged to what is termed Society as did also some of the other actors in this bewildering drama. The world, social, financial, legal and, shall we say also, the underworld, leaving to this word its generally accepted literal meaning, knows them. So many Jekylls and Hydes stalk about unsuspectingly in our midst!

From such an example I have been led to the conclusion that, among others, three factors can help one from being completely destroyed by the combined forces of that "underworld": a flawless life, independent means and real friends, all three of which must be backed by a fearless determination to fight evil on all points of the Masonic compass.

In these days when apparently vice triumphs and virtue must be penalized, it may be well for all of us to fight the undertow by which our children may be dragged under and must of necessity perish. Vice rings and secret societies form but one vortex into which youth is drawn and destroyed whilst the "good people", because of their ignorance, look on helplessly in despair.

It is for their instruction that this book has been written. Its compilation has taken several years and, had it not been for the generous efforts of one of my friends, Mme de Shishmareff, and of several other persons, I would never have been able to complete the task which I set out to accomplish.

What must concern us all now is the protection of decency or, in other words—*Equal rights*—for such as are not vice adepts.

This book is not complete. It will never be complete, but for the present it must remain as a study of the root conditions which have led to present day subversive upheavals and the overthrow of the principles of Christian civilization.

EDITH QUEENBOROUGH

Occult Theocrasy
Part I

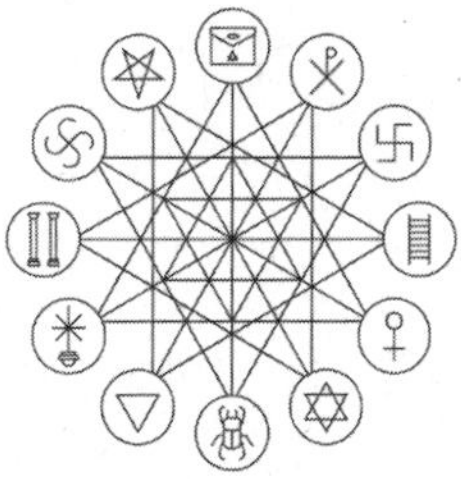

The Mysteries of Freemasonry

"My final work is a word of warning to American women: Keep away from the Swamis, the Yogis, the traveling teaching men. You would need no such bidding if, for an instant, you guessed the truth. In your good faith, in your eager-minded receptivity of high-sounding doctrine, in your hunger for colour, romance, glamour, and dreams come true , you expose yourself, all unsuspecting, to things that, if you knew them, would kill you dead with unmerited shame."

Katherine Mayo in *Why I wrote Mother India.*

CHAPTER I

THE RELIGION OF THE SECRET

MAN IS A creature of mind and matter. To the realm of mind belongs metaphysical thought which, whether trained or untrained, is peculiar to each individual and is subject for its development or restraint to his will. It is the basis of religion in the generally accepted sense of this word; it is purely spiritual and can reach the height of mysticism. From it issue creeds or doctrines and the erection of a theological system of beliefs.

Imparted to other individuals and accepted by them, the metaphysical thought of a few great minds has become the basis of religious systems. Upon its teaching was grafted a Ritual or Law, disciplining the life, mystic, moral, social and even physical, of its adherents or believers. From the exercise of such laws, theocracy or the rule of priesthood was evolved. It is to be found in every religion regardless of the fact that in some instances like in the Buddhist doctrine of Gautama and in the teaching of Jesus Christ, nothing is further removed than ritualism from the metaphysical thought or religious conception of the founders.

The power of theocrasy or exercise of government rule over the masses by a hierarchy of priests or adepts rested on its dual system of teaching, namely: Exoterism and Esoterism, the former a code of discipline of the thought and mode of life of the masses, the latter the hierarchic school wherein were trained the chosen adepts destined to safeguard the rules imposed upon the people by the high priests.

Upon a close study of the manifold religious systems, the corruption of which led to theocratic rule, namely, Brahminism, the Ancient Egyptian Cult, Mosaism or Judaism, Christianism and Mahometanism, one finds the accepted belief of Monotheism as the basis of esoteric or secret belief or doctrine. Monotheism is here taken in the sense of First Principle.

Whereas the Egyptian high priesthood of Memphis kept this theory as the esoteric teaching of the high adepts, Moses, brought up as one of them, gave it as exoteric or popular belief to the Israelitic sect to which he belonged, embodying it in a deity, the terrible *Jehovah* of the Jews.

Another side of the esoteric teaching was that of occultism, the development of all human psychic forces which, when misused, lead to the practice of magic. The esoteric part of all religions or hermeticism, the teaching and practice of occultism, led to the development of what might be termed the religion of the secret, which eventually overshadowed and helped to dissimulate subversive activities.

It is with this that we are chiefly concerned and will endeavour, to some degree, to show its baneful influence on society of all creeds and nations. Let the reader bear in mind that it is not the object of this work to discuss the place occupied and the part played by either Metaphysics and Philosophy on the one hand, and Science and Ritualism on the other. The limitations of each and its encroachment upon the territory of the others, the ensuing conflicts, are matter for the history of fanaticism throughout the ages. Our aim is to follow the outgrowth of Esoterism and a few of its multiple ramifications in the realm of perversion and subversion.

CHAPTER II

THE MEANING OF OCCULTISM

A SUMMARY AND some explanation of the principal forms of occultism must precede the chapters which deal with the historical side of this subject, and the objections, those of the credulous as well as those of the sceptics, must be foreseen and forestalled. Many persons are tempted to deny, arbitrarily and without examination, statements on matters of which they have no previous knowledge, but even the possible criticism of such as these must have received due consideration.

In this age of wireless and aeroplanes, one of the fads of the modern highbrow is to scoff at such things as sorcerers, magic and evocations as old wives' tales. Tales of ancient history! There are people who refuse to believe in the existence of the supernatural, perhaps we should say supernormal, even when confronted with the evidence. Such are the sceptics who deny everything. Hidebound in their prejudice, they ignore the fact that magic, White or Black, has now as many adepts as ever, nor can they distinguish between the different schools of spiritism.

First, there are the charlatans whose tricks in the line of Spiritism are generally sooner or later unmasked.

Second, there are the Occultists who operate in secrecy and hide their meetings from all but initiates with the greatest care.

Many persons are duped by charlatans, so the sceptics persuade themselves of the absolute non-existence of all diabolical practices in modern times. They are wrong. For Occultism flourishes now in Europe, Asia, and America. The Black Mass is said today in Paris and London, and Satanism has its faithful followers. On this subject one of the most eminent writers was Carl Hackse, who, under the pseudonym of Dr. Bataille, made an extensive study of Occultism and gave his extremely exaggerated views of it in the book *Le Diable au XIXᵉ Siècle*

The following pages of this chapter are mostly either quotations or abridgements from that work:

"According to the teaching of the Christian churches, God allows demons certain limited powers, but they are not permitted to open the gates of hell and release a spirit at the request of one who evokes the dead. The dead, even damned, will not show themselves if evoked, nor would evocations be answered by those who had succeeded in attaining the kingdom of heaven, but devils can and do, says the Church, substitute themselves for the deceased. They will impersonate a dead person whose appearance is demanded by invocations.

"It is also admitted that the fallen angels or spirits will often manifest to people without being called, The theological hagiographa cite many cases of diabolical apparitions to saints, apparitions which these saints have been able to repel and conquer... but what sceptics and agnostic Christians alike ignore is that besides the drawing room mediums, mediums for diversion, there are occultists whose vile practices are veiled in the profoundest mystery. These men, whose moral sense is absolutely perverted, believe in Lucifer, but they believe him to be the equal of God and worship him secretly."[1]

Modern Occultism is on the one hand practical Cabala and on the other, Indian Yogism, both of which have always had their adepts more or less openly.

The Cabala is Occult Science itself. It is the secret theology of the initiates, theology essentially Satanic. In a word the counter-theology. Our God, the God of the Christians, is the power of evil in the eyes of the Cabalists; and for them the power of good, the real God, is Lucifer.

"The Cabala teaches magic or the art of intercourse with spirits and supernatural beings.

"One cannot be a convinced Cabalist without soon becoming a magician and devoting oneself to the practices of occultism.

"Not that our Cabalists or contemporary magicians practice all the different branches of occultism. Some of these have been abandoned and others are only used by charlatans for the exploitation of superstitious persons, but a great many, precisely the most criminal and perverse, are observed in the hidden dens of our modern Luciferians."[2]

Magic has two divisions:

The first is *divining* magic, subdivided into several branches of which the principal are:

- Astrology
- Aeromancy
- Palmistry
- Hydromancy
- Anthropomancy
- Pyromancy
- Oneirocritics
- Cartomancy

The second is *operative* magic, also subdivided into several branches of which the principal are:

- Alchemy
- Necromancy
- Mesmerism
- Theurgy
- Various miraculous feats

There are moreover some superstitious practices not specially classed.

Bataille thus defines some of the foregoing:

Astrology.—Divining the future by the stars. The casting of horoscopes is its most prevalent practice.

Palmistry.—Divining the future by the hand.

Anthropomancy.—This is one of the practices supposed at present to have fallen into disuse. It is a horrible, savage abomination and consists in disemboweling a human being for the purpose of divining the future by inspection of the entrails.

Mediaeval history accuses Gilles de Retz of perpetrating this crime on children, whom he lured to his castle for the purpose. Tacitus says that the Druids, in ancient Britain, used to consult their Gods by looking into the entrails of their captives.

Oneirocritics.—Divining the future through interpretation of dreams.

Aeromancy.—Divination by the study of aerial phenomena.

Hydromancy.—Divination by the study of liquids or aquatic phenomena.

Pyromancy.—Divination by fire.

Cartomancy.—Divination by cards.

There is no need to expatiate further on the more or less grotesque means employed by those who follow these false sciences. One must be somewhat erratic to imagine that the future can be foretold by coffee grounds, by the antics of flames in a grate, by the order in which shuffled cards will be drawn, or by the odd shapes assumed by wind-driven clouds! When events corroborate predictions made under these conditions, it can be attributed to the use of the power of *clairvoyance*, but these fortune tellers, some of whom have a thorough knowledge of the rules governing the practices of these absurdities, are the first to distrust their art.

Such expedients, disdained by the real occultists, are too unimportant to be worthy of note. It is quite another matter to expose the Satanists, ignored by the public, whose sects, bearing different names in different countries, constitute, in reality, *only one, single, secret religion* whose fanatics, imbued with the spirit of evil, will sacrifice themselves blindly to their cause.

Throughout the universe, all Luciferian and Satanic rites bear a basic similarity.

Dealing principally with the practices of contemporary operative magic, it is Bataille's opinion that as regards the mysterious art of Alchemy, its theory is called Hermetic Science and has a double objective, namely, the discovery of the philosopher's stone, a substance capable of transmuting base metals into gold and drinkable gold, or the Elixir of long life which is a magic potion endowed with the properties necessary to prolong human life indefinitely or, at least, to maintain in old age the faculties of youth. Alchemy as a science seems now obsolete.

The Alchemists knew the existence of microbes and toxins long before the medical discoveries of the present age. The laboratories of Satanic bacteriology have been working, for a long time, on cultures of bacilli or solutions of their toxic properties which, even when administered in infinitesimal doses, mixed with food or drink, disseminate disease and death where it is judged necessary by the "Masters" that life is to be destroyed. In these cases deaths occur from apparently natural causes!

He further says that *Magnetic Mesmerism* is the occult medicine of the Cabalists. One must naturally not confuse the scientists who are at present making researches in hypnotism and suggestion, in the interest of science, with the emulators of Cagliostro whose aim is to procure diversions, often wicked and immoral. Scientific magnetism is still an obscure question being studied by theologians, physiologists and criminologists, whereas that of the adepts of magic has nothing to do with this; it is a branch of the subterranean work that is nearing its goal today.

Necromancy is partly divining magic and partly operative magic. This practice consists in the evocation of the spirits of the dead. Spiritism and rapping of tables are necromancy, but if all spiritists are not necessarily Cabalists, all Cabalists are practicing necromancy. People are far from suspecting the progress made by necromancy along these lines. Freemasonry is yearly more and more invaded by the spiritist element to the extent that, in 1889, an international convention of spiritist Freemasons attended by about 500 delegates was held at the Hotel of the Grand Orient of France, rue Cadet, Paris.

This was only a beginning![3]

Eliphas Levi, a renowned occultist of the 19th century, writing in *Histoire de la Magie*,[4] in the following words, sounds a warning to those who, recklessly, would venture into the domain of the occult.

"The experiences of theurgy and necromancy are always disastrous to those who indulge in them. When one has once stood on the threshold of the other world one must die and almost invariably under terrible conditions. First giddiness, then catalepsy followed by madness. It is true that the atmosphere is disturbed, the woodwork cracks and doors tremble and groan in the presence of certain persons, after a series of intoxicating acts. Weird sounds, sometimes bloody signs, will appear spontaneously on paper or linen. They are always the same and are classed by magicians as *Diabolical writings*. The very sight of them induces a state of convulsion or ecstasy in the mediums who believe themselves to be seeing spirits. Thus Satan, the Spirit of Evil, is transfigured for them into an angel of light but, before they will manifest, these so-called spirits require sympathetic excitement produced by sexual intercourse on the part of their devotees. Hands must be placed in hands, feet on feet, they must breathe in each other's faces, these acts often being followed by others of an obscene character. The initiates, revelling in these forms of excesses believe themselves to be the elect of God and the arbiters of destiny. They are the successors of the fakirs of India. No warning will save them.

"To cure such illnesses, the priests of Greece used to terrify their patients by concentration and exaggeration of the evil in one great paroxysm. They made the adept sleep in the cave of Trophonius. After some preliminary preparations, he descended to a subterranean cavern in which he was left without light soon to be prostrated by intoxicating gases. Then the visionary, still in the throes of ghastly dreams caused by incipient asphyxia, was rescued, being carried off prophesying on his tripod. These tests gave their nervous systems such a shock that the patients never dared mention evocations of phantoms again.

"Theurgy is the highest degree of occultism. Necromancy is limited to the summoning of dead souls, but the Theurgists of the nineteenth century evoke entities qualified by them as genii, angels of light, exalted spirits, spirits of fire etc. In their meetings, scattered throughout the world, they worship Lucifer. The three mysterious letters J… B… M…, that the common initiates see in the Masonic Temples, are reproduced in the meeting rooms of the Luciferians, but they no longer mean Jakin, Bohaz,

Mahabone, as in the Lodges, nor Jacques Bourguignon Molay, as with the Knights Kadosch ; in Theurgy these three letters mean ; Jesus Bethlemitus Maledictus. Theurgy is therefore pure Satanism."[5]

"Moreover it is important to note that the Cabalists, admitted to the mysteries of Theurgy, never mention the word Satan. They look upon certain dissident adepts who invoke the devil under the name of Satan as heretics, whose system they call Goety or Black Magic. They call their own practices Theurgy or White Magic."[6]

Between these two types of Devil worshippers, the Luciferian occultists and the Satanists, there is a difference which must not be overlooked.

Luciferians never call their infernal master "Spirit of Evil" or "Father and Creator of Crime". Albert Pike even forbade the use of the word Satan under any circumstances.

There is indeed a distinction between the Satanists and Luciferians. The Satanists, described by Mr. Huysmans in his book, *Là Bas*, are chiefly persons mentally deranged by the use and abuse of drugs who, while suffering from a peculiar form of hysteria, accuse the God of the Christians of having betrayed the cause of humanity. They are persons who recognize that their God Satan occupies a position in the supernatural sphere, inferior to that of the Christian deity. On the other hand the Luciferians or the initiates of kindred rites, while still labouring under a strange delusion, act deliberately and glorify Lucifer as the principle of good. To them he is the equal of the God of the Christians whom they describe as the principle of evil.

It is necessary to recognize the distinction which exists between Luciferians and Satanists, for their two cults bear each other no resemblance, although Lucifer-Satan manifests indiscriminately to his faithful followers of both denominations. One must not, however, imagine that the pride and satisfaction he derives from this adulation acts as an inducement to making him appear whenever he is called! Occultists of all schools agree that nothing is more capricious than the conduct of spirits when evoked!

It is well moreover to remember that Luciferian occultism is no novelty, nor must one make the mistake of confusing it with ordinary Freemasonry, the Lodges of which are only private clubs.[7]

Many authors have published books on Freemasonry, some printing the rituals, some their personal observations on certain facts, but few of these authors, having themselves passed into occult masonry, the real masonry of the Cabalistic degrees which is in touch with all secret societies, Masonic as well as non-Masonic, have been able to state that *Luciferian Occultism controls Freemasonry.*

Though this is indeed the case, neither the President of the Council of the Order of the Grand Orient of France, the supreme chief of French Freemasonry, nor the president of the Supreme Council of Scottish Rites will be received at the meeting of a simple Luciferian ceremony just on account of his title and dignity unless, at the same time, he possesses a diploma of Cabalistic grade which requires another initiation. On the other hand, the first Oddfellow from Canada, a member of the Chinese San-ho-hui of China, a Luciferian Fakir from India, all these can visit at their pleasure all lodges and inner shrines of ordinary Freemasonry in all countries because, in each one of the Satanic sects, the directing authority is exercised by heads who belong to the most exalted masonic degrees of the different rites, degrees which are for them of secondary importance. These chiefs, at the request of their subordinates of the Luciferian societies, deliver to them freely the diplomas necessary to obtain admittance everywhere, as well as the sacred words and yearly and half yearly passwords of all the masonic rites of the globe.[8]

Luciferian Occultism, as has been said before, is therefore not a novelty, but it bore a different name in the early days of Christianity. It was called Gnosticism and its founder was Simon the Magician.

The Gnostics were not ordinary heretics but constituted an antichristian sect. To deceive the multitude, they affected disagreement with certain doctrines of the Apostles, and the chiefs selected from among the initiates those destined to receive, in secret council, the Satanic revelation. Gnosticism is marked with the seal of Lucifer. It is contemporary with the Apostle Peter and has continued, without interruption, down to the present day, periodically changing its mask.

The seven founders of Freemasonry were all Gnostics, Magi of the English Rose Croix, whose names were: Theophile Desaguliers, named

Chaplain of the Prince of Wales by George II, Anderson, the clergyman, an Oxford graduate and preacher to the King of England, George Payne, James King, Calvert, Lumden-Madden, and Elliott.

Gnosticism, as the Mother of Freemasonry, has imposed its mark in the very centre of the chief symbol of this association. The most conspicuous emblem which one notices on entering a masonic temple, the one which figures on the seals, on the rituals, everywhere in fact, appears in the middle of the interlaced square and compass, it is the five pointed star framing the letter G. Different explanations of this letter G are given to the initiates. In the lower grades, one is taught that it signifies Geometry. To the brothers frequenting the lodges admitting women as members, it is revealed that the mystic letter means Generation, but the revelation is attended with great secrecy. Finally, to those found worthy to penetrate into the sanctuary of Knights Kadosch, the enigmatic letter becomes the initial of the doctrine of the perfect initiates which is Gnosticism. This explanation is no longer an imaginary fabrication. It is Gnosticism which is the real meaning of the G in the flamboyant star, for, after the grade of Kadosch (a Hebrew word meaning consecrated) the Freemasons dedicate themselves to the glorification of Gnosticism (or anti-christianity) which is defined by Albert Pike as "the soul and marrow of Freemasonry."[9]

Let us add that the ancient mysteries of Gnosticism have been known and published in the past. There is no difference between the Gnosticism of the early ages of Christianity and modern occultism.

The fundamental principle of Gnosticism was the double divinity (dual principle) and this is exactly the theological theory of modern occultism. The Gnostics claimed that the good God was Lucifer and that Christ was the devil, that what the Christians call vice was for them virtue, and to the Christian dogma they opposed Gnosticism, a word meaning human knowledge.

Early Gnosticism had its doctors; the Basilideans, Ophites and Valentinians. Basilide of Alexandria, one of them, lived at the end of the first century. He taught metempsychosis and the principles underlying present-day Theosophy. His system resembles that of the spiritists of the nineteenth century who have invented nothing, for they copy Gnosticism even in its theory of the transmigration of souls. Basilide affirmed that he was the reincarnation of Plato. Whoever has penetrated into assemblies of modern theurgists can attest that one of its current theories is that of reincarnation.

After Basilide came Montanus who died in 212. Montanus was a grand master of the art of divination. The Bite of Mizraim (a Freemasonry said to be Egyptian) copies slavishly, in its Cabalistic grades, all the phantasmagoria of Montanus. This Gnostic doctor plunged himself into ecstasies and, according to history, he had two women, Maximilla and Priscilla, trained to act as his accomplices. The Gnostics came in crowds to admire their contortions worthy of epileptics. They had the sacred illness,[10] and were considered two saints of Satan. In the assemblies of the sect, when they went into frenzies and prophesied, their oracular sayings were listened to with veneration by the adepts.

Were they acting a part, were they just mediums or somnambulists, or were they what the Roman Catholics call "possessed"?

This is a hard question to answer.

A modern example of the influence exercised by occult organizations on the destinies of mankind is to be found in the history of The Holy Alliance, founded in 1815 by Alexander I, Emperor of Russia. This was originally a union of monarchs pledged to support the Christian Church and to stem the rising tide of radicalism, revolution and subversion.

In *L'Histoire de la Magie* (p. 467), Eliphas Levi states that the spiritist sect of "The Rescuers of Louis XVI", wishing to penetrate this organization to use it for their own purposes, succeeded in insinuating one of their illumines into the good graces of the Czar. This was Madame Bouche, known to the adepts as Sister Salome. After eighteen months spent at the Russian Court, during which she had many secret interviews with the Emperor, she was supplanted by another medium-somnambulist of the sect, the famous Madame de Krudner who acquired so great an influence over the Czar that his ministers became alarmed at the situation thus created.

Levi thus describes the fall of the favorite;

"One day, as the emperor was leaving her, she barred his passage crying 'God reveals to me that your life is in great danger. An assassin is in the palace'. The Emperor, alarmed, caused the palace to be searched and a man, armed with a dagger, was found. He confessed, when questioned, that he had been introduced into the palace by Madame de Krudner herself."

One wonders if the whole affair was not simply the result of a clever intrigue calculated to get rid of the prophetess. As such it was singularly successful for Madame de Krudner was summarily banished from the Russian Court.

In *De la Maçonnerie Occulte* (pp. 87–88), J. M. Ragon tells us that "science counts four kinds of Somnambulism: The natural, the symptomatic, the magnetic and the ecstatic.

"Natural and symptomatic somnambulism are two essentially different states, one occurring only at night, the other by day as well as by night. The conduct of the subject is different under the two conditions.

"Magnetic and ecstatic somnambulism differ from one another insomuch as the one is commanded (willed) and the other is not. The first is artificial, the other natural. In the first, the subject is dependent; in the second, he acts independently. That is why induced somnambulism cures the natural when substituted for it.

"A lucid somnambulist bears no more resemblance to a man asleep than he does to an active man awake".

When the Gnostics practised magic, they evoked the spirits of the dead exactly as do the occultists of today. Dawning Christianity was prolific in miracles so, in order to fight it, the disciples of Gnosticism had recourse to diabolical marvels. In this respect, are not contemporaneous spiritists, with their rapping tables and apparitions, Gnostics under another name?

Secret Gnostic meetings lead to depravity, as the adepts indulge in every kind of turpitude and obscenity, often under the influence of drugs such as Indian Hemp *(Cannabis indica)* or Opium, the medicinal properties of which, when administered under certain conditions, are provocative of mediumistic phenomena.

Thus debauched, their moral sense weakened, initiates are ready to work. They work, they fall, and, as they fall the Occult power grasps its prey. Their life, henceforth, is subject to the will of the Hidden Masters who, according to their secret designs, will lead their slaves to power, or a semblance of power, or else to their downfall. To use the words of "Inquire Within" in *Light-bearers of Darkness* (p. 118) ... "These masters, doubtless identical with the terrible power behind the horrors of Russia's sufferings and World Revolution, have in reality no interest in soul or astral development, except as a means of forming passive illuminised tools, completely controlled in mind and actions."[11]

"Inquire Within" further suggests that there is a group of flesh-and-blood men, who can form etheric links, from any distance, with the leaders of these societies and who secretly work by means of that light which can slay or make alive, intoxicating, blinding, and, if need be, destroying unwary men and women, using them as instruments or 'Light-bearers' to bring to pass this mad and evil scheme of World Dominion by the God-People—the Cabalistic Jew."[12]

A further explanation of the phenomenon of induced mediumship is given us by the same author who quotes the following lines from Eliphas Levi's *History of Magic:*

"This may take place when, through a series of almost impossible exercises... our nervous system, having been habituated to all tensions and fatigues, has become a kind of living galvanic pile, capable of condensing and projecting powerfully that Light (astral) which intoxicates and destroys.

"Inquire Within" comments further:

"It attempts to show that it leads to mastership and self-control, but on careful consideration it proves to be merely conscious mediumship inspired by crafty and wilful deception, giving the adept a false confidence, inducing him to let go his physical senses and work upon the astral, where, enclosed by formulae given by these masters themselves, he is completely at their mercy."

A recent practical illustration of these methods is the teaching contained in a book *Asia Mysteriosa* by Zam Bhotiva, (published by Dorbon Ainé) which suggests ways and means of communication with the "Hidden Masters".

It will be recognised by anyone having taken an interest in the progress of science along certain lines that there is nothing impossible or even improbable in the suggestion that telepathy may be exploited by organisations for their own particular ends.

Forty years ago William Gay Hudson wrote on telepathy as follows:

If the power exists in man to convey a telepathic message to his fellow-man, it presupposes the existence of the power in the percipient to repeat the message to a third person, and so on indefinitely, until someone receives it who has the power to elevate the information above the threshold of his consciousness, and thus convey it to the objective intelligence of the world. Nor is the element of time necessarily an adverse factor in the case; for there is no reason to suppose that such messages may not be transmitted from one to another for generations. Thus, the particulars of a tragedy might be revealed many years after the event, and in such a way as to render it difficult, if not impossible, to trace the line through which the intelligence was transmitted. For the spiritist the easy and ever-ready explanation of such a phenomenon is to ascribe it to the intervention of spirits of the dead. But to those who have kept pace with the developments of modern scientific investigation, and who are able to draw the legitimate and necessary conclusions from the facts discovered, the explanation is obvious, without the necessity of entering the domain of the supernatural."[13]

On the subject of Hypnotism and Crime, Hudson, writing further, reaches however a fatally false conclusion which for many years remained unchallenged. He states (p. 140) "It is true that, on ordinary questions, the truth is always uppermost in the subjective mind. A hypnotic subject will often say, during the hypnotic sleep, that which he would not say in his waking moments. Nevertheless, he never betrays a vital secret… That this is true is presumptively proved by the fact that in all the years during which the science of hypnotism has been practised, no one has ever been known to betray the secrets of any society or order. The attempt has often been made, but it has never succeeded."

Hudson attributes this reticence to auto-suggestion opposing the suggestion of another. This however is not the case, for, where a member of a secret society or order is concerned, that member was already hypnotized during initiation and it is not his will that guards the secret, it is the will of another, the will of the Lodge.

How many people know that hypnotism is about all there is to initiation? Hypnotism and fear. The rest is camouflage.

In the event of this statement being doubted, we quote herewith from *Freemasonry Universal* an article which needs no further comment:[14]

"The Stewards prepare the candidate; the Tyler first, and afterwards in turn the I. G., Deacons and Junior Wardens should inspect the candidate to see that everything is strictly correct.

"The preparation symbolises poverty, blindness (or ignorance) and poverty of spirit, but it may also signify a purification, i.e., that the riches and pleasures which bind one to the material side of life are discarded and the spirit blinded to their attractions. The baring of the right arm, left breast, left knee and right heel being slipshod, are apparently a reference to the awakening of occult centres in one's being which may only become active when purification of the whole nature has begun.

"The very specific character of the preparation points to real knowledge of the occult physiology of the process of initiation on the part of those who originated the method which has been so faithfully preserved. Certain Forces are sent through the candidate's body during the ceremony, especially at the moment when he is created, received and constituted an Entered Apprentice Freemason. Certain parts of the Lodge have been very *heavily charged* with *magnetic force especially* in order that the Candidate may *absorb as much as possible of this force*. The first object of this curious method of preparation is to expose to this influence those various *parts of the body* which are especially used in the ceremony. In ancient Egypt, there was another reason for these preparations, for a weak current of physical electricity was sent through the candidate by means of a rod or sword with which he was touched at certain points. It is partly on this account that at this first initiation the candidate is *deprived of all metals since they may very easily interfere with the flow of the currents.*"

All kinds of nice inspiring symbolical interpretations of the ritual are generally given for the benefit of people who seem to want them, but it is here evident that the candidate, unknown to himself or herself, has acted throughout the ceremony of initiation under the stress of hypnotism. No longer a free agent, the initiate takes the oath under hypnotic force which, has also been used to instill into him the feeling of fear. Fear guards the secret of initiation, fear born under the power of hypnotism to serve henceforth as the controlling agent of the initiators over the initiated.

The Right Worshipful Master must be a genuine occultist, as it is up to him to *charge* (hypnotise) the candidate, for to give this in the words of *Freemasonry Universal*: "The R. W. M. gives the light, the pure white light of truth and illumination."[15]

Illumination, alias Kundalini, alias Serpent power, alias Electro-magnetic force, alias the Sex force, etc.!

Even in our western world anyone wishing to study Hatha Yoga can learn to neutralize the action of gravity and go some yards up in the air. This stunt, and the assumption of any size at will, are tricks for which training is essential, and if one works at it hard enough, one will eventually be able to mesmerize people for one's own purposes, business, political or other, thus following the lure of the occult to a sinister end i.e. Black Magic.[16]

We would here observe that the miracles performed by Jesus Christ bore a distinctive feature, often overlooked, namely, that in every case altruism was the source of their inspiration. Thus they were a symbol of charity.

This gives us the esoteric explanation of His silence when taunted on the cross. "He saved others, himself he cannot save." Sooner than use this power for personal advantage He chose death!

Gnostic miracles, such as that of being buried alive for a period of time which constitutes the Hindu religious rites of Samadhi have no ulterior charitable purpose. They are chiefly performed for the object of creating wonderment, curiosity or faith in magic, and as such, failing the altruistic motive, are classifiable under the general term of Black Magic.

As a stimulus to popular faith, they are, however, sanctioned by most

Pagan religions, though where such a custom prevails, the magical performers themselves are not privileged to withhold their gains for themselves, as these are claimed by the Temple.

Having dealt with the preliminaries of the subject, we will now proceed along the thorny paths of history not the history of wars, battles, heroes, but that of the agents of their being!

CHAPTER III

BRAHMINISM

FOR A BRIEF study of Brahminism, the religion practised in India, we can hardly do better than quote from the work of such recognized authorities as Messrs. Stillson and Hughan.[17] In attempting to trace the origin of Brahminism, they make the following observations: "After being conquered by the Cuthites under Rama, the son of Cush, referred to in Genesis x, 2, 7, the Mysteries of the Deluge were introduced. The worship soon became divided into two sects. We are not fully apprised when was first introduced the Brahminic system, composed of Brahma, Vishnu, and Siva, constituting the Trimurti... one branch of which was mild and benevolent, and addressed to Vishnu, the Preserver, while the other proclaimed the superiority of Siva, who was called the Destroyer and the representative of terror and penance, barbarity and blood; in Egypt, represented by Typhon.

"These Mysteries, whatever may have been their origin, or for what purposes they were then instituted, were certainly a corruption of the original worship of the one Deity. They bore a direct reference to the happiness of Man in Paradise, where he was first placed; his subsequent deviations and transgressions, and the destruction of the race by the general deluge... The great cavern of Elephanta, perhaps the most ancient temple in the world made by man, in which these rites were performed and remaining to the present day, is an evidence of the magnitude of that system...

"The caverns of Salsette, of which there are three hundred, all have within them carved and emblematic characters. The different ranges of apartments are connected by open galleries, and only by private entrances could the most secret caverns, which contained the ineffable symbols, be approached, and so curiously contrived as to give the highest effect upon the neophytes when in the ceremonial of initiation. A cubical *cisia*, used for the periodical sepulture of the aspirant, was located in the most secret recesses of the cavern. The consecrated water of absolution was held in a carved basin in every cavern, and on the surface floated the flowers of the lotus. The Linga or Phallus appeared everywhere most conspicuous, and oftentimes in situations too disgusting to be mentioned…

"Sacrifices to the sun, to the planets, and to household gods, were made accompanied with ablutions of water, purifications with dung and urine of the cow. This last was because the dung was the medium by which the soil was made fertile and reminded them of the doctrine of 'Corruption and reproduction' taught in the worship of Siva."

An initiation is thus described:

"Amidst all the confusion, a sudden explosion was heard, which was followed by a dead silence. Flashes of brilliant light were succeeded by darkness. Phantoms and shadows of various forms, surrounded by rays of light, flitted across the gloom. Some with many hands, arms, and legs; others without them; sometimes a shapeless trunk, then a human body with the head of a bird, or beast, or a fish; all manner of incongruous forms and bodies were seen, and all calculated to excite terror in the mind of the postulant.

"A gorgeous appearance, with unnumbered heads, each having a crown set with resplendent jewels, one of which excelled the others; his eyes gleamed like flaming torches, but his neck, his tongues and his body were black; the skirts of his garments were yellow, and sparkling jewels hung in all of his ears; his arms were extended, and adorned with bracelets, and his hands bore the holy shell; the radiated weapon, the war mace, and the sacred lotus. This image represented Mahadeva[18] himself, in his character of the Destroyer."

Among other learned authorities, writing on these subjects, is Jacolliot who gives the following description of perverted Brahminism:

"The study of philosophic truth does not relieve the Nirvanys and Yogys from the necessity of the tapassas, or bodily mortifications. On the contrary, it would seem that they carry them to the greatest extremes everything that affects or consumes the body, everything that tends to its annihilation, without actually destroying it, is thought to be meritorious.

"Several centuries previous to the present era, however, these bodily mortifications had assumed a character of unusual severity.[19]

"To the contemplative dreamers of the earliest ages in India, who devoted the whole of their time to meditation, and never engaged in practices involving physical suffering oftener than once a week, had succeeded a class of bigoted fanatics, who placed no limit to their religious enthusiasm, and inflicted upon themselves the most terrible tortures.[20]

"A spiritual reaction, however, occurred, and those who had been initiated into the higher degrees took that opportunity to abandon the practice of the tapassas, or corporal mortification. They sought rather to impress the imagination of the people by excessive asceticism in opposition to the laws of nature. A profound humility, an ardent desire to live unknown by the world, and to have the divinity as the only witness to the purity of their morals, took possession of them, and though they continued the practice of excessive abstemiousness, they did so perhaps more that they might not seem to be in conflict with the formal teachings of the sacred scriptures.

"That kind of austerity is the only one now enjoined upon all classes of initiates.

"The Fakirs appear to have gradually monopolized all the old modes of inflicting pain, and have carried the m to the greatest extremes. They display the most unbounded fanaticism in their self-inflicted tortures upon all great public festivals

" The Nirvanys live in a constant state of ecstatic contemplation, depriving themselves of sleep as far as possible, and taking food only once a week, after sunset.

"They are never visible either in the grounds or inside the temples, except on the occasion of the grand festival of fire, which occurs every five years. On that day, they appear at midnight upon a stand erected in the centre of the sacred tank. They appear like spectres, and the surrounding atmosphere is illumined by them by means of their incantations. They seem to be in the midst of a column of light rising from earth to heaven.[21]

"The seven degrees of initiation in the sacerdotal cast of the Brahmins are:[22]

Grihasta—or House-Master.

Pourohita—or Priest of Popular Evocations.

Fakir—Performing.

Sanyassis—or Naked Cenobites, Superior Exorcists. Nirvanys—Naked Evocators.

Yogys—Contemplative.

Brahmatma—Supreme Chief.

"Upon reaching the third degree of initiation, the Brahmins were divided into tens, and a superior Guru, or professor of the occult sciences, was placed over each decade. He was revered by his disciples as a god.

"Seventy Brahmins more than seventy years old are chosen from among the Nirvanys to see that the law of the Lotus, or the occult science, is never revealed to the vulgar, and that those who have been initiated into the sacred order are not contaminated by the admission of any unworthy person." (Quoted from the *Agrouchada-Parikchai*).

"In addition to its attributes as an initiatory tribunal, the council of the elders also had charge of administering the pagoda property, from which it made provision for the wants of its members (of the three classes) who shared everything in common. It also directed the wanderings of the Fakirs, whose duty it is to give manifestations of occult power outside.

It also elected the Brahmatma from its own members.

With regard to the rise to power of the Brahmin caste in India, Mr. Jacolliot writes in *Les Fils de Dieu:*

"Doubtless, in the midst of this new society discontent and discord were unavoidable. Happy in the power they had secured, the chiefs of the Brahmins, however, had to consider means for preserving and insuring it against a reversal of popular favour. At this distance, it is impossible for us to judge the mental influences at work during a period covering about two thousand years, that is to say, from the day when the priests united into a kind of corporation to the time when, enjoying unchallenged authority, they published the *Vedhas*. This was a collection of prayers and ancient ceremonies interspersed with the texts necessary to maintaining their supremacy under the name of *Manou* (Sanscrit meaning: wise law giver), a new code of law which, rejecting all the ancient customs of equality and dividing the people into castes, invested the Brahmins with world power and established the dogma of the Trimourti or Trinity of God, from which eventually was to spring polytheism and a host of the most monstrous superstitions.

"This religious revolution occurred about twelve thousand years before our era, under the Brahmatma Vasichta-Richi.

"The *Vedhas* and *Manou*, collected and codified by the Brahmins were given as coming from Brahma himself, and anyone doubting the truth of this origin was liable to the penalty of death."

As among the Ancient Egyptians the teaching of monotheism was restricted to the highest initiates alone. Jacolliot emphasises this when he writes:

"The worship of the one God or Zeus unrevealed, reserved to the priests, was forbidden to the lower classes, but three temples dedicated to the three persons of the Trimourti, Brahma, Vishnu, Siva, opened their doors to the adoration of the people, all of whom were allowed to select one of the three personages of the trinity they would prefer to worship."

This division in religious worship which eventually led to the caste system shows the power of theocratic tyranny, the Brahmins, seeking to justify the method whereby the control of the masses is vested in the hands of a few, when preaching in the pagodas, even now say: "See how logical is this system of division of the people into castes. It was formed in the likeness of the divinity, Zeus, sovereign master of all things, but taking no action himself. This is the Brahmin priest Brahma, the God who creates, who acts, who directs, that is the aristocrat or the prince; Vishnu, the God who preserves, that is the artisan, the merchant, who produces taxes, preserving and assuring the prosperity of the State by his work and industry. As for Siva, the terrible God, he keeps the Soudra (peasant) in a state of humility and obedience appropriate to his station in life.

"Another very important function appears however to have been early assigned to him, on which much more stress is laid in his (Siva) modern worship—that of destroyer—viz., the character of a generative power, symbolized in the phallic emblem (Linga) and in the sacred bull (Nandi), the favourite attendant of the god. This feature being entirely alien from the nature of the Vedic god, it has been conjectured with some plausibility, that the Linga-worship was originally prevalent among the non-Aryan population, and was thence introduced into the worship of Siva.[23]

One of the most curious facts in the Theocratic System ruling India is that the principle of equality is evidenced only in the teaching and practice of Occultism. Members of all castes are admitted on the same footing to learn magic or fakirism and compose the class known under the name of Fakirs. This system of equality is similar to the brotherhood principle and teaching of democracy advocated in Freemasonry which was so effectively exploited in all the lodges that fomented the French Revolution.

"As all castes are admitted to the congregation of the Fakirs, the lowest of the soudras on entering it becomes the equal of the Brahmins. In spreading the belief that whosoever consented to enrol among the high initiates of the pagoda, and to die for the faith, was transported to the abode of Brahma without accomplishing further migration on earth or having to pass through hell, the Brahmins provided for an inexhaustible supply of fakirs."

"Before entering the category of fakir, those who are destined to illustrate the ceremonies of the cults by their tortures and death, the new recruits practise the occult sciences under the direction of initiated Brahmins in the innermost recesses of the pagodas."

While "there are indeed extraordinary phenomena in what is termed by the Brahmins occult science, there are none which cannot be explained and which are not in accordance with the law of nature."

"To become expert in magic, like the believers in the philosophic doctrine of the Pitris, the pupil must learn, from a magician whom the sorcerers call their Guru, the formulas of evocation, by means of which the malign spirits are brought into complete subjection.

"Some of these spirits the magician evokes in preference to others, probably on account of their willingness to do anything that may be required of them."

"An intimate connection exists between the doctrine of the ancient Jewish Cabalists and those of the Hindu votaries of the Pitris—or spirits—whose scientific book is the *Agrouchada-parikchai.*[24]

"It would be impossible to enumerate the different drugs, ingredients and implements that compose the stock-in-trade of a magician."[25]

The standard Indian book on magic is the *Oupnek'hat*. Therein is to be found a detailed description of methods available for producing catalepsy, somnambulism, hallucination and ecstasy by strength of will and fatigue of the nervous system.[26]

This is what is known to the modern common-sense mortal as "Yogi Stuff", and it is mostly based on breathing exercises.

We will now quote from Mr. Sellon:

"It is a little remarkable that of the host of Divinities, especially in Bengal, Siva is the God whom they are especially delighted to honour. As the Destroyer, and one who revels in cruelty and bloodshed, this terrible deity, who has not inaptly been compared to the Moloch of Scripture, of all their Divinities suggests most our idea of the Devil. It may therefore be concluded that the most exalted notion of worship among the Hindus is a service of Fear. The Brahmins say that the other Gods are good and benevolent, and will not hurt their creatures, but that Siva is powerful and cruel, and that it is necessary to *appease him.*

"Although this deity is sometimes represented in the human form in his images, it is not thus that he is most frequently adored. The most popular representation of him is unquestionably the *Linga*; a smooth stone rising out of another stone of finer texture, *simulacrum membri virilis, et pudendum muliebre.* This emblem is identical with Siva in his capacity of 'Lord of all'.[27]

"It is necessary, however, to observe here that Professor Wilson, while admitting that 'the Linga is perhaps the most ancient object of homage adopted in India' , adds, 'subsequently to the ritual of the *Vedhas*, which was chiefly, if not wholly, addressed to the Elements, and particularly to fire. How far the worship of the Linga is authorized by the *Vedhas* is doubtful, but that it is the main purport of several of the *Puranas* there can be no doubt'.'[28]

"The worship of Siva under the type of the Linga is almost the only form in which that deity is reverenced. Its prevalence throughout the whole tract of the Ganges as far as Benares is sufficiently conspicuous. In Bengal, the Lingam Temples are commonly erected in a range of six, eight, or twelve on each side of a Ghaut leading to the river. At Kalma is a circular group of one hundred and eight temples erected by the Rajah of Burdwan. These temples, and indeed all those found in Bengal, consist of a simple chamber of a square form surmounted by a pyramidal centre; the area of each is very small. The Linga of black or white marble, and sometimes of alabaster slightly tinted and gilt, is placed in the middle."[29]

"Benares is the peculiar seat of this form of worship. The principal Deity, Siva, there called Viweswarra, is a Linga; and most of the chief objects of pilgrimage are similar blocks of stone. No less than forty-seven Lingas are visited, all of preeminent sanctity; but there are hundreds of inferior note still worshipped, and thousands whose fame and fashion have passed away. It is a singular fact, that upon this adoration of the procreative and sexual Sacti (or power) seen throughout nature, hinges the whole gist of the Hindu faith.[30]

"Bacchus or Osiris was represented by an equilateral triangle, and the sectarian mark of the worshippers of Siva is this hieroglyphic. The worship of Bacchus was the same as that which is paid to Siva, it had the same obscenities, the same cruel bloodthirsty rites, and the same emblem of the generative power.[31]

"Durga, Kali, or Maha Kali as the Sacti, spouse or energetic will of Siva, the destructive power, bears a remarkable analogy with the Moloch of Scripture, as well as with Typhon, Saturn, Dis, Pluto, and other divinities of the West.[32]

"When the attributes of the Supreme Being began to be viewed in the light of distinct individuals, mankind attached themselves to the worship of the one or the other exclusively, and arranged themselves into sects: the worshippers of Siva introduced the doctrine of the eternity of matter. In order to reconcile the apparent contradiction of assigning the attribute of creation to the principle of Destruction, they asserted that the dissolution and destruction of bodies was not real with respect to matter, which was in itself indestructible, although its modifications were in a constant succession of mutation; that the power must necessarily unite in itself the attributes of creation and apparent destruction; that this power and matter are two distinct and co-existent principles in nature; the one active, the other passive; the one male, the other female; and that creation was the effect of the mysterious union of the two.

"This Union is worshipped under a variety of names: Bhava, Bhavani, Mahadeva, Mahamaya, etc. Thus the attribute of creation was usurped from Brahma, by the followers of Siva, to adorn and characterise their favourite divinity."

"This seems to have been a popular worship for a great length of time, out of which sprang two sects: the one personified the whole Universe and dispensations of providence (in the regulation of it) under the name of Prakriti, and which we from the Latin call nature. This sect retains the Sacti only, and were the originators of the Sactas sects, or worshippers of Power. The other sect took for their symbol the Male emblem (Linga) unconnected with the female Sacti (or Yoni). There was also a third sect, who adored both male and female.

"According to Theodoret, Arnobius, and Clemens of Alexandria, the Yoni of the Hindus was the sole object of veneration in the mysteries of Eleusis.[33]

"It is not only the votaries of Siva who adore their God under the symbolic form of the Linga; the Vaishnavas, or followers of Vishnu, use the same medium. They also are Lingayetts, one of the essential characteristics of which is wearing the Type on some part of their dress or person.[34]

"The Vaishnavas are divided into many sects. They comprise the Ghoculasthas, the Yonijas, the Ramani, and Radha-balluthis.

"The Ghoculasthas adore Krishna, while the Ramani worship Rama; both have again branched into three sects—one consists of the exclusive worshippers of Krishna, and these only are deemed true and orthodox Vaishnavas... As Parameswarra, Krishna is represented of a black or dark blue colour. Now the Tulasi is the black Ocymum, and all animals or vegetables of a black or blue colour are sacred to him. His linga also is always either black or dark blue, and may thus be distinguished from that of Siva, which is generally white.

"This divinity, as Parameswarra, is Janan'nauth (Juggernaut), or 'Lord of the Universe', and it is under the wheels of his sacred car that so many misguided beings annually immolated themselves.

"To return, however, to the Vaishnavas. Another of their sects adore Krishna and his mistress Radha united. These are the Lingionijas, whose worship is perhaps the most free of all the Pujas. A third, the Radha-ballubhis, dedicate their offerings to Radha only. The followers of these last mentioned sects have adopted the singular practice of presenting to a naked girl the oblation intended for the Goddess, constituting her the living impersonation of Radha. Rut when a female is not to be obtained for this purpose, the votive offerings are made to an image of the Yoni, or emblem of the feminine power. These worshippers are called Yonijas, in contradistinction to the Lingayats, or adorers of the Krishna (Vishnu) Linga.

"As the Saivas are all worshippers of Siva and Bowannee (Pavati) conjointly, so the Vaishnavas also offer up their prayers to Laksmi-Nayarana. The exclusive adorers of this Goddess are the Sactas.

"The caste mark of the Saivas and Sactas consists of three horizontal lines on the forehead with ashes obtained, if possible, from the hearth on which a consecrated fire is perpetually maintained. The adoration of the Sacti is quite in accordance with the spirit of the mythological system of the Hindus. It has been computed that, of the Hindus in Bengal, at least three-fourths are Sactas, of the remaining fourth, three parts are Vaishnavas, and one, Saivas.

"Independently of the homage paid to the principal Deities, there are a great variety of inferior beings, Dewtas, and demi-gods of a malevolent character and formidable aspect, who receive the worship of the multitude. The bride of Siva, however, in one or other of her many and varied forms, is by far the most popular goddess in Bengal and along the Ganges.

"The worship of the female generative principle, as distinct from the Divinity, appears to have originated in the literal interpretation of the metaphorical language of the *Vedhas*, in which Will, or purpose to Create the Universe, is represented as originating from the Creator and co-existent with him as his bride, and part of himself."

"Although the adoration of the Sacti (the personified energy of the Omnipotent) is authorized by some of the *Puranas*, the rites and formulae are more clearly set forth in a voluminous collection of books called *Tantras*. These writings convey their meaning in the similitude of dialogue between Uma (or Siva) and Pavati. "The followers of the *Tantras* profess to consider them as a fifth Vedh, and attribute to them equal antiquity and superior authority."

"The *Tantras* are too numerous to specify them further, but the curious reader will find them under the heads of Syama Rahasya, Anandra, Rudra, Yamala, Mandra, Mahodahi, Sareda, Tilika, and Kalika-Tantras. "Although any of the goddesses may be objects of the Sacta worship, and the term Sacti comprehends them all, yet the homage of the Sactas is almost restricted, in Bengal, to the consort of Siva. The Varnis, or Vamacharis, worship Devi as well as all goddesses. Their worship is derived from a portion of the *Tantras*. "According to the immediate object of the worshipper is the particular form of worship; but all the forms require the use of some or all of the five Makaras—Mansa, Matsya, Madya, Maithuna, and Mudra—that is: flesh, fish, wine, women, and certain mystical gesticulations with the fingers. Suitable Muntrus, or incantations, are also indispensable, according to the end proposed, consisting of various unmeaning monosyllabic combinations of letters, of great imaginary efficacy.

"When the object of worship is to acquire an interview with, and control over, impure spirits, a dead body is necessary. The adept is also to be alone, at midnight, in a cemetery or place where bodies are burnt. Seated on the corpse he is to perform the usual offerings, and if he do so without fear or disgust, the Dhutas, the Yoginis, and other male and female demons become his slaves.[35]

"In this and many of the observances practised, solitude is enjoined, but all the principal ceremonies comprehend the worship of Sacti, or Power, and require, for that purpose, the presence of a young and beautiful girl, as the living representative of the goddess. This worship is mostly celebrated in a mixed society; the men of which represent Bhairavas, or Viras, and the women, Bhanravis and Nayikas. The Sacti is personified by a naked girl, to whom meat and wine are offered, and then distributed among the assistants. Here follows the chanting of the Muntrus and sacred texts, and the performance of the Mudra, or gesticulations with the fingers. The whole terminates with orgies amongst the votaries of a very licentious description. This ceremony is entitled the Sri Chakra or Purnabisheka, The Ring or full Initiation.[36]

"This method of adoring the Sacti is unquestionably acknowledged by the texts regarded by the Vanis as authorities for the impurities practised.

"The members of the sect are sworn to secrecy, and will not therefore acknowledge any participation in Sacta-Puja. Some years ago, however, they began to throw off this reserve, and at the present day they trouble themselves very little to disguise their initiation into its mysteries, but they do not divulge in what those mysteries consist.

"The Kauchiluas are another branch of the Sactas sect; their worship much resembles that of the Caulas. They are, however, distinguished by one particular rite not practised by the others, and throw into confusion all the ties of female relationship; natural restraints are wholly disregarded, and a community of "women among the votaries inculcated.

"On the occasions of the performance of divine worship, the women and girls deposit their "julies", or bodices, in a box in charge of the Guru, or priest. At the close of the rites, the male worshippers take each a "julie" from the box, and the female to whom it belongs, even were she his sister, becomes his partner for the evening in these lascivious orgies.

"In every temple of any importance in India we find a troupe of Nautch or dancing girls attached.

"These women are generally procured when quite young, and are early initiated into all the mysteries of their profession. They are instructed in dancing and vocal and instrumental music, their chief employment being to chant the sacred hymns, and perform nautches before the God, on the recurrence of high festivals. But this is not the only service required of them, for besides being the acknowledged mistresses of the officiating priests, it is their duty to prostitute themselves in the courts of the temple to all comers, and thus raise funds for the enrichment of the place of worship to which they belong... A Nautch woman esteems it a peculiar privilege to become the Radha Dea on such occasions. It is an office indeed which these adepts are, on every account, better calculated to fulfil with satisfaction to the sect of Sacteyas, who require their aid, than a more innocent and unsophisticated girl.

"The worship of Sacti is the adoration of Power,[37] which the Hindus typify by the Yoni, or womb, the Argha or vulva, and by the leaves and flowers of certain plants thought to resemble it.[38]

"In *Ananda Tantram*, cap. VII, 148, and other passages, reference is made to Bhagamala. She appears to be the goddess who presides over the pudendum muliebre, i.e. the deified vulva; and the Sacti is thus personified.

"Such are some of the peculiar features of the worship of Power (or Gnosticism), and which, combined with the Linga Puga (or adoration of the Phallus), constitutes at the present day one of the most popular dogmas of the Hindus."

Heckethorn tells us that the Maharajas constitute another sect of priests and adds: "It appears abundantly from the works of recognized authority written by Maharajas, and from existing popular belief in the Vallabhacharya sect, that Vallabhacharya is believed to have been an incarnation of the god Krishna, and that the Maharajas, as descendants of Vallabhacharya, have claimed and received from their followers the like character of incarnations of that god by hereditary succession. The ceremonies of the worship paid to Krishna through these priests are all of the most licentious character. The love and subserviency due to a Supreme Being are here materialized and transferred to those who claim to be the living incarnations of the god. Hence the priests exercise an unlimited influence over their female votaries, who consider it a great honour to acquire the temporary regard of the voluptuous Maharajas, the belief in whose pretensions is allowed to interfere, almost vitally, with the domestic relations of husband and wife."[39]

Miss Mayo, in her book *Mother India*, published in 1927, gives an interesting description of a temple of Kali. "Kali Ghat"—place of Kali—is the root-word of the name Calcutta. "Kali is a Hindu goddess, wife of the great god Siva, whose attribute is destruction and whose thirst is for blood and death-sacrifice." Kali has thousands of temples in India, great and small.

Heckethorn further explains that "the association of Thugs, after having existed in India for centuries, was only discovered in 1810. The names by which the members were known to each other, and also to others, was Funsiegeer, that is, 'men of the noose'. The name Thug is said to be derived from thaga, to deceive, because the Thugs get hold of their victims by luring them into false security. One common mode of decoying young men having valuables upon them is to place a young and handsome woman by the wayside, and apparently in great grief, who, by some pretended tale of misfortune, draws him into the jungle, where the gang are lying in ambush, and on his appearance strangle him. The gang consists of from ten to fifty members; and they will follow or accompany the marked-out victim for days, nor attempt his murder until an opportunity, offering every chance of success, presents itself. After every murder they perform a religious ceremony, called Jagmi; and the division of the spoil is regulated by old-established laws—the man that threw the handkerchief gets the largest share, the man that held the hands the next largest proportion, and so on. In some gangs their property is held in common. Their crimes are committed in honour of Kali who hates our race, and to whom the death of man is a pleasing sacrifice.[40]

"Kali, or Bhowany, for she is equally well known by both names, was, according to the Indian legend, born of the burning eye which Shiva has on his forehead, whence she issued, like the Greek Minerva, out of the skull of Jupiter, a perfect and full-grown being. She represents the Evil Spirit, delights in human blood, presides over plague and pestilence, and directs the storm and hurricane, and ever aims at destruction. She is represented under the most frightful effigy the Indian mind could conceive; her face is azure, streaked with yellow; her glance is ferocious; she wears her dishevelled and bristly hair displayed like the peacock's tail and braided with green serpents. Her purple lips seem streaming with blood; her tusk-like teeth descend over her lower lip; she has eight or ten arms, each hand holding some murderous weapon, and sometimes a human head dripping with gore. With one foot she stands on a human corpse. She has her temples, in which the people sacrifice cocks and bullocks to her, but her priests are the Thugs, the 'Sons of Death', who quench the never-ending thirst of this divine vampyre."[41]

As regards the sect of Kali's worshippers, Heckethorn gives the following details:

"A newly admitted member takes the appellation of Sahib-Zada. He commences his infamous career as lughah, or gravedigger, or as belhal, or explorer of the spots most convenient for executing a projected assassination, or bhil. In this condition he remains for several years, until he has given abundant proof of his ability and good will. He is then raised to the degree of Bhuttotah, or strangler, which advancement, however, is preceded by new formalities and ceremonies. On the day appointed for the ceremony, the candidate is conducted by his guru into a circle, formed in the sands and surrounded by mysterious hieroglyphics, where prayers are offered up to their deity. The ceremony lasts four days, during which the candidate is allowed no other food but milk. He occupies himself in practising the immolation of victims fastened to a cross erected in the ground. On the fifth day the priest gives him the fatal noose, washed in holy water and anointed with oil, and after more religious ceremonies, he is pronounced a perfect bhuttotah. He binds himself by fearful oaths to maintain the most perfect silence on all that concerns the society, and to labour without ceasing towards the destruction of the human race. He is the rex *sacrificulus*, and the person he encounters, and Bhowany places in his way, the victim. Certain persons, however, are excepted from the attacks of the Thugs."[42]

The political significance of such a sect in any Theocrasy can be easily understood when one realizes what it means to the rulers of a land to have at their disposal a staff of fanatics trained to kill anyone on the order of a priest! The utility of such organizations is obvious in a hierarchy where the rulers are also priests reigning by "Divine Right".

CHAPTER IV

MAZDEISM (ZOROASTRIANISM)

WHILE THE ORIGIN of Mazdeism seems shrouded in mystery, one may nevertheless recognize its antiquity, probably the same as that of the *Rig-Vedha*, for it has been proved by Eugene Bournouf and Spiegel that certain parts of the *Avesta* are as old as the Rig, and the many similarities of this religion with that of the Vedhas proves that Mazdeism must have had its origin at the time when the Aryans undertook the conquest of India, that is to say seventeen to eighteen centuries before our era.

From *Le Mazdeisme, l'avesta* of G. de Lafont, we extract the following facts:[43] The historic role of Media began with Ouwakshatara, a name written by the Greeks Kyouxares, the founder of the Median empire. After defeating the Scythians, Kyouxares went to Assyria where he laid siege to Nineveh, after the destruction of which the Assyrian empire came to an end. (612 B. C.)

Kyouxares left a son Astyage whose daughter Mandane married the Persian Cambyses and from their union sprang the great Cyrus the founder of the Persian empire.

The Parthian dynasty of the Arsacides, who reigned from 256 B. C. until 226 A. D., marks a fatal period for Mazdeism. It was only on the accession of Ardeschir Babejan, the founder of the Sassanide dynasty, that Mazdeism regained its strength. With Ardeshir, Mazdeism became the state religion and Shapour II caused all the Avesta texts treating of philosophy, medicine, cosmogony and astronomy to be collected.

Under the last Sassanides appeared several heretical sects, the most celebrated of which were those of Manes and of Mazdeck. However, in the seventh century, came the Arab conquest; with Yesdegirt the Persian empire of the Sassanides disappeared and with it the influence of Mazdeism.

Towards the tenth century, a few thousand Persians, faithful to the old cult, went into exile taking with them their laws and altars. Some of these took refuge in the Kirman in the Yezd while the others fled to India where they now constitute the well-known sect of the Parsees.

The *Zend Avesta*, the sacred book of Persia and of the modern Parsees, contains the teaching of Zoroaster (Zarathustra), a reformer, said to have lived some 7000 years before Christ. It was first translated into French by Hyacinthe-Anquetil Duperron in 1761.

The Chevalier de Ramsay, giving Plutarch as his authority, says: "Zoroaster taught that there are two Gods contrary to each other in their Operations, the one the Author of all the Good, the other of all the Evil in Nature. The good Principle he calls Oromazes, (Ahura-Mazda) the other the Daemon Arimanius (Agra-Mainyus). He says that the one resembles Light and Truth, the other Darkness and Ignorance.

There is likewise a middle God between these two named Mythras, whom the Persians call the Intercessor or Mediator. Mythras is the Yazata (spirit) of light and the guardian of justice and truth."

For the benefit of the reader we compile the following interesting information from the previously mentioned author, G. de Lafont:

Pure Zoroastrianism was monotheistic, for in the beginning Ahura-Mazda was recognized as infinitely more powerful than Agra-Mainyus, thus dualism, or the potential equality of these two deities, was actually the development of a later corruption of the Zoroastrian teaching.

The *Avesta*, the bible of Mazdeism, containing the revelations of Ahura-Mazda to the Prophet Zoroaster, is composed of two principal parts—the *Avesta*, containing the *Vendidad*, the *Yacnca* and the *Vispered*, and the *Khorda Avesta*, or little *Avesta*, itself composed of six parts.

Mazdeism taught the immortality of the soul, a compensating justice in another world of Heaven or Hell, the resurrection of the body, the last judgment and the freedom of the soul to choose between right and wrong as a free agent, as opposed to the Islamic theory of fatalism.

Oromazes is the Universal Creator of all that is good, eternal, he created the Good Genii, the spiritual and material world; man is his creature, and at the end of time he will resurrect him to endow him with eternal happiness and will cause the powers of evil and evil itself to vanish from the earth. No cult is rendered to Agra-Mainyus (Lucifer) who, with his Devas (evil spirits) fights Ahura-Mazda (God) through the ages.

Fire, in the Mazdean religion, was worshipped as the luminous and pure element, the work of Ahura-Mazda and for that reason always burns sheltered from defilement. But it is not material fire that in this case is to be considered as a Yazata. The *Avesta* distinguishes several kinds of fire:

1. Berezucavanha, or internal fire of the earth.
2. Vohufryana or fire of the human body and animals. (Kundalini, Sex-force, Serpent Power).
3. Urvazista or fire of vegetation.
4. Vazista or fire of lightning.
5. Cpenista or fire of Ahura-Mazda, represented by the fire on the Altar.

The Fravashis (modern Ferouers) are supposed to be the souls of the dead deified. Their cult also forms the basis of the Ancestor worship, of the Pitris of India and the Manes of Latin Countries.

According to Geiger, by "Fravashis" must be understood the immortal, divine part in man, which unites with a body for a limited time only. Consequently there are Fravashis of those who are dead, of those who are living, and of those who are still unborn. Darmstater further explains that the Fravashis are the spiritual form of a being, independent of its material life and anterior to it. According to Mazdean teaching, Oromazes offered to the Ferouers of men the choice of remaining in the spiritual world or of descending on earth to incarnate in human bodies.

At the advent of death, corpses were supposed immediately to become the prey of the Demon Druge Nacus, the demon of the impurity of corpses. Thus, it being most essential never to allow the elements of fire, water and earth to be sullied by contact with anything unclean, the funeral rites and ceremonies of the Mazdeans differ from those of other religions.

Their ancient customs persist today among the Parsees of India where the bodies of the dead are carried to "The Towers of Silence" there to be exposed and devoured by the birds of prey.

Besides the many other parallels between Mazdeism and Christianity, the deity of the Mazdeans, their personal God, Ahura-Mazda, was not a god of vengeance as was the Jehovah of the Jews. He was the essence of universal love, charity, justice and activity and the ideal of Mazdean virtue in early times was similar to that of the Christians of today.

JAINISM

Jainism, which like Buddhism denies the authority of the Vedhas and is therefore regarded by the Brahmins of India as heretical, may have been founded by Parsva whose death is placed at 250 years before that of Vardhamana Mahavira, the last of the prophets of the Jains and a contemporary of Buddha.

Vardhamana Mahavira died at the age of 72 at Pava 527 B. C. He had eleven disciples to whom he preached the law. Many authorities however believe the Jain Church to be as old as Brahminism itself.

The following paragraph quoted from Hastings' *Encyclopaedia of Religions and Ethics*, article on *Jainism*, describes the Jain theory of the Transmigration of Souls as opposed to the orthodox theory of Reincarnation. It is here referred to as "a peculiarity of the Jains which had struck all observers more than any other, viz. their extreme carefulness not to destroy any living being, a principle which is carried out to its very last consequences in monastic life, and has shaped the conduct of the laity in a great measure.

No layman will intentionally kill any living being, not even an insect, however troublesome: he will remove it carefully without hurting it. It goes without saying that the Jains are strict vegetarians. This principle of not hurting any living being bars them from some professions, *e. g.* agriculture, and has thrust them into commerce and especially into its least elevating branch of money-lending. Most of the money lending in Western India is in the hands of the Jains, and this accounts in a great measure both for their unpopularity and for their wealth. A remarkable institution of the Jains, due to their tender regard for animal life, is their asylums for old and diseased animals, the panjarapolas, where they are kept and fed till they die a natural death."

The reluctance on the part of an orthodox Jain to discourage vermin on the theory that a louse may actually be his reincarnated grandmother or a scorpion some other reincarnated relative is only a logical development of his religious belief in the transmigration of souls.

The Jains are subdivided today into numerous schools each following the teachings of a certain master but united in certain fundamental beliefs.

CHAPTER V

CONFUCIANISM AND TAOISM

PREVIOUS TO THE Christian era, China, judging from the available annals, presented the spectacle of a country whose social life was based almost solely on what might be called the family cult. The metaphysical tradition, overshadowing the life of the people, leading to a monotheistic belief in a Supreme Being, was the knowledge and belief of a few. Vaguely, the people believed that the Monarch alone held communication with the Sublime Sovereign or God. The rites had nothing of a religious character, they were purely social. Then in 1122 B. C, when the Chinese dynasty of Chang-Yin was overthrown by the Tcheou, there were introduced in China numerous innovations, most of them appertaining to magic and occultism, also brahminic and avestic dogmas and beliefs. The whole construction of social ideology in China had undergone a slow but radical change. The ground was prepared for the pantheistic teaching of the philosopher Lao-Tse whose doctrine was bitterly fought by Confucius (551–479) who opposed the dualist theory, and strove to regenerate the former state of Chinese social life, the cult of the family and ancestors. Moreover, the whole moral code of Confucius was contained in a few words: loyalty and good feeling towards one's neighbour.

Only in about 65 A. D. was Buddhism introduced in China, followed in turn by Mazdeism, Manicheism and Mahomedanism.

CHAPTER VI

EGYPTIAN ESOTERISM

MORE THAN ANY other country, Ancient Egypt was an illustration of theocratic power. There, priesthood ruled and adumbrated royalty. Depositories of the Indo-Iran tradition of Ra, Zarathustra and Manu, the priests of Thebes and Memphis made of Egypt the fortress of antique esoterism. Their Sovereign Lord God and Teacher bore the name of Hermes or Thoth, the Great Initiator. In him were typified the three great powers of royalty, law-giving or legislative and high priesthood which made the Greeks, disciples of the Egyptians, surname him Hermes Trismegistus or thrice great.

To Hermes was credited a large number of books containing the secrets of Indo-Aryan occult science. Fire was the first Principle, the basis of all teaching and the law of Ammon-Ra, the Sun God of Thebes.

Only after the conquest of Egypt by the Hyksos (2000 B. C.) did the priests spread among the people the cult of Osiris and Isis and their son Horus. This popular religion served as a screen which most effectively shielded the Hermetic mysteries from intrusion and disclosure and safeguarded ancient and Aryan esoterism which had to fear annihilation at the hands of the priesthood of the black or Ethiopian race whose esoterism was based upon a different conception of occult and psychic knowledge.

A striking example of the rivalry of the two esoteric schools is given in the Bible when Moses and Aaron, practising the magic taught them by the Ethiopian Jethro, failed to confound the Egyptian priests before Pharaoh.

Concealed behind the popular cult of Osiris and Isis was the soul of Egyptian esoterism which no one could reach, except after having been deemed worthy to penetrate the most sacred mysteries of Isis whose statue, with its face veiled, stood before the door of the temple of occultism.

The trials of initiation which a candidate had to withstand before he beheld the light of Osiris and understood the "Vision of Hermes" were long and terrible. They were interspersed, however, by states of trance induced by special beverages, during which the initiate had voluptuous visions of Isis preceded by the five-pointed flamboyant star or the Rose of Isis.

Two great flowing currents issued from the esoteric wisdom, jealously safeguarded by the Egyptians, namely: Mosaism or Judaism, taught by Moses whose God was Jehovah, and Orpheism taught by Orpheus whose God was Zeus or Jupiter. The former adapted his beliefs to suit the mentality of undisciplined, rebellious masses of Israelites in Egypt, hence a god of Fear and Vengeance; the latter legislated for a people whose hellenic genius touched sublime heights of philosophic wisdom on the one hand, and sought on the other to carry it's irrepressible sense of beauty and lightheartedness in its pursuit of material pleasures. Hence the great difference between the two currents which had derived their initial teaching from the same source.

CHAPTER VII

JUDAISM (THE PHARISEES)

JUDAISM HAS BEEN described by Moses Mendelssohn, a learned Jew, in this way: "Judaism is not a religion but a Law religionized." This definition does away effectively with the erroneous belief prevalent among the non-Jews that Judaism is a religion.

In spite of the loud and frequent assertions, made by Jews and Christian divines alike, contending that the Jews were the first monotheists, it is a well proven fact that the high initiates of the Memphis priesthood were monotheists long before the Jews ever went to Egypt.

Judaism would be best described as a rite or compendium of rites, for, if one lends belief to the existence of the Jewish Lawgiver, Moses, one must bear in mind that he first studied among the high initiates of Egypt, and later, became the pupil and son-in-law of black Jethro, the Ethiopian magician whom one might call the Father of Voodooism, name given to the magic practices and rites performed by the negroes.

The closer one studies the history of the Jews, the clearer it appears that they are neither a religious entity nor a nation. The absolute failure of Zionism which was a desperate effort on the part of certain Jewish leaders to bind all the Jews of the world into a national entity, whose territory would have been Palestine, proves the futility of such an effort.

Judaism is not a religion and the Jews are not a nation, but they *are a sect with Judaism as a rite.*

The obligations and rules of the rite for the Jewish masses are contained in the *Talmud* and *Schulchan Aruk*, but the esoteric teachings for the higher initiates are to be found in the Cabala.

Therein are contained the mysterious rites for evocations, the indications and keys to practices for conjuration of supernatural forces, the science of numbers, astrology, etc.

The practical application of the Cabalist knowledge is manifested in the use made of it, through the ages, by Jews to gain influence both in the higher spheres of Gentile life and over the masses. Sovereigns and Popes, both, usually had one or more Jews as astrologers and advisers, and they frequently gave Jews control over their very life by employing them as physicians. Political power was thus gained by Jews in almost every Gentile country alongside with financial power, since Jewish court-bankers manipulated state funds and taxes.

Through the ages also, can be followed the spreading power of the sect, and no more awful example of the devastating and destructive power of the penetration of a secret subversive society has ever been witnessed.

With its B'nai B'rith Supreme Council as the directing head, the sect with its members swarming among all nations has become the sovereign power ruling in the councils of all nations and governing their political, economic, religious and educational policies.

In his book *Nicholas II et les Juifs, Netchvolodow* explains that "the Chaldean science acquired by many of the Jewish priests, during the captivity of Babylon, gave birth to the sect of the Pharisees whose name only appears in the Holy Scriptures and in the writings of the Jewish historians after the captivity (606 B. C) . The works of the celebrated scientist Munk leave no doubt on the point that the sect appeared during the period of the captivity.

"From then dates the Cabala or Tradition of the Pharisees. For a long time their precepts were only transmitted orally but later they formed the Talmud and received their final form in the book called the *Sepher ha Zohar*."[44]

The Pharisees were, as it were, a class whose tendency was to form a kind of intellectual aristocracy among the Jews. At first, they formed a sort of brotherhood, a *haburah*, the members being called *haburim* or brothers. They were a subversive element, aiming at the overthrow of the Sadducean High-priesthood, whose members prided themselves on their aristocracy of blood and birth, to which the Pharisees opposed an aristocracy of learning. The war waged by the latter extends over a long period of time, and the rivalry was bitter. The Pharisees, who, although they professed, as one of their chief tenets, the utmost contempt of the *am-haretz* or simple people, did not overlook the fact that they needed their mass support for the attainment of their own aim, and they enlisted it by opposing the Sadducean strictness of the Law in many instances, namely, in the observance of the Sabbath.

The power of the Sadducees fell with the destruction of the Temple by Titus and thenceforth the Pharisaic element held supremacy among the Jews.

Quoting an acknowledged authority on Judaism, Mr. Flavien Brenier, Lt. Gen. Netchvolodow further describes the policy of the sect as follows:[45]

"Before appearing proudly as the expression of Jewish aspirations, The Tradition of the Pharisees had serious difficulties to surmount, the chief of which was the revival of the orthodox faith stimulated in the Jewish people by the Captivity. To the exiles, bemoaning the fall of the Temple of Jerusalem and begging Jehovah to end the misfortunes of their homeland, the revelation that Jehovah was only a phantom, entailed not only certain defeat, but also their own exposure to perils the least of which would have been the loss of all authority over Israel.

"The Pharisees then, judging it wiser to capture the confidence of their compatriots by taking the lead of the religious movement, affected a scrupulous observance of the slightest prescriptions of the law and instituted the practice of complicated rituals, simultaneously however cultivating the new doctrine in their secret sanctuaries. These were regular secret societies, composed during the captivity of a few hundred adepts. At the time of Flavius Josephus which was that of their greatest prosperity they numbered only some 6,000 members.

"This group of intellectual pantheists was soon to acquire a directing influence over the Jewish nation. Nothing, moreover, likely to offend national sentiment ever appeared in their doctrines. However saturated with pantheistic Chaldeism they might have been, the Pharisees preserved their ethnic pride intact. This religion of Man divinised, which they had absorbed at Babylon, they conceived solely as applying to the profit of the Jew, the superior and predestined being. The promises of universal dominion which the orthodox Jew found in the Law, the Pharisees did not interpret in the sense of the reign of the God of Moses over the nations, but in that of a material domination to be imposed on the universe by the Jews. The awaited Messiah was no longer the Redeemer of original Sin, a spiritual victor who would lead the world, it was a temporal king, bloody with battle, who would make Israel master of the world and 'drag all peoples under the wheels of his chariot'. The Pharisees did not ask this enslavement of the nations of a mystical Jehovah, which they continued worshipping in public, only as a concession to popular opinion, for they expected its eventual consummation to be achieved by the secular patience of Israel and the use of human means.

"Monstrously different from the ancient law were such principles as these, but they had nothing one could see, which might have rendered unpopular those who let them filter, drop by drop, among the Jews.

"The admirably conceived organization of the Pharisees did not fail soon to bear fruit.

"One cannot better define its action in the midst of Jewish society before Jesus Christ," said Mr. Flavien Brenier, "than in comparing it with that of the Freemasons in modern society."

"A carefully restricted membership tightly bound, imposing on their members the religion of 'the secret', the Pharisees pursued relentlessly their double aim which was:

"1. The seizure of political power, by the possession of the great political offices (the influence of which was tremendous in the reconstituted Jewish nation) and the conquest of the Sanhedrin (Jewish parliament).

"2. To modify gradually the conceptions of the people in the direction of their secret doctrine."

The first of these aims was achieved when Hillel, a Pharisee of Babylon who claimed Davidic descent, was elected president of the Sanhedrin.

Thus ended the bitter fight between the Pharisees and the Sadducees. Opposed to Hillel was Shammai, a Sadducee, supporter of the Sadducean High Priest who was made Chief Judge of the assembly. The attitude of the two men towards each other is a matter of long record in the Talmud

Among the most noted Pharisees, after Hillel, are:—Yochanan ben Zakkai, founder of the school of Yamnai, Akibah who, with Bar Cochba, fomented the revolt against the Romans under Hadrian, rebellion ending with the order for the dispersion of Jews (132 A. D.) Also Simon ben Yohai, who might be termed the great Magician and Father of the Cabala, lastly Juda h the Prince who compiled the Babylonian Talmud. Under these chiefs, the Pharisaic power was definitely established in the Sanhedrin. Those among the Jews who clung to the Sadducean tradition and refused to acknowledge the dominion of the Pharisees, remained as dissidents. Such were the Samaritans and the Karaites who rejected the Talmud.

The second of the aims and its method of attainment is exposed in the so-called *Protocols of the Wise Men of Zion* so loudly denounced by the descendants of those who devised The Secret Doctrine in Israel, Israel here meaning the Jews as a religious community, most of whom remain quite ignorant of the intricate subversive schemes imputed to them.

The attitude of Jesus Christ to this sect is definitely expressed in the New Testament (see Luke xi and John viii).

Exoteric Judaism, the Jewish religion as practised in the twentieth century, is based on the Old Testament, and on equally ancient commentaries on it, preserved for ages as oral traditions, and known, as above stated, under the general name of *The Talmud.* All copies of this book were ordered to be burned by Philip IV, the Fair, King of France, in 1306, but the book survived the holocaust.

We know that the Jewish God is not the father of all men and the ideal of love, justice and mercy, like the Christian God, or even like Ahura-Mazda or Brahma. On the contrary, he is the God of vengeance down to the fourth generation, just and merciful only to his own people, but foe to all other nations, denying them human rights and commanding their enslavement that Israel might appropriate their riches and rule over them.

The following quotations will serve to illustrate this point:

"And when the Lord thy God shall deliver them before thee; thou shalt smite them, and utterly destroy them; thou shalt make no covenant with them, nor shew mercy unto them." Deut. vii, 2.

"For thou art a holy people unto the Lord thy God: the Lord thy God hath chosen thee to be a special people unto himself, above all people that are upon the face of the earth."—Deut. vii, 6.

The Talmud comments upon it: "You are human beings, but the nations of the world are not human beings but beasts." Baba Mecia 114, 6.

On the house of the Goy (non-Jew) one looks as on the fold of cattle." Tosefta, Erubin viii.

From The Talmud (a prayer said on the eve of Passover, to the present day) "We beg Thee, 0 Lord, indict Thy wrath on the nations not believing in Thee, and not calling on Thy name. Let down Thy wrath on them and inflict them with Thy wrath. Drive the m away in Thy wrath and crush them into pieces. Take away, O Lord, all bone from them. In a moment indict all disbelievers. Destroy in a moment all foes of Thy nation. Draw out with the root, disperse and ruin unworthy nations. Destroy them! Destroy them immediately, in this very moment!" (*Pranajtis; Christianus in Talmudas Judeorum*, quotations from: *Synagoga Juda*ica, p. 212. *Minhagin*, p. 23. *Crach Chaim* 480 Hagah).

"When one sees inhabited houses of the 'Goy' one says, 'The Lord will destroy the house of the proud'. And when one sees them destroyed he says, 'The Lord God of Vengeance has revealed himself' (*The Babylonian Talmud*, Berachot 58, 6.)

"Those who do not own Torah and the prophets must all be killed. Who has power to kill them, let him kill them openly with the sword, if not, let him use artifices till they are done away with." (*Schulchan Aruch: Choszen Hamiszpat*, 425, 50).

The Jewish Sages soon understood that Christ's way of commenting upon the old Law introduced, instead of hatred towards foreign nations, brotherly feelings and equality of all men in the face of God, thus denying the Jews their privileged position as masters of the world.

At the same time, Christ's reforming the very primitive and rough moral ideas of the Old Testament, deprived the Jews of their very convenient-in-the-battle-of-life, unscrupulous, double morality. Thence the Jewish hatred for the Christian faith is conspicuous in the following quotations from Talmudic sources:

"The estates of the Goys are like wilderness, who first settles in them has a right to them. (*Baba Batra*, 54 b.)

"The property of the Goys is like a thing without a master." (*Schulchan Aruch: Choszen Hamiszpat,* 156, 5).

"If a Jew has struck his spade into the ground of the Goy, he has become the master of the whole." (*Baba Batra,* 55 a.)

In order to enhance the authority of the Old Testament equally recognized by the Christians, while simultaneously augmenting that o the Talmud and the Rabbis, its commentators and authors teach:

"In the law (the Bible) are things more or less important, but the words of the Learned in the Scripture are always important.

"It is more wicked to protest the words of the rabbis than of Torah" (*Miszna, Sanhedryn* xi, 3.) "Who changes the words of the rabbis ought to die." (*Erubin*, 21, b.) "The decisions of the Talmud are words of the living God. Jehovah himself asks the opinion of earthly rabbis when there are difficult affairs in heaven." (Rabbi Menachem, *Comments for the Fifth Book.*)

"Jehovah himself in heaven studies the Talmud, standing: he has such respect for that book." (Tr. Mechilla).

To enhance the dignity of religions dogmas the following commandments are given:

"That the Jewish nation is the only nation selected by God, while all the remaining ones are contemptible and hateful.

"That all property of other nations belongs to the Jewish nation, which consequently is entitled to seize upon it without any scruples."

"That an orthodox Jew is not bound to observe principles of morality towards people of other nations, and on the contrary, he even ought to act against morality, if it were profitable for himself or for the interest of Jews in general."

"A Jew may rob a Goy (Goy means unclean, and is the disparaging name for a non-Jew), he may cheat him over a bill, which should not be perceived by him, otherwise the name of God would become dishonoured." (*Schulchan Aruch, Choszen Hamiszpat*, 348.)

"Should a Goy to whom a Jew owed some money die without his heirs knowing about the debt, the Jew is not bound to pay the debt." (*Schulchan Aruch, Choszen Hamiszpat* 283, 1.)

"The son of Noah, who would steal a farthing ought to be put to death, but an Israelite is allowed to do injury to a goy; where it is written, Thou shalt not do injury to thy neighbour, is not said, Thou shalt not do injury to a goy." (*Miszna, Sanhedryn*, 57.)

"A thing lost by a goy may not only be kept by the man who found it, but it is forbidden to give it back to him." (*Schulchan Aruch, Choszen Hamiszpat*. 266, 1.)

"Who took an oath in the presence of the goys, the robbers, and the custom-house officer, is not responsible." (*Tosefta Szebnot*, 11.)

"In order to annul marriages, oaths and promises, a Jew must go to the rabbi, and if he is absent, he must call three other Jews, and say to them that he is sorry to have done it, and they say, 'Thou art allowed to'." (*Schulchan Aruch*, 2, 1. 247.)

The Kol Nidre prayer on the Day of Judgment, that acquits beforehand from the nonfulfilment of all kinds of oaths and vows, is given here.

"All vows, oaths, promises, engagements, and swearing, which, beginning this very day of reconciliation, we intend to vow, promise, swear, and bind ourselves to fulfil, we are sorry for already, and they shall be annulled, acquitted, annihilated, abolished, valueless, unimportant, our vow shall be no vows, and our oaths no oaths at all."(*Schulchan Aruch*, edit. I., 136).

"If a goy wants a Jew to stand witness against a Jew at the Court of Law, and the Jew could give fair evidence, he is forbidden to do it, but if a Jew wants a Jew to be a witness in a similar case against a goy, he may do it." (*Schulchan Aruch, Choszen Hamiszpat*, 28 art, 3 and 4.)

"Should a Jew inform the goyish authorities that another Jew has much money, and the other will suffer a loss through it, he must give him remuneration." (*Schulchan Aruch. - Ch. Ha.*, 338.)

"If there is no doubt that someone thrice betrayed the Jews, or caused that their money passed to the goys, a means and wise council must be found to do away with him."

"Every one must contribute to the expense of the community (Kahal) in order to do away with the traitor." (*Ibid.* 163, 1.)

"It is permitted to kill a Jewish denunciator everywhere it is permitted to kill him before he has denounced.... though it is necessary to warn him and say, 'Do not denounce'. But should he say, 'I will denounce,' he must be killed, and he who accomplishes it first will have the greater merit." (*Ibid.* 388, 10.)

"How to interpret the word 'robbery'. A goy is forbidden to steal, rob, or take women slaves, etc., from a goy or from a Jew, but he (a Jew) is not forbidden to do all this to a goy." (*Tosefta, Aboda Zara*, viii, 5.)

"If a goy killed a goy or a Jew he is responsible, but if a Jew killed a goy he is not responsible." (*Ibid.* viii, 5.)

The authors of the Talmud, having issued this horrible moral code, that acquits all kinds of crimes, in order to make easier the strife with foreigners to their own nation, understood the necessity of keeping its contents a secret and thus legislated:

"To communicate anything to a goy about our religious relations would be equal to the killing of all the Jews, for if the goys knew what we teach about them, they would kill us openly." (*Book of Libbre David*, 37.)

"It is forbidden to disclose the secrets of the Law. He who would do it would be as guilty as if he destroyed the whole world" (*Jaktu Chadasz*, 171, 2). The restrictions and commandments bearing this in view were raised to the dignity of dogmas of faith. It is not astonishing that in face of such prohibitions the secrets of the Talmud have been so little known to other nations, especially to the Western ones, and till the present day, even the most progressive and citizen-like Jews think the disclosure of the principles of the Talmud a proof of the most outrageous intolerance, and an attack on the Jewish religion.

In order to separate the Jewish nation from all others, and thus prevent it from mixing with them, and losing their national peculiarities, a great many precepts of the ritual and rules for every-day life, prejudices and superstitions, the remainder of the times of barbarism and obscurity, have been gathered in the Talmud and consecrated as canons. The precepts observed by Eastern Jews till the present day deride even the most simple notions of culture and hygiene. For instance they enjoin:

"If a Jew be called to explain any part of the rabbinic books, he only ought to give a false explanation, that he might not, by behaving differently, become an accomplice in betraying this information. Who will violate this order shall be put to death." (*Libbre David*, 37.)

"It is forbidden to disclose the secrets of the Law."

"One should and must make false oath, when the goys ask if our books contain anything against them. Then we are bound to state on oath that there is nothing like that." (*Szaalot-Utszabot. The book of Jored' a*, 17.)

"Every goy who studies Talmud, and every Jew who helps him in it, ought to die." (*Sanhedryn* 59 a. *Aboda Zora* 8–6. *Szagiga* 13.)

"The ears of the goys are filthy, their baths, houses, countries are filthy." (*Tosefta Mikwat*, v. 1.)

"A boy-goy after nine years and one day old, and a girl after three years and one day old, are considered filthy." (*Pereferkowicz: Talmud* t. v., p. 11.)

These principles afford an explanation of the action of governments in excluding Jews from judicial and military positions. They also explain that mysterious phenomenon known as Antisemitism.

In his *Manual of Freemasonry* Richard Carlile makes the following observations:[46]

"The disposition of the mistaken Jew is to monopolise his portion of the Sacred Scriptures as a charm or benefit prepared and presented to his people in their sectarian character.

"That there was no such nation as the Israelites, is a truth found in the consideration that they are not mentioned beyond the Bible in any records whatever. Egypt knew them not, Persia knew them not, Hindostan knew them not, Scythia knew them not, Phoenicia knew them not, Greece knew them not, as a nation. And in the first general notice that we have of the Jews, they are introduced to the world as a sect, or a series of sects, being Pharisees, Sadducees, and Essenes; and in that general notice, beyond that sort of mistaken allegorical history which Josephus has copied from the books of the Old Testament, and which is not otherwise corroborated, and no better authority than the book of the Old Testament, there is no presentation of the Jews as the descendants of a larger nation of Israelites; as a religious or philosophical sect of distinction, mixed up with, and found in real human history, they are not to be traced higher than the century before the Christian era. It is satisfactory to be able to show the origin of anything, for such a knowledge is a common passion and curiosity among mankind; and I think the Rev. Robert Taylor has discovered and developed the origin of the titles of Hebrew, Israelite, and Jew.[47]

"Hebrew, Israelite, and Jew, are Syriac, Phoenician and Egyptian terms used in the mysterious degrees; and it would be as reasonable to argue that the Freemasons are a dispersed nation, as that the Jews are, or were, a dispersed nation. The Rev. Mr. Taylor has beautifully explained this in his discourses.[48]

"The scenes and characters of the mysterious drama, as found in the Eleusinian Orgies of Greece, were:

Eleusis.—The Advent, or coming-in light—the birth and character of the subject of the drama—the title of the whole play or mystery.

Hierophant.—The Expounder of the Mysteries, the High Priest, the Pope, the Archbishop.

Hupereet.—The Minister, or Ordinary Priest.

Diaconos.—The Deacon, or Lower Officer.

Diadochos.—The Torch-bearer.

Photagogue.—The Bringer-in of Light.

Autoptos.—The Candidate admitted to see the sight. The visitor of the Temple—the Church and Chapel goer.

Autopsy.—The sight itself.

Hebrew.—The initiated Candidate who had passed through all the degrees of the mystery.

Teleios.—The adept, or perfected.

Israelite.—God-seer, purified from all guile.

Jew.—The God himself, or the mysterious perfection and deification of the human character.

"The whole type of what may be made of human nature by cultivation of mind, which is the conditional promise of paradise, or kingdom of heaven. This is the revelation of all the mysteries."

Carlile further states[49] "We are prepared with historical disproofs of the existence of such a people as Israelites or Jews as a nation. They were a religious or philosophical sect, who had been made adepts in the higher Pagan Mysteries: a sect among nations; but not a nation among sects."

Judaism sanctions Gnosticism which is further elaborated in their books of the Cabala. For further study of this subject we refer the reader to Chapter XIII.

CHAPTER VIII

ORPHEISM AND THE PAGAN MYSTERIES

THERE IS NO greater or more erudite authority than Fabre d'Olivet (1768–1825) on Orpheus or Dyonisius[50] and to such an eminent source, among many others, must the reader be referred.

The feats of the white Dorian race of Greece and the mysticism of its priests of Thrace as well as the centuries-long rivalry between the solar or male cult and the lunar or female cult, have provided inexhaustible sources of religious and literary lore.

The legendary birth of Orpheus adorned with his descent from Apollo, his flight from Thrace, initiation in the temple of Memphis and return to his own country as a high adept of the most profound mysteries, constitute but the first part of his life.

After his return to Greece, he united the cults of Dyonisius and Zeus, reformed that of Bacchus and instituted the Mysteries. To him was allotted the task of reducing the power of the Bacchantes, priestesses of Hecate, by a magic superior to theirs, and their vengeance, which caused his death, has been the theme of many a poet.

One follows the evolution of Greece from Orpheus to Pythagoras, Socrates and Plato and one searches for the remnants of Egyptian esoterism in the utmost recesses of the Delphic temples and in the ceremonies of initiation to the Eleusinian mysteries. These, having still been practised until the Emperor Theodosius I, the Great, (379–395) prohibited them and ordered the destruction of the Eleusinian Temple, much material is available for their description.

We are indebted to Bishop Lavington, an erudite member of the Anglican Church, for a graphic description of the perversion to which they gave rise, but we preface this article with that author's apology to the reader, which, like the text of most of this chapter, we quote verbatim from the Bishop's book *The Enthusiasm of Methodists and Papists compared*, Part III:

"We wallow indeed in the mire, by publishing these things. But lest anyone should fall into the mire of these heretics, from mere ignorance, I purposely and knowingly defile my own mouth, and the ears of the auditors, because it is beneficial. For it is much better to hear absurdity and filthiness in accusing others, than to fall into them out of ignorance. Much better to be informed of the mire, than, for want of information, to fall into it."

Bishop Lavington then proceeds with the explanation of the Pagan Mysteries from which we quote:[51] "The Gods and Goddesses each had their special mysteries. Even Cotytto, the Goddess of Turpitude, had her rites and devotees.

"A high opinion of the Mysteries was very far from being general, or received by great and good Persons. Those great Men, Agesilaus and Epaminondas, would not submit to an Initiation The Athenians asking Diogenes to be initiated because such had the Precedency in a future State; he replied, 'Ridiculous thing! that Agesilaus and Epaminondas must rowl in dirt; and every Scoundrel initiated, such as Patecion the Thief, be happy in the Elysian Fields'. Nor shall we entertain the better Notion of the Mysteries when we find so wise and good a Man as Socrates refusing initiation. For which (though perhaps he had stronger) he gives this Reason: 'If the Mysteries were bad, he should not be able to conceal the Secret, but must discourage every one from Initiation; and if good, Humanity would oblige him to discover it for the public Benefit'.

"Rut whether the Mysteries were good or bad, Authors are pretty well agreed as to the preparatory Ceremonies, and manner of Initiation:

whereby they were to Represent, and Act over again, the Actions and passions of the Deities, for whose Honour the Mysteries were instituted.

"That Initiation might seem a venerable and solemn Thing, the Devotees were taught to qualify themselves by Prayer to the Demons, Fastings, Watchings, Confession to the Priest, and other Lustrations. We read in Plutarch, 'that fasting is to precede the Mysteries of Ceres, and that Confession was required;' Antalcidas being examined by the Priest, in order to his initiation, what grievous crimes he had committed, made Answer, 'If I have been guilty of any such Crime, the Gods know it already'. The Confession was a trick of the Masters of the Ceremonies to get the people under their Girdle.

"Tertullian says, 'As to the superstition of the Eleusinian Mysteries, what they conceal is the Shame of them. Therefore they make the Admission tortuous, take Time in the Initiation, set a Seal on the Tongue, and instruct the Epoptae for five Years, to raise a high Opinion of them by Delay and Expectation. But all the Divinity in the sacred Domes, the Whole of what they aspire to, what sealeth the Tongue, is this: *Simulacrum membri Virilis revelatur*. But for a Cover of their Sacrilege, they pretend these Figures are only a mystical Representation of venerable Nature.' "The original Reason of such figures being exposed to View, and had in Veneration, in the Mysteries, we learn from others. Clemens Alexandrinus giveth a full account of this religion of the Mysteries, too prolix to be transcribed; 'Of their wicked Institution, Cruelty, Stupidity, Madness, making Goddesses of Harlots, corrupting Mankind: the Mysteries of Ceres are nothing but representations of incestuous Deities: their ridiculous Exclamations upon Admission were, I have eat out of the Timbrel, I have drank out of the Cymbal, I have carried the Chest, I have crept into the secret Chamber. 'In the Chest *Pudendum Bacchi inclusum erat.—Cistam et veretrum nova Religione colenda tradunt.*—It is a shame to mention the filthy circumstances in the story of Ceres...

"The Pagan Mysteries being of such an immoral Nature, and Tendency, it might justly be thought strange, were no Notice taken of them in the Holy Scriptures. And therefore, though such an Enquiry might carry us into too great a Length, yet I shall not entirely pass it over. There can be then little Doubt, but they are pointed out by St. Paul: 'It is a Shame even to speak of those Things that are done of them in Secret'. And where Christianity is termed the Mystery of Godliness, it is set, I am persuaded, in Opposition, not only to the Mystery of Iniquity that was to work in the Christian World, but likewise to the preceding Mysteries among the Gentiles. Nor is it improbable, that the Apostle writeth in direct Opposition to the Appearances, Pretences, and Impostures of those false Divinities: Without Controversy great is the Mystery of Godliness…

"In the Old Testament, Deut. xxiii. 17 (not indeed in the Hebrew, but in the Septuagint) after the Words, 'There shall be no Whore,—nor Sodomites of the Sons of Israel,' we find added Words of this Import, 'There shall not be an Initiator, nor an Initiated, of the Sons or Daughters of Israel'. 'Tis possible this additional Clause may have been inserted by the Seventy, by Way of Interpretation of the preceding Words. They knew the Nature of the Mysteries full well; and we are led to this Meaning by the Impurities forbidden, and by the Price of the Dog in the next Verse; the Egyptian God Anubis being usually figured with a Dog's Head. (Edit. Daniel. Schol.)

"We may observe also, that Philo the Jew (*de Sacrific.*) expressly ranketh the Prohibition of the Mysteries among the Laws of Moses. 'The Law, saith he, expressly excludeth the whole of the Mysteries, their Inchantments and execrable Scurrilities, from the Holy Ordinances: not permitting those educated in her Society to celebrate such Heathen Rites; nor, depending on such mystical Ceremonies, to disregard the Truth; and to follow the Works of Night and Darkness, omitting what deserveth the Light and the Day. Let none therefore among the Disciples of Moses either initiate, or be initiated: it being equally wicked either to teach, or to learn the Mysteries.

'Tis generally the Case with them, that no good Person is initiated; but Thieves, and Pirates, and mad Gangs of abominable and immodest women; after parting with their Money to the initiating Priests."

Several of the Fathers have taken Notice of the same Passage in the Septuagint, and explained it in the same manner.

"For further Proof of the Turpitude in the Mysteries of Isis and Osiris, and that it was so from the Beginning, we need only consult Diodorus Siculus, Lib. I. 'Isis being overwhelmed with Grief for the Loss of her Husband Osiris, took particular Care in deifying him to consecrate his Pudenda; which she ordered to be peculiarly honoured and adored in the Mysteries. And the same holy Institution was observed with the same Ceremonies, when carried into Greece by Orpheus: where the common People, partly from Ignorance, and partly from a Love of the new god (Phallus), were very fond of being initiated'.

"Much more might be collected (even from initiated Authors, however, generally shy) concerning the infamous Origin of the Mysteries, which I pass over "The celebration of the Eleusinian Mysteries commenced in Greece about 1400 years before Christ but 'whenever or however they were brought into Greece, and transferred to the Honour of Ceres and Proserpina, they were of the same Nature, and observed with equally chaste Ceremonies, with those of Isis…'

"One contrivance for 'giving the Initiated a Sight of the Divinities, was by means of a Looking-glass, wherein none could see their own Faces, but had a clear View of the Gods and Goddesses'. This we have from Pausanias: and Eusebius relates the same Thing.

So easily might weak People, and under the utmost Astonishment, be deluded by Figures behind a glass, in a proper Habit and Posture ; and especially by living Persons, personating the Deities in any Manner they thought fit.

'As a proof of the Indecencies, Sozomen writeth, that Theophilus, Bishop of Alexandria, egregiously ridiculed and exposed to public View the shameful Figures belonging to the Mysteries, the Phallus, etc. which he brought out of the Pagan Temple. For which the enraged Heathens raised a Tumult, and massacred a great Number of the Christians'. Even the initiated Pausanias (notwithstanding his usual Reservedness) sometimes blurts out a little too much, and intimates something shameful:' as frequent assignations; the proneness of the religious Females to venery; a Mixture of the Obscene and Miraculous; the continuance of the Eleusinian Festival for a week; on the third Day whereof all Males, even the Dogs, are excluded; but the next Day the Men are admitted among them, when they pass the Time in sporting, and light Discourse; the Amours of Ceres, of a very strange Kind; with the Secrecy enjoined; The Obscenities in the Mysteries of Cupid, and suitable Hymns'.

"A man initiated, and under an Oath of Silence, could not well have discovered more of the true Nature of the Mysteries, and the Reason why they ought not to be divulged. We are assured too, that one Day of the Eleusinian Festival was set apart for the Rites of Venus and Cupid, and another for those of Bacchus: both of which were confessedly beyond measure abominable. Nor will our Opinion be more favourable, when we remember what Athenœus writes;' Apelles, being extremely desirous of drawing a Venus from the famous Phryne, could find no Opportunity of seeing her naked, without going to the Eleusinian and Neptunian Games ; where she stripped herself in the Sight of all the Men, and went into the sea to wash herself...'

"I apprehend therefore that no great Stress is to be laid upon those initiated Authors, who have thought themselves obliged to say nothing but what was good of the Mysteries; or have talked of the Unity of the Deity, as the great Secret of them; perhaps to avoid the Shame of being thought Dupes to a foolery, or inquisitive into something worse."[52]

On the same subject the Chevalier de Ramsay, reputed founder of Scottish Rites, writes the following:[53] "About the fifteenth Olympiad, six hundred Years before the Christian era, the Greeks having lost the traditional Knowledge of the Orientals, began to lay aside the Doctrine of the Ancients, and to reason about the Divine Nature from Prejudices which their Senses and Imagination suggested. Anaximander lived at that time, and was the first that set himself to destroy the Belief of a supreme Intelligence, in order to account for everything from the Action of blind Matter, which by necessity assumes all Sorts of Forms. He was followed by Leucippus, Democritus, Epicurus, Strato, Lucretius, and all the School of the Atomical Philosophers.

"Pythagoras, Anaxagoras, Socrates, Plato, Aristotle, and all the great Men of Greece, opposed this impious Doctrine, and endeavoured to prove the ancient Theology of the Orientals. These Philosophers of a superior

Genius observed in Nature, Motion, Thought and Design. And as the Idea of Matter includes none of these three Properties, they inferred from thence, that there was another Substance different from Matter.

"Greece being thus divided into two Sects, they disputed for a long time, without either Party being convinced. At length about the 120th Olympiad Pyrrho formed a third Sect whose great Principle was to doubt everything, and determine nothing. All the Atomists who had laboured in vain to find out a Demonstration of their false Principles, presently struck in with the Pyrrhonian Sect. They ran wildly into the System of universal Doubt, and carried it almost to such an Excess of Frenzy, that they doubted of the clearest and most sensible Truths. They maintained without any Allegory, that everything we see is only an Illusion, and that the whole Series of Life is but a perpetual Dream of which those of the Night are only so many Images.

"At last Zeno set up a fourth School about the 130th Olympiad. This Philosopher endeavoured to reconcile the Disciples of Democritus with those of Plato, by maintaining that the first Principle was indeed an infinite Wisdom, but his Essence was only a pure Aether, or a subtile Light, which diffused itself everywhere, to give Life, Motion, and Reason to all Beings.

"In these last Ages the modern Freethinkers have done nothing but revive the ancient Errors. Jordano Bruno, Vannini and Spinoza, have vamped up the monstrous System of Anaximander; and the last of the three has endeavoured to dazzle weak Minds, by dressing it up in a geometrical Form.

"Some Spinosists, finding that they were every Moment at a Loss for Evidence in the pretended Demonstrations of their Master, are fallen into a senseless sort of Scepticism, called Egomism, where every one fancies himself to be the only Being that exists.

"Mr. Hobbes and several other Philosophers, without setting up for Atheists, have ventured to maintain, that Thought and Extension are Properties of the same Substance.

"Descartes, F. Malebranche, Leibnitz, Dr. Bentley, Clarke, and several Philosophers of a Genius equally Mile and profound, have endeavoured to refute these Errors, and brought Arguments to support the ancient Theology. Besides the Proofs which are drawn from the Effects, they have insisted on others drawn from the Idea of the first Cause. They shew plainly that the Reasons of believing, are infinitely stronger than any Arguments there are for doubting. This is all that can be expected in metaphysical Discussions." The History of former times is like that of our own Human Understanding takes almost the same Forms in different Ages, and loses its Way in the same Labyrinths."

CHAPTER IX

THE DRUIDS

WE HEARD, IN 1928, of a "Druid" celebration at Stonehenge. Shortly afterwards we read of another, an initiation ceremony, at Penzance where "12 bards of Britain, including Sir Arthur Quiller-Couch, the author, were initiated by the Archdruid of Wales into a sect revived after a lapse of 2000 years."[54]

Some of us might prefer the lapse to have continued and as the subject of the Druid Mysteries is here relevant we quote verbatim the chapter entitled "The Druids" from Mr. Charles William Heckethorn's interesting book *Secret Societies of All Ages and Countries*: The secret doctrines of the Druids were much the same as those of the Gymnosophists and Brahmins of India, the Magi of Persia, the priests of Egypt, and of all other priests of antiquity. Like them, they had two sets of religious doctrines, exoteric and esoteric. Their rites were practised in Britain and Gaul, though they were brought to a much greater perfection in the former country, where the Isle of Anglesey was considered their chief seat. The word Druid is generally supposed to be derived from δρυς "an oak", which tree was particularly sacred among them, though its etymology may also be found in the Gaelic word Druidh, 'a wise man' or 'magician'.

"Their temples, wherein the sacred fire was preserved, were generally situate on eminences and in dense groves of oaks, and assumed various forms.

"The adytum or ark of the mysteries was called a cromlech, and was used as the sacred pastos,[55] or place of regeneration. It consisted of three upright stones, as supporters of a broad, flat stone laid across them on the top, so as to form a small cell. Kit Cotey's House, in Kent, was such a pastos. Considerable space, however, was necessary for the machinery of initiation in its largest and most comprehensive scale. Therefore, the Coer Sidi, where the mysteries of Druidism were performed, consisted of a range of buildings, adjoining the temple, containing apartments of all sizes, cells, vaults, baths, and long and artfully-contrived passages, with all the apparatus of terror used on these occasions. Most frequently these places were subterranean.

"The system of Druidism embraced every religious and philosophical pursuit then known in these islands. The rites bore an undoubted reference to astronomical facts. Their chief deities are reducible to two,—a male and a female, the great father and mother, Hu and Ceridwen, distinguished by the same characteristics as belonged to Osiris and Isis, Bacchus and Ceres, or any other supreme god and goddess representing the two principles of all being. The grand periods of initiation were quarterly, and determined by the course of the sun, and his arrival at the equinoctial and solstitial points. But the time of annual celebration was May-eve, when fires were kindled on all the cairns and cromlechs throughout the island, which burned all night to introduce the sports of May-day, whence all the national sports formerly or still practised, date their origin. Round these fires choral dances were performed in honour of the sun, who, at this season, was figuratively said to rise from his tomb. The festival was licentious, and continued till the luminary ha d attained his meridian height, when priests and attendants retired to the woods, where the most disgraceful orgies were perpetrated. But the solemn initiations were performed at midnight, and contained three degrees, the first or lowest being the Eubates, the second the Bards, and the third the Druids. The candidate was first placed in the pastos bed, or coffin, where his symbolical death represented the death of Hu, or the sun; and his restoration in the third degree symbolized the resurrection of the sun. He had to undergo trials and tests of courage similar to those practised in the mysteries of other countries, and which therefore need not be detailed here.

"The Druids taught the doctrine of one supreme being, a future state of rewards and punishments, the immortality of the soul and a metempsychosis... Their doctrines were chiefly those of Pythagoras.

"Their authority in many cases exceeded that of the monarch. They were, of course, the sole interpreters of religion, and consequently superintended all sacrifices; for no private person was allowed to offer a sacrifice without their sanction. They possessed the power of excommunication, which was the most horrible punishment that could be inflicted next to that of death, and from the effects of which the highest magistrate was not exempt. The great council of the realm was not competent to declare war or conclude peace without their concurrence. They determined all disputes by a final and unalterable decision, and had the power of inflicting the punishment of death. And, indeed, their altars streamed with the blood of human victims. Holocausts of men, women, and children, enclosed in large towers of wicker-work, were sometimes sacrificed as a burnt-offering to their superstitions, which were, at the same time, intended to enhance the consideration of the priests, who were an ambitious race delighting in blood. The Druids, it is said, preferred such as had been guilty of theft, robbery, or other crimes, as most acceptable to their gods; but when there was a scarcity of criminals, they made no scruple to supply their place with innocent persons. These dreadful sacrifices were offered by the Druids, for the public, on the eve of a dangerous war, or in the time of any national calamity; and also for particular persons of high rank, when they were afflicted with any dangerous disease.

"The priestesses, clothed in white, and wearing a metal girdle, foretold the future from the observation of natural phenomena, but more especially from human sacrifices. For them was reserved the frightful task of putting to death the prisoners taken in war, and individuals condemned by the Druids ; and their auguries were drawn from the manner in which the blood issued from the many wounds inflicted, and also from the smoking entrails. Many of these priestesses maintained a perpetual virginity, others gave themselves up to the most luxurious excesses.

"As the Romans gained ground in these islands the power of the Druids gradually declined; and they were finally assailed by Suetonius Paulinus, governor of Britain under Nero, A. D. 61, in their stronghold, the Isle of Anglesey, and entirely defeated, the conqueror consuming many of them in the fires which they had kindled for burning the Roman prisoners they had expected to make—a very just retaliation upon these sanguinary priests. But though their dominion was thus destroyed, many of their religious practices continued much longer; and so late as the eleventh century, in the reign of Canute, it was necessary to forbid the people to worship the sun, moon, fires, etc. Certainly many of the practices of the Druids are still adhered to in Freemasonry; and some writers on this order endeavour to show that it was established soon after the edict of Canute, and that as thereby the Druidical worship was prohibited in *toto*, the strongest oaths were required to bind the initiated to secrecy."

There is no mystery as to the existence in Berlin of the "Druidenorden" today. It is a branch of Freemasonry and its Sovereign Grand Master, until late, was Dr. Hübbe-Schleiden.

CHAPTER X

CHRISTIANITY

TO DEFINE CHRISTIANITY, one could hardly do better than use the words of Frederic W. Farrar, Canon of Westminster and Chaplain to Queen Victoria, who in 1874 wrote a *Life of Christ.* In his preface are the following lines:

"We study the sacred books of all the great religions of the world; we see the effect exercised by those religions on the mind of their votaries; and in spite of all the truths which even the worst of the m enshrined, we watch the failure of the mall to produce the inestimable blessings which we have ourselves enjoyed from infancy, which we treasure as dearly as our life, and which we regard as solely due to the spread and establishment of the Christian faith. We read the systems and treatises of ancient philosophy, and in spite of all the great and noble elements in which they abound, we see their total incapacity to console, or support, or deliver, or regenerate the world. Then we see the light of Christianity dawning like a tender spring day amid the universal and intolerable darkness. From the first, that new religion allies itself with the world's utter feeblenesses, and those feeblenesses it shares; yet without wealth, without learning, without genius, without arms, without anything to dazzle and attract the religion of outcasts and exiles, of fugitives and prisoners—numbering among its earliest converts not many wise, not many noble, not many mighty, but such as the gaoler of Philippi, and the runaway slave of Colossae—with no blessing apparently upon it save such as cometh from above—with no light whatever about it save the light that comes from heaven—it puts to flight kings and their armies; it breathes a new life, and a new hope, and a new and unknown holiness into a guilty and decrepit world. This we see; and we see the work grow, and increase, and become more and more irresistible, and spread 'with the gentleness of a sea that caresses the shore it covers'."

Words fail when attempting to speak of Jesus Christ, the Founder of Christianity. His birth, life and death are known to all. His teaching was public and accessible to the humblest. Long years of learning, awful initiation ceremonies striking terror in the adept's soul were not required from the followers of Christ. Himself, the bearer of that Light which He taught was not to be found in man's earthly nature but was to be sought from without, He invoked God with humble prayer and faith, and performed all miracles.

Therein, is Christ's teaching diametrically opposed to that of the high adepts whose secret doctrine was that man had divinity in himself and could bring it out by exercise of will, by concentration of thought and scientific psychic development. Fear, the predominant feature attendant upon the gaining of knowledge in all other religious systems, was foreign to the adherents of Christ who were repeatedly told: 'Fear not'... 'Be not afraid'. No bonds, no fetters were imposed by Him in the shape of ritualism. Love of God and love of neighbour were the only precepts, Faith and Charity the only means through which the divine Spirit gave man transcendental power over moral evil and physical ills.

No purer and simpler doctrine, no greater knowledge of the communion possible between God and man had ever been given. Yet, within a very short time after the death of Christ, Christian ritualism began to appear. A theological system of dogmas and beliefs was devised, modes of worship elaborated and a hierarchy arose with all its attendant evils. However, the Christian faith, under the lash of persecution, had shown the world the power of Faith and Charity.

And against this power the forces of evil have ever been unfurled. Blow after blow was dealt to the rising church. Both its beliefs and practices were attacked by those who professed other views and worshipped other gods and who designed all schemes to subvert and pervert Christianity. Henceforth, as it has ever been with all religions, the history of Christianity and of Gnosticism will develop side by side, the perversion and destruction of the former being the aims of the latter.

The Tree of Christianity gave forth three main branches, the Catholicism of Rome, Greek Catholicism, and in the XV I Century, Lutherism. The two former bodies remained homogeneous but Lutherism gave birth to innumerable sects all dissenting from the parent church.

CHAPTER XI

MANICHEISM

MANICHEISM IS THE religion of the followers of Manes, a slave who was sold to a widow who freed and adopted him, thus making him the "son of the widow" a name which after him passed to all his followers and is still used in Masonic Lodges.

Of Manicheism, C. W. Olliver, considered an authority on all masonic matters, writes:

"Manicheism was one of the most important attempts to found a universal religion and to reconcile the Christian, Buddhist, and Mazdean with the Greek philosophy. It presented the same syncretic ideas found later among Moslem Druzes and among Sikhs. It failed in the first place because Islam presented a much simpler system in the East, and because in the West Christianity was already developing, in the time of Manes, a religion which aimed at reconciling the Paganism of Italy and Gaul with the ethics of Christ, this presenting a simpler and more familiar faith. But the one achievement of Manes was the creation of the Devil which led to an afterwards unremovable taint throughout religion. Manes was a notable philosopher and religious teacher born about the year A. D. 216, and he was crucified and flayed alive by the Persian Magi under Bahram I in the year A. D. 277. His Persian name was Shuraik, rendered Cubricus in Latin."[56]

He was the slave of the wife of a certain Terebinth who was a disciple of Scythianus of the race of the Sarrasins.

Olliver tells us further that: "His *Acta Archdei* became the Manichean Bible with sundry added epistles. He taught the Mazdean dualism of the powers of light and darkness, as representing good and evil beings, and an asceticism which aimed at the control of all passions. Manes repudiated Judaism, and like the Gnostics, regarded Jehovah as an evil God. The Manicheans were more hated and feared by Catholic Christians than any other sect. They were still in existence in spite of constant persecution as late as our tenth century, and their influence was felt from China to Spain and Gaul. It still lingers in Asia, and among the 'Christians of St. Thomas' in Madras it survived till the fifteenth century. St. Augustine had listened for nine years to Manes, but the Roman Empire felt the force of this system chiefly in A. D. 280. The Romans knew it themselves in A. D. 330, and Faustus became its missionary among them. Many clung to Manicheism till A. D. 440, when Leo the Great found that he must stamp it out if the Roman creed was not to be extinguished. It was the basis of the Paulican heresy, and of that of the Albigenses in the South of France which was only quenched by blood in the thirteenth century.

"The doctrine of Manes can be summed up as follows. He believed in two gods, or, more exactly, principles, the principle of good and that of evil. Before the creation of the world the 'people of darkness' revolted against the God, and God, incapable of with-standing the attack, gave to them a portion of His essence. The people of darkness having within them the principle of evil by their very nature, and the principle of good which they had just acquired, were able to constitute the world, where both these principles are combined, but where the principle of evil predominates as the natural characteristic of its originators. Man is a mixture of two natures, the spiritual being the work of God, the body, and especially sex, the work of the Devil."[57]

Summers, another authority, further explains that "it must be clearly borne in mind that these heretical bodies with their endless ramifications were not merely exponents of erroneous religious and intellectual beliefs by which they morally corrupted all who came under their influence, but they were the avowed enemies of law and order, red-hot anarchists who would stop at nothing to gain their ends. Terrorism and secret murder were their most frequent weapons.... The Manichean system was in truth a simultaneous attack upon the Church and the State, a desperate but well-planned organization to destroy the whole fabric of society, to reduce civilization to chaos."[58]

Manicheism possessed its dogmas, liturgies, devotees, and churches.

But again to quote Olliver: "First and foremost amongst the manifestations of what had become Devil worship we find the Black Mass or Devil Masses of the Middle Ages, from which the ceremonial and ritual of Black Magic are derived. The principle which forms the very essence of the Devil, the idea of opposition, also underlies the whole ceremonial and ritual of Black Magic and Black Masses. Such ideas as repeating prayers backwards, reversing the cross, consecrating obscene or filthy objects, are typical of this sense of opposition or desecration, which is also a recognised form of mental disease. The key-word to the whole of the practices of Black Magic is desecration."[59]

Yet another authority not to be overlooked, namely Abbe Baruel, author of *Memoires pour servir à l'histoire du Jacobinisms* shows the remarkable analogy between the dogmas and rituals of Freemasonry, Templarism and those of Manicheism. Grades concur in number and signs are identical. The mourning for Jacques Molay is a ceremony analogous to that practised by the Manicheans in remembrance of Manes and known as Bema. The term MacBenac still used in Masonic lodges was the reminder of the execution of Manes which all Manichean adepts sought to avenge. The practice of so called Fraternity or Brotherhood was in Manicheism extended only to adepts of the sect, just as it is similarly practised by Freemasons towards one another only.

The question which naturally comes up to one's mind when one follows closely the links of the Manichean chain is this:—Is not Freemasonry, such as we see it today, the full development of the idea of Cubricus or Manes the slave, the apotheosis of Manicheism as achieved by Albert Pike, Sovereign Pontiff of Universal Freemasonry?

CHAPTER XII

WITCHCRAFT

MARGARET ALICE MURRAY, writing in *The Witch-cult in Western Europe* establishes both the phallic and religious character of the "craft", in her remarkable book from which we extract part of the following valuable information:

The deity worshipped by the witches was in some cases Lucifer, as the Good God in opposition to Adonay, the Christian God in His character of the benefactor of humanity, and in other instances Satan, the same spirit, as the Principle of Evil.

This is evident from the various references to their deity adduced in the trials of persons accused of this heresy. In both cases however, the devotees, whether of Lucifer or Satan, were obliged formally to renounce Christ, the Holy Ghost and the Christian God, before embracing the Devil faith which was the logical outgrowth of the Mazdean-Manichean Dualist doctrine of the double divinity.[60]

The God of the witches seems to have been generally represented either as the double faced God Janus or the goat-headed Baphomet, the latter variously modified but usually bearing between the horns on its head the phallic emblem of a lighted candle.

Esoterically, this candle symbolized the sex-force or Kundalini risen to the pineal gland.

Cotton Mather stated that the witches "form themselves after the manner of Congregational Churches," and M. A. Murray gives the following description of their leader:

"The Chief or supreme Head of each district was known to the recorders as the 'Devil'. Below him in each district, one or more officers—according to the size of the district—were appointed by the chief. The officers might be either men or women; their duties were to arrange for meetings, to send out notices, to keep the record of work done, to transact the business of the community, and to present new members. Evidently these persons also noted any likely convert, and either themselves entered into negotiations or reported to the Chief, who then took action as opportunity served. At the Esbats the officer appears to have taken command in the absence of the Grand Master; at the Sabbaths the officers were merely heads of their own Covens, and were known as Devils or Spirits, though recognized as greatly inferior to the Chief. The principal officer acted as clerk at the Sabbath and entered the witches' report in his book; if he were a priest or ordained minister, he often performed part of the religious service; but the Devil himself always celebrated the mass or sacrament."[61]

From Lemoine in *La Tradition,* published 1892, we learn that the garter is the distinctive mark of the witch leader, for a woman shared this honour with the Grand Master as the Grand Mistress and in some cases occupied the office of deacon.

Animal masks seem to have been a popular form of disguise adopted by the witches and wizards attending meetings, and this custom is probably responsible for many of the stories of witch lycanthropy.

Among other obscene and phallic witch-rites was the Black Mass, celebrated by a renegade priest upon the naked body of the adept for whose benefit it was performed. It symbolized the perversion of all the rites of the Catholic church. Black candles instead of white, inverted crosses, chalices containing the blood of new-born infants sacrificed for ritual purposes, urine for holy water, all these were part of the paraphernalia needed, according to historians, to propitiate the Prince of Darkness and his retinue of minor Devils. Besides evocations, casting of spells and sexorgies, devil worship entailed such inanities as desecration of the hosts stolen from catholic churches and the kissing of the Grand Master (devil) on the tail or *membrum virile.*

Only hosts consecrated in Roman Catholic churches could serve for Black Màss purposes as it was essential, in order to achieve desecration, that the miracle of transubstantiation should have taken place. The host had actually to be, not merely to represent, the body and blood of Christ.

As regards the Black Mass, M. Emile Caillet makes the following astute observation in *La Prohibition de L'Occulte*, page 113.

"One may wonder if it was not in order to canalize such an overflow of sacrilege that the church, in the Middle Ages, tolerated the 'Feast of Fools', a last vestige of the saturnalia of Ancient Greece. Before the altar, upon the communion table, writes C. Lenient,[62] were spread pell mell, grilled hogs puddings, sausages, playing cards and dice. For perfumes, old shoe-leather burned in the incense burners. Even the text of the divine service... becomes the butt of an interminable parody..., a confused jumble of jests and nonsense, of grotesque alleluias and latin buffooneries.... an indescribable charivari of cat calls, cries and whistles. etc. A few days afterwards the church, purged of all these impurities, washed and cleaned, resumed its usual appearance; God again became master of His Altar; the flood of human folly had passed!"

In 1484, Pope Innocent VII I issued a bull against the craft couched in the following terms:

"It has come to our ears that numbers of both sexes do not avoid to have intercourse with demons, Incubi and Succubi; and that by their sorceries, and by their incantations, charms and conjurations, they suffocate, extinguish, and cause to perish the births of women, the increase of animals, the corn of the ground, the grapes of the vineyard and the fruit of the trees, as well as men, women, flocks, herds, and other various kinds of animals, vines and apple trees, grass, corn and other fruits of the earth; making and procuring that men and women, flocks and herds and other animals shall suffer and be tormented both from within and without, so that men beget not, nor women conceive; and they impede the conjugal action of men and women."

Eliphas Levi, in *Histoire de la Magie*, (p. 116) gives the following explanation of the supposed origin of "elementals" known by spiritists as "dwellers on the threshold."

He states that; "according to the best authorities, these spirits (larves) possess an ethereal body formed of the vapour of blood. That is why they seek blood and why they were supposed, formerly, to feed on the smoke of sacrifices.

"They are the Incubi and Succubi, the monstrous children of impure dreams.

"When sufficiently condensed to be visible, they are only a vapour coloured by the reflection of a picture and, having no independent life, they imitate the life of him who evokes them as the shadow does the body." They generally manifest around the persons of idiots and beings devoid of morality whose isolation has led them to develop irregular habits.

"Owing to the feeble cohesion of the parts of their fantastic bodies, they fear the open air, fire, and above all, the point of swords, and as they live only by the life of those who have created or evoked them, they become the vaporous appendices of the real body of their parents. So it can happen that an injury inflicted on them might actually react upon the parent body, as the unborn child is really wounded or disfigured by an impression made upon its mother.

"These elementals draw the vital heat from persons in good health and quickly exhaust those who are weak.

"They are the source of the stories of vampires, stories only too true and periodically recurrent, as everyone knows.

"That is why one feels a chill of the atmosphere when approaching mediums who are persons obsessed by these spirits that never manifest in the presence of anyone able to unveil the mystery of their monstrous birth. They are children of an exalted imagination or unbalanced mentality…"

In politics, throughout the ages, witchcraft, as practised by subversive sects, has played a prominent part.

Illustrations of this are to be found in the case of the North Berwick Witches who were tried for treason in 1592 when their Devil or Grand Master, Francis Stewart, Earl of Bothwell, attempted to supplant James VI as King of Scotland. The Black Masses held by the infamous Abbe

Guibourg for Madame de Montespan, with the object of regaining for her the favour of Louis XIV, are famous in history.

Eliphas Levi, the great initiate, has thus defined the aims of magic and witchcraft:

"To deceive the peoples for the purpose of exploiting them, to enslave them and delay their progress, or prevent it even if possible, such is the crime of black magic."[63]

Proof of the foregoing devil worship and contact with spirits or devils is found in history, even as late as 1819 when we read that; "The Devil met Margaret Nin-Gilbert etc..." Studying the history of the Mopses in 1761 we find its Grand Masters, Grand Mistresses and Deacons, adorned with the distinctive "Garter" of the witch, performing the ceremonial of kissing the Devil's tail as part of the ritual of 18th Century Masonry. The "Coven" of the Middle Ages is the Masonic "Lodge" of today, but the "Craft" remains the "Craft".

CHAPTER XIII

THE GNOSTICS (THE HERETICS)

GNOSTICISM, LIKE THE Ancient Mysteries, was founded on Spiritism, their mediums giving instructions purporting to come from the Gods or Spirits.

In the Christian era, one of the earliest prominent Gnostics was Simon Magus, a Jew and an adept of the sect of Dosithians.

This article is composed of certain passages transcribed verbatim from *The Moravians Compared and Detected by Lavington*. (See pages XIII, 59, 105 to 109 and 133).

Among the successive disciples of Simon Magus were—Basilides, Valentinius, Carpocrates, Marcus, Marcion, Cerdo, Epiphanes, Montanus, etc., and according to Bishop Lavington, "these were Heretics, and, that they were Heretics of the worst Kind that ever defiled and disgraced the Christian Name, is allowed by all Denominations of Christians.

"Some of these lived in the first Century and even in the Apostles' Days, but the second Century was most fruitful in the Production of this Generation of Vipers and we must receive our Knowledge of their abominable Tenets from the early Ecclesiastical writers such as Irenoeus... Epiphanius... Theodoret... and many others...

"The Spirit among these Heretics went by different Names, Ogdoas, Sophia, Terra, Jerusalem and Lord in the masculine Gender:—is particularly called both Prunicus and Prunica; Mother Prunica the bold, and

Mother Achamoth:—Their Mother is a Woman from a Woman. Sometimes their celestial Beings are neither Male nor Female: sometimes interchangeably either male or female.

"Such was the Excellency of their Knowledge and Illumination, who arrogantly styled themselves Gnostics that they are superior to Peter or Paul or any of Christ's other disciples. They only, have drunk up the supreme Knowledge, are above Principalities and Powers, secure of Salvation: and for that very Reason are free to debauch Women, or indulge all manner of Licentiousness—This Knowledge is of itself perfect Redemption, and sufficient."—"Simon Magus, who taught that his Harlot Helena was the Holy Ghost, instituted certain foul and infamous Mysteries inexpressibly filthy and had Assemblies equally filthy to celebrate them: These being the Mysteries of Life, and of the most perfect Knowledge."

"The Carpocratians... practised all manner of Philtres and Enchantments: in order, as they speak, to have full Power in all Things, and to do whatever they please.—Hence they spend their Time in Luxury and Pleasure and bodily Enjoyments: nor ever come among us, unless it be to ensnare unstable Souls, and entice them into their impious Doctrine."

"For this end they taught Incontinence to be obligatory, as a Law: and not only lawful, but necessary to Salvation; not only compatible with the Saviour's Religion, but an essential Part of it: and those were the best Men, who in the common Opinion were the most vicious.

"The Carpocratians grew to that Degree of Madness, that being unable to conceal their Debaucheries, they made Incontinence to be a Law"—"Prodicus added this to the Tenets of Carpocrates, that Fornication ought to be open and public, and the Use of Women common. For which Reason, in their Feasts, the Candles were extinguished, each lay with the Women, as Chance appointed; and they called this Lasciviousness a mystical Initiation, a mystical Communion."

"Clemens Alex. gives a long Passage from the Writings of Epiphanes, contending for a Community of Women, as being the Law of Heaven; and that Men and Women ought no more to be confined in their Amours than other Animals. 'For', says Epiphanes, 'he hath implanted a strong and vehement Desire in Man of propagating his Species; which neither

Law, nor Custom, nor any Thing else, can abolish; for it is the Decree of God'.

"The Ophites, or Cainites, say, that Cain was the Progeny of a higher Principality than Abel; and they confess that Esau, Corah, and the Sodomites, and all such, were their Relations:—That Vulva was the Creator of the Universe; and that none could be saved, unless he passed thro' all. So also Carpocrates taught.—Most of the Gnostics, with wonderful Artifice of Improbity, taught what is not fit to be named, in the promiscuous Use of Women, and to roll in all manner of filthy Communication. The Banquet being over, says the Man to the Woman, Arise, and shew thy Love to a Brother. So they proceed to Copulation".—"Some of them, by a most horrible Abuse of Scripture, apply the Words, Give to every one that asketh thee, towards enticing the Women."—"Take hold, says Isidorus, of some robust woman, that you be not plucked away from Grace; and when you have spent your seminal Fire, you may pray with a good Conscience."

"Both Epiphanius, and Irenoeus before him, say of the Founder of the Nicolaitans: 'Being ashamed of his own Remissness, he audaciously pronounced, that no one, who was not lascivious every Day could be Partaker of eternal life'. Therefore those Gnostics, after a Debauchery, were used to boast of their Happiness, as having done a meritorious Thing: and when they had their Will on a complying Female, they told her 'she was now a pure Virgin'; though she was daily corrupted, and for many Years together."

"This may be a proper Place to introduce The Confession of Epiphanius; who in his Youth had fallen into the Gnostic Heresy; whence he received what he writes concerning them, from the professed Teachers' own Mouths: when their Women, one in particular, used all their Arts to debauch him. But by the Help of the divine Grace he overcame their temptations. I was then, says he, reproached by those pestilent Women, who thus scoffingly talked with each other, 'We would have saved this Youth, but not being able, we have suffered him to perish in the Hands of the Principalities'. For the most beautiful among them makes herself the bait; and those whom she enticeth, she is said not to destroy, but to deliver. Whence the handsomest are used to upbraid those who are less so;

'I am an elect Vessel, able to save those whom I attempt; which you have not Power to do'.

The most beautiful of them were employed to seduce me; but God delivered me from their Wickedness; so that, after reading their Books, I escaped from among them, and discovered the several Names of them to the Bishops of those Parts; and near eighty of them were sent into Banishment."

"The Valentinians, says Irenoeus, being in Love with certain Women, would, without a Blush, seduce them from their Husbands, and make them their own Wives. Others of them, seemingly modest at first, pretended to live with them as Sisters; and in Process of Time were discovered, Sister being found pregnant by Brother."

"And to aggravate their wickedness, they esteemed Copulation as a most sacred Mystery, known only to themselves; and which the Profane were not allowed to put in Practice: What was abominable in others being highly meritorious in themselves. For, saith Irenoeus again, 'They have this Grace descending to them from the unspeakable and unnameable Copulation above. For which Reason they ought always to be meditating on the Mystery of Copulation'. And thus they persuade silly People, addressing them in Discourse, 'Whoever is in the World and of the World, and mingleth with a Woman is not of the Truth, nor shall pass into the Truth; because he mingleth in Concupiscence. 'Therefore Continence, say they, is necessary to us natural Men; but by no means to themselves, who are spiritual and perfect; among whom the Seed, small from above, is perfected here." Compare Tertullian, p. 261.

"To quote Clemens Alexandrinus. 'I will bring in to open Light your most secret Mysteries: not ashamed to speak what you are not ashamed to worship" i. e. the secrets of both Sexes'. For I may well call them Atheists, who impudently worship those Parts, which modesty forbids to mention."

CHAPTER XIV

LAMAISM

LAMAISM WAS FOUNDED about 407 A. D. by a Bodisatva called, it is said, Chomschim, in Chinese Boyanchi-yin, (the voice which reflects the world) on the mountain Bouthala around which was built the sacred city of Lhassa.

Lamaism is not only a religion, it is a theistic government.

In 1206, when Tibet was conquered by Ghengis Khan (Mongol), Buddhism became the established religion but in 1368 when Tibet fell from the hands of the Mongols into those of the Chinese, Lamaism, losing its temporal power, became merely a religion, its spiritual power remaining however the same and the religion of more than 250 million men.

The Lamas are Priests of Buddha among the Mongols and Tibetans, but Lamaism is not orthodox Buddhism.

Gautama Buddha, the founder of Buddhism, laid down the following laws governing the attainment of Nirvana (state of not being). Their enumeration will serve to show how Buddhism and Lamaism differ.

According to that great teacher the ten obstacles which prevent people from attaining the supreme liberation are:

1. The belief in the "Ego",
2. Doubt,
3. The belief in the efficacity of rites and ceremonies,
4. Sensual desires,

5. Anger,
6. The wish to live in a world less coarse than our own,
7. The wish to live in a more subtle world than our own,
8. Pride,
9. Agitation,
10. Ignorance.

The few quotations given hereafter from the very remarkable books of Madame Alexandra David-Neel can only serve to show students of these subjects the great value of the books themselves.

Quoting *Bhagavad Gita*, she writes:

"Orthodox Buddhism denied the existence of a permanent soul which transmigrated, and considered this theory as the most pernicious of errors but the great majority of Buddhists have fallen back into this old belief of the Hindus concerning the 'jiva' (self) which periodically changes its old body for a new one, as we cast off old clothes for new."[64]

The Tibetan clergy comprises a theocratic aristocracy the members of which are called Lamas, "tulkous". "According to popular belief, a tulkou is either the reincarnation of a saint or dead sage or else the incarnation of a superhuman being, a god or a demon.

In answer to a question she put to the Dalai Lama on the definition of the word "tulkou" Madame David-Neel quotes him as saying: "A Bodhisattva is the base from which can spring numberless magical forms. The force he engenders by a perfect concentration of thought enables him simultaneously to show a phantom similar to himself in thousands and thousands of worlds. He is not only able to create human forms, but every other kind as well, even to inanimate objects such as houses, enclosures, forests, roads, bridges, etc. etc. and he can produce atmospheric phenomena, as well as the elixir of immortality which quenches all thirst. (This expression, he explained, was to be taken both in a literal and symbolic sense.)[65]

"In fact, concluded the Dalai Lama, his power to create Magic forms is limitless."

"The Kandhomas are reincarnated women, fairies, and may either be married or in holy orders."[66]

The usual method employed for locating the new body appropriated by an old soul is the following: "A child answering to the prescribed conditions is discovered and a lama diviner is consulted. Should he pronounce in favour of the candidate the following form of trial takes place: Some personal belongings of the deceased lama are mixed with other similar ones, and the child must point out the first, thus proving that he recognizes the things that were his in his former existence.[67]

"This system assumed its present form towards the year 1650 when the fifth Grand Lama Lobzang Gyatso, having become sovereign of Tibet, but wishing to acquire a higher dignity, proclaimed himself the reincarnation (avatar) of Tchenrezigs, a dignitary of the Mahayanist Pantheon. Simultaneously he established his master as Grand Lama of the monastery of Trachilhumpo, proclaiming him the reincarnation of Eupamed, a Mystic Buddha of whom Tchenrezigs was the spiritual son.

"The example thus given by the lama-king stimulated the creation of tulkous. Soon all monasteries made a point of having at their head the incarnation of some celebrated personage. Thus the Dalai Lama, the political head of Tibet today, is said still to be a reincarnation of Tchenrezigs and the present Trachi Lama one of Eupamed."[68]

The palace of the Dalai Lamas is the monastery of Gahlden situated some twenty kilometres from Lhassa. It was founded by Tsong Khapa in the XV century. Tsong Khapa, the reformer, forbade marriage and the use of fermented beverages to the clergy. His followers called Gelougspas are known as the Yellow Sect and their favourite God is Jigsdjied, the destroyer (the terrible), another version of the Hindu god Siva. The Red Sect, the Sakyapas, those distinguished by their red hats, are their religious opponents.

As regards the Tibetan gods and the ritual pertaining to their worship Madame David-Neel gives us the following most illuminating description:

"To the respiratory exercises repeated several times a day the recluse often joins meditation-contemplation assisted by Kyilkhors.

"A Kyilkhor, or magic circle, is a kind of diagram drawn on paper or stuff or engraved on metal, stone or wood... Deities or lamas are generally represented on them by little pyramids of paste called 'torma'.[69] "Kyilkhors are also designed with coloured powder on boards or on the floor, but only such persons as have received a special initiation may compose or draw them. Each Kyilkhor, moreover, requires a particular initiation and that erected by a non-initiate would remain a dead thing impossible to animate and powerless. An advanced student, wishing to evoke a Bodhisatva or deity, seeks to animate the Kyilkhor which has hitherto only served as a focus for concentration.

"The Hindus endow magical diagrams as well as the statues of deities with life before worshipping them. The object of this rite, called pranapratishtha, is to convey to the inanimate object, by means of psychic currents, the energy of the worshipper. The life thus infused into the latter is kept up by the daily cult which is rendered it, for it lives on the concentration of thought which has given it birth. Should it suddenly be deprived of this subtle food, the living soul within it will perish and die of inanition the object reverting to its former condition of inert matter."[70]

The Tibetan mystics animate their Kyilkhor by a similar method, but they do not aim at making it an object of worship and the material representation of the Kyilkhor is abolished when, after a certain amount of practice, it becomes purely a mental image.

A tradition of the Kahgyudpas relates that the founder of their sect, Marpa, was blamed by his master (guru) Narota for having paid homage first to the Kyilkhor.

"It is I who constructed the Kyilkhor", declared Narota. "Its life and energy were infused in it by me. Without me, those figures would be only inert objects. The gods that inhabit it are born of my spirit therefore, it is to me that homage is primarily due."[71]

"According to Tibetan occultists, these beings, (the gods) have acquired a kind of real existence due to the innumerable thoughts which have been concentrated on them.[72]

"According to the Tibetans, during the celebration of a rite, the thoughts of the officiating evocator, concentrated on the deities who 'exist already', cause these to become more powerful and more real for him. By identifying himself with them the evocator establishes contact with an accumulation of energy infinitely greater than that which he alone might generate."[73]

Thus we must conclude that the gods of Eastern Magic correspond to what our occidental scientists call thought-forms. That these thought-forms can be projected and reabsorbed into the person of their creator is a theory with which all students of spiritism and psychic science are familiar, but that they can detach from their makers and lead separate existences, empowered for good or evil by the collective thought force of their worshippers, is an idea with which the western world is still unfamiliar.

"Gods, Demons, the whole universe is a mirage, a fantasy of the brain issuing therefrom and resolvant thereto."[74]

"Thus the aim of the teaching is to bring the student to understand that the world and all its phenomena are but phantasms born of our own imagination. This in short is the fundamental teaching of the Mystics of Tibet."[75]

Among the various tricks taught to initiates and described by Madame David-Neel in her books are:—

	Pages	
Yoga breathing exercises	119 in *Initiations Lamaiques.*	
Levitation	209 in *Parmi les Mystiques et les Magiciens du Thibet.*	
Loung-gom (fast walking)	211	"
Toumo (self heating)	219	"
Telepathy	231	"

Buddha who, after a thorough investigation of them, rejected the physical practices of the Brahmins, pays little heed to the breathing exercises of Yoga, in his spiritual teaching.[76]

Madame David-Neel tells the following anecdote of the Great Master.

"One day Buddha, travelling with one of his disciples, met an emaciated Yogi alone in a hut in the middle of the forest.

The master stopped, enquiring how long the ascetic had lived in that place practising such austerities. "Twenty-five years", answered the Yogi.

"And what results have you obtained after such dire efforts"? queried the Buddha further.

"I am able to cross a river walking on the water", proudly declared the anchorite:

"Ah, My poor friend!" answered the Sage sympathetically, "have you really wasted so much time for that, when for a pittance you can get taken across it on the ferry!"

On page 157 of her remarkable book *Initiations* Lamai*q*ues Madame David-Neel explains further the existence of another school of curious rites, presumably a development of degenerate Hindu Tantric Buddhism, to the practice of which may be ascribed much that seems objectionable in the Oriental occultism, which has filtered through to the Western world. There we are told that: "A certain class of Tibeta n occultists teach a method of semi-physical semi-psychic stimulation, which consists in such singular practices as that of causing the seminal flow, ejected in the course of sexual union, to be reabsorbed etc. etc."

Tibet is indeed the land of Demons where Official Lamaism competes with Unofficial Sorcery, and Magic, white and black, still remains the law of the land.

CHAPTER XV

THE YEZIDEES (DEVIL WORSHIPPERS)

THE SECT OF the Yezidees was founded by Sheik Adi in the fifth century.

Mr. W. B. Seabrook's observations on the Yezidees, as recorded in his book, *Adventures in Arabia*, form a basis for the study of the beliefs of this sect.

According to his informant, the Yezidee faith is briefly this:[77]

"God created seven spirits 'as a man lighteth one lamp after another', and the first of these spirits was Satan, whom God made supreme ruler of the earth for a period of ten thousand years. And because Satan was supreme master of the earth, those who dwelt on it could prosper only by doing him homage and worshipping him.

"Since the true name was forbidden", Mechmed Hamdi told me, "they referred to Shaitan as Melek Taos (Angel Peacock) and worshipped him in the form of a brass bird"

"While the name of Shaitan was forbidden", he said, "so much so that if a Yezidee hears it spoken, their law commands him either to kill the man who uttered it or kill himself—yet we could talk as freely with the m about Melek Taos as we could to a Christian about Jesus."

A priest of the cult also volunteered the following information to Mr. Seabrook on the Yezidee divinity. "Our difference from all other religions is this—that we know God is so far away that we can have no contact with Him—and He, on his part, has no knowledge or interest of any sort concerning human affairs. It is useless to pray to him or worship Him. He cares nothing about us.

"He has given the entire control of this world for ten thousand years to the bright spirit Melek Taos, and Him, therefore, we worship. Moslems and Christians are wrongly taught that he whom we call Melek Taos is the spirit of evil. We know that this is not true. He is the spirit of power and the ruler of this world. At the end of the ten thousand years of his reign—of which we are now in the third thousand—he will re-enter paradise as the chief of the Seven Bright Spirits, and all his true worshippers will enter paradise with him."

The Grand Priest of the order, the "Mir", receives one-seventh part of the harvests of the land. He is the arbiter of all religious matters and under him rank seven ecclesiastical orders.

The doctrine of the Yezidees is contained in three sacred books *The Black Book, The Revelation and The Contract with the Devil*; but a knowledge of reading and writing is restricted to the priests of the first order and is classified by the sect as a serious sin.

CHAPTER XVI

ORTHODOX ISLAM

THE ARABIAN PENINSULA was the home of nomads and mountaineers when, in the seventh century, Mahomet arose as a self-styled Prophet and the creator of Islamism. The doctrine of Islam has three dogmas:

1. Monotheism.
2. Belief in the Prophet, namely Mahomet.
3. The law of retribution.

The sacred book of Islamism, the Koran, was devoid of mystic teaching. The Figh, for every believer, is the code of morals and obligations such as fast, prayer, pilgrimage to Mecca, etc. Mysticism was interjected into Islamism by Sufism.

Mahomet aimed at the establishment of a religion which, he declared, was revealed to him during periods of trance which he frequently underwent. He was determined to impose this religion on all the Arabs and, through much bloodshed, he succeeded in stamping out the Koraishites from whom he took Mecca.

The death of Mahomet was the signal for disruption among his followers and innumerable divisions both political and religious, from the history of the Arabs during their periods of conquest which began immediately after the death of Mahomet during the Khalifate of Omar (634–644).

CHAPTER XVII

UNORTHODOX ISLAM, THE ISHMAELITES, THE LODGE OF CAIRO

MANICHEISM WAS NOT the only secret association that sprang from the initiations of the Magi. In the seventh century of our era we meet with similar societies, possessing an influence not limited to the regions in which they arose, variations of one single thought, which aimed at combining the venerable doctrines of Zoroaster with Christian belief. Of these societies or sects the following may be mentioned: the followers of Keyoumerz; the worshippers of Servan, certain Zoroastrians, so-called "Dualists"; Gnostics and, lastly, the followers of Mastek, the most formidable and disastrous of all, preaching universal equality and liberty, the irresponsibility of man, and the community of property and women.

The Arabs having rendered themselves masters of Persia in the seventh century, the sects of that country set to work to spread their tenets among Islam in order to undermine it.

This is corroborated by Heckethorn who writes: "The Persian sects examined the Koran, pointed out its contradictions, and denied its divine origin. And so there arose in Islamism that movement which attacks dogmas, and destroys faith, and substitutes for blind belief free enquiry."[78]

In Persia and in Mesopotamia had spread the new rationalism, the philosophical heresy of the Mutazilites (schismatics) exposed by Hassan al-Basri.

The Jew Abdallah Ibn Saba[79] presented himself as the prophet of the future Imam, who was to manifest. He meant to overthrow the caliphate and to uphold the rights of Mahomet al-Hanafi, the son of Ismael, the descendant of the prophet by his daughter Fatima, the wife of Ali. Thus was founded the Shi'a sect.

The Fatmite dynasty (from Fatima, daughter of Mahomet) was founded in 909 A. D. when Ahmed Said, the son of a Jewess who had married the Shi'a chief al-Hussain,[80] conquered Egypt and Syria, establishing the centre at Cairo. Declaring himself to be the long expected Imam, Said, on coming to power, assumed the name of Obaid Allah el-Mahdi.[81] The Fatmite dynasty lasted from 909 to 1171. Heckethorn informs us that "The Doial-Doat, or supreme missionary or judge, shared the power with the prince.[82]

"Meetings were held in the Lodge at Cairo, which contained many books and scientific instruments; science was the professed object, but the real aim was very different. The course of instruction was divided into nine degrees... the ninth degree... as the necessary result of the teaching of all the former, taught that nothing was to be believed, and that everything was lawful.

"Egypt, especially, seems as if predestined to be the birthplace of secret societies, of priests, warriors and fanatics. It is the region of mysteries... Cairo has succeeded the ancient Memphis, the doctrine of the Lodge of Wisdom that of the Academy of Heliopolis... The throne of the descendants of Fatima was to be surrounded with an army of assassins, a formidable body-guard; a mysterious militia was to be raised, that should spread far and wide the fame and terror of the caliphate of Cairo, and inflict fatal blows on the abhorred rule of Bagdad. The missionaries spread widely, and in Arabia and Syria, partisans were won, to whom the designs of the order were unknown, but who had with fearful solemnity sworn blind obedience."

The Fatmites had received from the sect the mission of destroying, or at least of disrupting Islam. The successor of Obaid-Allah continued this work, having himself proclaimed a Shi'a while in reality he was sceptic. It was under the Caliph Hakim that the Druses came into being.

The Shi'a sects who recognized Mohammed al-Hanafi as the last living "Imam" were called Ismaelites or Septimans. From their midst sprang a secret body, the Khoja, which, in spite of persecution still exists in Persia and India, where its exoteric chief is the Anglicised Indian, the Aga Khan, whose followers are the moneylenders of Islam, a profession forbidden by Mahomet.

Still another Shi'a sect, the Duodecimans or Imanites, recognize Mohamed al-Muntazar the twelfth Imam.

Under the Fatmite Caliph Hakim, a new religion sprang out of Ismailism, that of the Druses, so called from its inventor, a certain Darosi. This religion differs little from Ismailism, except that it introduces the dogma of the incarnation of God himself on Earth, under the form of the Caliph Hakim.

When the Fatmite Caliph Mostansir ascended the throne, he re-established the Ismailian belief: and the Druses, driven from Egypt, took refuge in Lebanon, where they still exist.

CHAPTER XVIII

THE DRUSES

THE DRUSES, AS afore stated, are a gnostic sect among the Ismaelite Mahommedans. It was founded in the tent h century during the reign of the Fatimite Caliph al-Hakim Biambellalu.

The founder is usually recognised as Mohammed al Darazi or al Druzi (Nouchtegin ben Ismail al Bokhari) born near Bokhara cir. 960. He adopted the doctrine then preached by al-Hakim of the successive reincarnations of the divinity under human form[83] and wrote a treatise in which he established the continuous series of divine incarnations ending with the statement that the last living manifestation was al-Hakim, the Caliph of Egypt. So pleased was al-Hakim with the book that he called Mohammed al-Druzi to him, and gave him great authority in the conduct of affairs. From that time, al-Hakim who hitherto had been known as Biambellalu that is "the one governing by the order of God," changed his name to Biam-Eh meaning "the one governing by his own right." He then caused himself to be worshipped as God. The public reading of Mohammed al-Druzi's book, in one of Cairo's mosques, caused popular riots and its author was obliged to flee from Egypt. He took refuge in the mountains of Syria and made many proselytes by allowing his adepts the use of wine, condoning licentiousness and encouraging the propagation of ideas tending to the confiscation of property. Later, he returned to Egypt but was confronted by the power gained by one of his disciples,

Hamza al-Hadi, who had become leader of the Druses there. In the conflict that ensued, Mohammed al-Druzi took up arms against his rival and adversary and was killed in 1019.

Hamza, later, went to Syria and Lebanon and preached to the Druses the doctrine of al-Hakim such as prevailed in Egypt. Hamza was declared the prophet, the Imam of al-Hakim who, being the divine incarnation, will yet manifest himself to the Druses, be their Messiah and give them all earthly power. The sect is divided into three degrees: Profanes, Aspirants and Wise.

The Druses, from a political point of view, are divided into two parts, the Djumblatiehs and the Yezbekiehs and religiously they have their own rites, mysteries, and exoteric and esoteric doctrines. The high initiates or priests rule the people and through religious fanaticism have reduced the Druses to a state of theocrasy with all its attendant law of fear and numerous restrictions upon which theocratic power can alone be edified.

In his book on Secret Societies, Heckethorn comments on the similarity existing between the law of the Druses and that of the Jews whereby "to a brother, perfect truth and confidence are due but it is allowable, nay, a duty, to be false towards men of another creed." Subsequently, he draws yet another comparison between the Druses and the Freemasons and mentions the Masonic degrees of "The United Druses "and "Commanders of Lebanon".

CHAPTER XIX

THE ASSASSINS

THE JUDEO-SHI'A SECT of the Assassins or Hashishims was founded in 1090 by Hassan Sabah, a Persian, who had been initiated into Ismailism at Cairo, in the household of the Fatimite Caliph, al-Mostansir. He was known as "The Old Man "or rather "The Lord of the Mountain". His influence in Egypt having excited the envy of many, he was sent into exile. Caliph al-Mustansir's "vizir was a Jew named Abu Mansur Sadakah ibn Yussuf",[84] under whose protection Hassan traversed Persia as a missionary, preaching and making proselytes, and, having seized the fortress of Alamut, on the borders of Irak and Dilem, which he called the "House of Fortune", he there established his rule.

The history of his time is full of his name. Kings in the very centre of Europe trembled at it; his powerful arm reached everywhere.

According to Heckethorn, "he reduced the nine degrees into which the adherents of the Lodge of Cairo were divided to seven, placing himself at the head, with title of Seydna or Sidna, whence the Spanish Cid, and the Italian Signore. The term Assassins is a corruption of Hashishim, derived from Hashish (Indian hemp) with which the chief intoxicated his followers when they entered on some desperate enterprise.[85]

"To regulate the seven degrees he composed the Catechism of the Order. The first degree recommended to the missionary attentively to watch the disposition of the candidate, before admitting him to the order.

The second impressed it upon him to gain the confidence of the candidate, by flattering his inclinations and passions; the third, to involve him in doubts and difficulties by showing him the absurdity of the Koran; the fourth, to exact from him a solemn oath of fidelity and obedience, with a promise to lay his doubts before his instructor; and the fifth, to show him that the most famous men of Church and State belonged to the secret order. The sixth, called 'Confirmation', enjoined on the instructor to examine the proselyte concerning the whole preceding course, and firmly to establish him in it. The seventh finally, called the 'Exposition of the Allegory', gave the keys of the sect.

"The followers were divided into two great hosts, 'self-sacrificers' and 'aspirants'. The first, despising fatigues, dangers, and tortures, joyfully gave their lives whenever it pleased the master, who required them either to protect himself or to carry out his mandates of death."

According to the legend "the man selected by the lord to perform the dangerous exploit was first made drunk, and in this state carried into a beautiful valley where he was, on waking, surrounded by lovely sylph-like women who made him believe he was in Elysium; but ere he wearied or became satiated with love and wine, he was once more made drunk, and in this state carried back to his own home. When his services were required, he was again sent for by the lord, who told him that he had once permitted him to enjoy paradise, and if he would do his bidding he could luxuriate in the same delights for the rest of his life. The dupe, believing that his master had the power to do all this, was ready to commit whatever crime was required of him."

"Several Christian princes were suspected of conniving at the deeds of the Assassins. Richard of England is one of them; and it has been the loyal task of English writers to free him from the charge of having instigated the murder of Conrad of Montferrat... There also existed for a long time a rumour that Richard had attempted the life of the King of France through Hassan and his Assassins. The nephew of Barbarossa, Frederick II , was excommunicated by Innocent II for having caused the Duke of Bavaria to be slain by the Assassins; and Frederick II, in a letter to the

King of Bohemia, accuses the Duke of Austria of having by similar agents attempted his life."

The corruption of the Order of The Templars which brought about its downfall has been imputed by most historians to this sect which was suppressed in 1256, when the Mongolians, led by Prince Hulagu, attacked and overthrew them.

CHAPTER XX

THE KNIGHTS TEMPLAR

THE FIRST KNIGHTS Templar Order, founded in 1118 by Hugh de Payens, had 13 degrees. So has its modern successor; these are:—

BLUE DEGREES

1. Entered Apprentice.
2. Fellow Craft.
3. Master Mason.
4. Mark Mason.
5. Past Master.

CHAPTER DEGREES

6. Most Excellent Master.
7. Royal Arch.
8. Royal Master.
9. Select Master.
10. Super Excellent Master.
11. Knights of the Red Cross
12. Knights Templar.
13. Knights of Malta.

It is chronicled that several of the founders of the Templar Order were initiates in the sect of The Assassins.

Blanchard, writing of it, says:—

"During the middle ages, the most eminent warriors and noblemen of Europe entered its ranks. The Knights of the Temple became the bulwark of the Holy Land against the Saracens. France, England and other countries formed associations (Priories) of Templar Knights, each with its own Grand Master and other officers. Such great wealth was accumulated in the treasuries of the order that in the year 1185 its annual income represented a sum equal to thirty millions of dollars. The Templars were bankers and loaned money on their own terms. But wealth and prosperity naturally led to licentiousness, neglect of Templar law and in the end destruction."[86]

Having embraced Gnosticism while in Palestine, and in touch with the sect of the Assassins, the Templar order degenerated, and some of its members under the influence of that sect, were said to practice Phallicism or sex-worship and Satanism and to venerate "The Baphomet", the idol of the Luciferians. The crime of Sodomy was a rite of Templar initiation.

It is here interesting to note that the Phallus holds the lowest rank in Brahmin theology for, in countries where the people are virtually enslaved by superstition, this kind of heresy is useful to the ruling classes.

Morris thus summarizes the fall of the Templars. "In the year 1307, the Grand Master of the order, Jacques de Molay, was arrested in Paris with sixty of his knights and imprisoned upon charges of idolatry and other crimes. Shortly afterward, all the Knights Templar in France were put in prison in Paris. May 12, 1310, fifty-four of them were burnt alive. March 18, 1314, the Grand Master, with three of his most eminent officers, suffered in like manner. The great possessions of the order were now confiscated and the society suppressed both by the Pope and the leading monarchs of Europe."[87]

In England, the Knights Templar were dissolved in the reign of Edward II, and after the grant of their properties to the Knights Hospitallers, these in their turn were dissolved by Henry VIII.

After the death of Molay, the Knights Templar found a protector in King Dinis II of Portugal who reformed the order in 1317, under the name Knights of Christ.

A complete bibliography of literature both in print and in manuscript, dealing with the subject of the Knights Templar has been compiled by M. Dessubré and the student is referred to his book: *Bibliographie de I Ordre des Templiers.*

CHAPTER XXI

KNIGHTS OF MALTA

THE KNIGHTS OF St. John of Jerusalem, or Hospitallers of St. John, afterward called Knights of Rhodes and finally Knights of Malta, were founded about the commencement of the Crusades, as a military and religious order.[88]

CHAPTER XXII

THE ROSICRUCIANS

SPECULATION HAS BEEN rife as to the origin of the Rosicrucians, and the many fables and legends connected with the subject have but little historical value.

Owing to the great discrepancy between the information contained in the following article and that given in the more modern editions of the Encyclopaedia Britannica, it has been deemed advisable to reprint the former. (See Enc. Brit., 3r d Edition, Vol. 16, year MDCCXCVII (1797) Edinburgh. Bell and Macfarquhar.)

"Rosicrucians, a name assumed by a sect or cabal of hermetical philosophers; who arose, as it has been said, or at least became first taken notice of in Germany, in the beginning of the fourteenth century. They bound themselves together by a solemn secret, which they all swore inviolably to preserve: and obliged themselves, at their admission into the order, to a strict observance of certain established rules. They pretended to know all sciences, and chiefly medicine: whereof they published themselves the restorers. They pretended to be masters of abundance of important secrets, and, among others, that of the philosopher's stone: all which they affirmed to have received by tradition from the ancient Egyptians, Chaldeans, the Magi, and Gymnosophists.

They have been distinguished by several names, accommodated to the several branches of their doctrine. Because they pretend to protect the period of human life, by means of certain nostrums, and even to restore youth, they were called *Immortals*; as they pretended to know all things, they have been called *Illuminati*; and because they have made no appearance for several years, unless the sect of Illuminated which lately started up on the continent derives its origin from them, they have been called the Invisible Brothers. Their society is frequently signed by the letters F. R. C. which some among them interpret fratres roris cocti; it being pretended that the matter of the philosopher's stone is dew concocted, exalted, etc. Some, who are no friends to free-masonry, make the present flourishing society of free-masons a branch of Rosicrucians; or rather the Rosicrucians themselves, under a new name or relation, viz. as retainers to building. And it is certain, there are some free-masons who have all the characters of Rosicrucians; but how the aera and original of masonry, and that of Rosicrucianism here fixed from Nadaeus, who has written expressly on the subject, conflict, we leave others to judge... Notwithstanding the pretended antiquity of the Rosicrucians, it is probable that the alchemists, Paracelsists,[89] or fire-philosophers, who spread themselves through almost all Europe about the close of the 16th century, assumed about this period the obscure and ambiguous title of Rosicrucian brethren, which commanded at first some degree of respect, as it seemed to be borrowed from the arms of Luther, which were a cross placed upon a rose. But the denomination evidently appears to be derived from the science of chemistry. It is not compounded, says Motheim, as many imagine of the two words rosa and crux, which signify rose and cross, but of the latter of these words, and the Latin ros, which signifies dew... At the head of these fanatics were Robert Fludd, an English physician, Jacob Behmen, and Michael Mayer; but if rumour may be credited, the present Illuminated have a head of higher rank. The common principles, which serve as a kind of centre of union to the Rosicrucian society, are the following: They all maintain that the dissolution of bodies, by the power of fire, is the only way by which men can arrive at true wisdom, and come to discern the first principles of things. They all acknowledge a certain analogy and harmony between the powers of nature and the doctrines of religion; and believe that the Deity governs the kingdom of grace by the same laws with which he rules the kingdom of nature; and hence they are led to use chemical denominations to express the truth of religion. They all hold that there is a sort of divine energy, or soul, diffused through the frame of the universe, which some call the argheus, others the universal spirit, and which others mention under different appellations. They all talk in the most superstitious manner of what they call the signatures of things, of the power of the stars, over all corporeal beings, and their particular influence upon the human race, of the efficacy of magic, and the various ranks and orders of demons—These demons they divide into two orders, sylphs and gnomes."[90]

This article having been written in 1747 only hinted at what the Rose Croix might have been. Subsequent research upon the organization of the Fraternity, its tenets and its achievements, shows it to have been a medium for the propagation of Gnosticism and a centre for political activities. Before it conquered Freemasonry, which was officially instituted in 1717, many names were already associated intimately with this esoteric organization. Among others were Faustus Socinius, Cesare Cremonini, Michael Maier, Valentin Andrea, Thomas Vaughan (Philaletes), Charles Blount, Frederich Helvetius, Richard Simon, and Theophilus Desaguliers.

It is claimed that Faustus Socinius, named after Faustus, the Manichee, nephew of Lelius Socinius, whose teacher was Camillo Renato, was an intimate of Rosicrucianism and the founder of the Socinians.

Catholics and Protestants alike opposed Faustus Socinius in his efforts to graft a secret cult on the existing orthodox religions, and in 1598, the people of Cracovia, revolted by his doctrines, pillaged his house, burned his books and manuscripts and almost massacred their author. He had sworn hatred to the church and busied himself in founding an association the aims of which were to be subversive to all its teachings, and two years before his death, he was obliged to take refuge from his enemies with one Abraham Blonski.

The membership of the Rose Croix was composed of Alchemists, Astrologers and Spiritists whose quest was the search for a process for transmuting base metals into gold and the secret of life. To most of these "generation was the root principle of Achemy."[91]

The order of the Rose Croix revealed itself in 1614 with the appearance of two books, *Fama Fraternitatis* and the *Confessio* attributed to Valentin Andrea giving the legend of the travels of Christian Rosenkreutz.

According to Charles T. MacClenachan 33°, Historian, Grand Lodge State of New York, this same legend had appeared as the work of Raymond Lulli, who died in 1315.

In this legend, translated into English in 1616 by Robert Fludd, a symbolic personage called Christian Rosenkreuz, destined to live 106 years on earth, travelled in the East where he studied the Cabala and, on his return to his native Germany, he revealed to three disciples the secret of secrets, the great secret of theosophy.[92] Finally, he retired to a cave to finish his days in solitude, dying in 1484 at the age of 106. His disciples came, enshrouded him and disappeared. His grave was to be unknown for six times twenty years at the end of which period it was to become the hearth of the light destined to illuminate the world at the time appointed by God. In 1604, chance brought men to this cave. On entering, great was their surprise to find it resplendent with a bright light. It contained an altar bearing upon a copper plate the inscription "Living, I reserved this light for my grave." One mysterious figure was accompanied by this epigram "Never vacant". A second figure "The Yoke of the Law". A third figure "The Liberty of the Gospels".

A fourth "The Glory of the Whole God". The hall still contained lamps burning without fuel, mirrors of various shapes and boks. Upon the wall was written "In six times twenty years I will be discovered". The prophecy was fulfilled, adds the fable, by way of conclusion.

The movement was greatly furthered by the impulse given it when, after the appearance of the *Fama Fraternitatis* and *Confessio*, a German Alchemist, Michael Maier, an English Physician, Robert Fludd and a Pietist, Julius Sperber, wrote treatises in defence or explanation of the order of the Rose Croix.

It has repeatedly been stated that Michael Maier, who frequently visited England, was a friend of Robert Fludd. He was the author of *Themis Aurea* and *Silentium post Clamores*, both Rosicrucian works. His political influence may be judged from his career. Physician to Rudolf II, he was created by him Count of the Palatinate, and acted as adviser to his sovereign. In 1609, Rudolf II issued an Imperial Charter granting religious liberty to the Moravians.[93]

Masonic authorities state that Maier, as a Rosicrucian, changed his official title to *Summus Magister*, Sovereign Master, which is that used by all his successors and borne by the principal Socinian Rose-Croix documents, dating from the time of Faustus Socinius to that of Johann Wolff, which are preserved in the Sovereign Patriarchal Council of Hamburg. (That is the Supreme Jewish Lodge secretly affiliated to International Masonry.)

In his book *Themis Aurea*, written in 1616 and 1617 and printed in 1618, Maier, the Grand Master, refers to a resolution passed at a meeting in 1617 in which it was formally agreed that the Brotherhood of the Rose Croix must maintain the strictest secrecy for a hundred years. On October 31, 1617, the Convention of the Seven at Magdebourg had indeed agreed to qualify its members during the ensuing one hundred years of secrecy as "The Invisibles". It had renewed its oath to destroy the church of Jesus Christ and had decreed that, in the year 1717, it would transform the fraternity into an association which could carry on a more or less open propaganda, while adopting such measures of prudence as might then be deemed expedient by the leaders of the sect. Finally, the Seven adopted definitely, as being sufficiently original to appeal to the popular imagination, Valentin Andrea's curious story of the Rose Croix which had been secretly printed in Venice towards 1613.

Robert Fludd was the author of *Tractatus Apologeticus* (1617) and *Clavis Philosophiae et Alchymiae* (1633). He was greatly helped in the foundation of the Rose Croix order in England by Francis Bacon, author of *Nova Atlantis*[94] (1624).

Valentin Andrea to whom, as we have seen, are ascribed the works *Fama and Confessio,* as well as *Chemycal Nuptials*, had, in 1640, been appointed preacher to the Duke of Brunswick Wolfenbuttel, who was soon to make him his chaplain.

To those who know the important part played by a Duke of Brunswick during the French Revolution, this entrance of the Brunswick family into the sect is very interesting. As a Rosicrucian, Andrea was the teacher of Comenius (Amos Kominsky), who frequently visited England during his mysterious political career. Bishop of a Moravian community, Comenius was the leader of the Moravian Brethren, a sect pledged to achieve the extermination of the Catholic church and which, being considered heretical, was also suspected of practising secret satanism. The Moravians were imbued with Socinianism that is the doctrine of Lelius Socinius which had been spread among them by his nephew Faustus Socinius who had found refuge in Moravia when persecuted by the Church. Their link with Rosicrucianism had already been established in the person of the pietist, Julius Sperber, who was also one of their leaders. When Kominsky was persecuted, he first went to London in 1641 and, early the next year, went to Sweden where he was granted refuge and help by the powerful Swedish Minister, Count Axel Oxenstiern, himself a Rosicrucian adept and protector of another initiate, Ludwig van Geer from Holland.

The combination of the pursuit of alchemy and hermeticism with political aims was frequently evidenced even before the official appearance of Rosicrucianism. The influence of adepts on the destinies of nations was immense.

To Queen Elizabeth, the advice of John Dee, her alchemist, was always considered in matters affecting national policy, and to Dee, his crystal gazer, Edward Kelly, was indispensable as a medium.[95]

Ludwig van Geer, (one of the Seven present at Magdebourg) had settled in Sweden and had won over the chancellor, Count Axel Oxenstiern, then the real regent, in view of the minority of Queen Christina. A great industrialist of Dutch birth, with a colossal fortune made in the manufacture of cannon, he had become a Baron, and as owner of 20 ships of the Swedish fleet, he was an indispensable man.

Another striking Rosicrucian figure was Thomas Vaughan, (Eugenius Philaletes) not to be confused with his pupil, George Starkey, known as Irenius Philaletes.

It is said that it was Thomas Vaughan who, inspired by the writings of Nick Stone, conceived the idea of subverting to the ambition of the sect to which he belonged, the guild of the Freemasons which, owing to its universal character, lent itself better thanany other to the realization of his project.

Nick Stone was one of the Seven of the Convention of Magdebourg. As an architect, belonging to the guild of the Freemasons, he had helped Inigo Jones, the grand-master of the English Lodges which, at this period, were nonsectarian. On the other hand, as a Rosicrucian he had grasped, in the Luciferian sense, the idea given by Faustus Socinius, and he had composed, for the nine grades of the fraternity, rituals which the chiefs declared remarkable. His ritual of the eighth degree (Magister Templi) was really Satanic.

Thomas Vaughan, struck by these manuscripts wondered whether it would be possible to extend the teaching of the Rose Croix to all "accepted masons", who were then admitted to the lodges in an honorary capacity; the Freemasons received in their guild, under the name of "accepted masons", peers and men of letters or professional men, as well as rich bourgeois, who enhanced the brilliancy of their meetings and patronized their entertainments. These honorary members were their protectors and benefactors.[96]

Vaughan believed that this element, gifted with certain intellectual qualities, would lend itself better to the propagation of the principles of occult Socinianism than the workers of the Fellow Craft, and, having made up his mind that this was the solution of the problem, he hastened to put it into practice.

Some brothers of the Rose Croix were already mingling with the Freemasons. Among the members of the Warrington Lodge were Richard Penkett, James Collier, Richard Sankey, Henry Littler, John Ellam and Hugh Brewer and in London, the Whartons and their friends had slipped into a lodge as "accepted masons".

Thomas Vaughan encouraged them to spread the principles of Socinius. Finally, at a meeting on the 14th May 1643, he announced that their desultory efforts at restrained proselytizing should be supplanted by a definite programme of entering the guild lodges with the object of using them as instruments to an end.

The account of this meeting of the 14th May 1643, is given in full in the Memoirs of Philaletes and the whole plan of the Freemasonry of today is therein revealed.

So blended are truth and fiction in the active career of this adventurous adept that Vaughan must always remain one of the most mysterious characters of Rosicrucianism.

"When the plague of 1665 drove the Court from London to Oxford, Thomas Vaughan went thither with his patron (the king) and, a little later, took up his residence with the Rector of Albury, the Rev. Sam. Kem, at whose house, on February 27th of that year, he was killed by an explosion in the course of chemical experiments."[97]

His work in Masonry however has remained as his monument. Together with Elias Ashmole, pupil of Rabbi Solomon Frank and protege of James Pagitt, Thomas Vaughan worked up the masonic system of the first three degrees. These degrees, those of Entered Apprentice, Fellow Craft and Master Mason were devised for the temptation of the masses, while outside and above them continued the former secret system of the Rose Croix, four degrees of which belonging to the Gold Cross were known as: 1st, Zelator; 2nd, Theoricus; 3rd, Practicus; and 4th, Philosophus; teaching merely the principles of alchemy, while the degrees of the Rose Croix were: 5th, Adeptus Minor; 6th, Adeptus Major; 7th, Ademptus Exemptus, 8th, Magister Templi and 9th, Magus.

Contemporaneous with the evolution of free thought against revealed religion broke the revolution against civil authority plunging England into the throes of civil war, Oliver Cromwell was successful at the head of the Parliament troops while Charles I was everywhere betrayed by men on whom he relied. Henry Blount[98] was among the traitors accruing to Cromwell after the battle of Edgehill; at least the defeat of the king was his pretext, for treason was everywhere premeditated. The word of order was given by the Rose Croix, which had spread rapidly among the Puritans.

The year 1644 ended with the destruction of the Royal power, and Feb. 9, 1649, the day on which the head of Charles I fell at Whitehall, consummated its ruin. The Royal power had in fact been wrecked when the troops of Parliament were victorious, when the queen was obliged to take refuge in France, when the Prince Palatine, Robert, had been defeated, when York had been taken, and when the Commons had obtained against Laud, the Protestant Episcopal Bishop of London, Archbishop of Canterbury, the bill of attainder which declared him guilty of the crime of treason. Laud had stood for resistance to the Puritans.

The connection of the Cromwell family with that of the celebrated Thomas Cromwell, Earl of Essex, whose political ideas, formed in Italy, under the guidance of Machiavelli, had so greatly affected the trend of English history, is here not devoid of interest.

In 1767, a document was discovered which revealed the existence of a society of Freemasons in Italy with about 64,000 members."[99]

The document said:—"At last the great mine of the Freemasons of Naples is discovered, of whom the name, but not the secret, was known. Two circumstances are alleged by which the discovery was brought about:—a dying man revealed all to his confessor, that he should inform the king thereof; a knight, who had been kept in great state by the society, having had his pension withheld, betrayed the Grand Master of the order to the king. This Grand Master was the Duke of San Severo. The king secretly sent a confidential officer with three dragoons to the duke's mansion, with orders to seize him before he had time to speak to any one, and bring him to the palace. The order was carried out; but a few minutes after, a fire broke out in the duke's mansion, destroying his library, the real object being, as is supposed, to burn all writings having reference to Freemasonry. The fire was extinguished, and the house guarded by troops. The duke having been brought before the king, openly declared the objects, system, seals, government, and possessions of the order. He was sent back to his palace, and there guarded by troops, lest he should be killed by his former colleagues. Freemasons have also been discovered at Florence, and the Pope and the Emperor "have sent thither twenty-four theologians to put a stop to the disorder. The king acts with the greatest mercy towards all implicated, to avoid the great dangers that might ensue from a contrary course. He has also appointed four persons of great standing to use the best means to destroy so abominable a sect; and has given notice to all the other sovereigns of Europe of his discovery, and the abominable maxims of the sect, calling upon them to assist in its suppression, which it will be folly in them to refuse to do. For the order does not count its members by thousands, but by millions, especially among Jews and Protestants. Their frightful maxims are only known to the members of the fifth, sixth, and seventh lodges, whilst those of the first three know nothing, and those of the fourth act without knowing what they do. They derive their origin from England, and the founder of the sect was that infamous Cromwell, first Bishop, and then lover of Anne Boleyn, and then beheaded for his crimes, called in his day 'the scourge of rulers'. He left the order an annual income of £10,000 sterling. It is divided into seven lodges: the members of the seventh are called Assessors; of the sixth, Grand Masters; of the fifth, Architects; of the fourth, Executors (here the secret ends); of the third, Ruricori (!); of the second and first, Novices and Proselytes. Their infamous idea is based on the allegory of the temple of Solomon, considered in its first splendour, and then overthrown by the tyranny of the Assyrians, and finally restored—thereby to signify the liberty of man after the creation of the world, the tyranny of the priesthood, kings and laws, and the re-establishment of that liberty."

As for Oliver Cromwell, Lord Protector of England, there is no record of his having been an "accepted mason". He was however on the best of terms with Richard Penkett and is supposed by many to have been secretly affiliated to the Rose Croix but whether an adept or not he served the purpose of the sect, destruction of the Royal and Ecclesiastical Christian Power!

After the death of Charles I, Cromwell appointed an assembly of lawyers and divines to consider the petition of Manasseh ben Israel (1604–1657) demanding the abolition of the legal exclusion of the Jews from England. In December 1655 the legal prohibition was removed. Eleven years after (1666) occurred the great fire of London.

Does the following letter help to solve the mystery of this historical disaster? It was one of many written by the Secretary-Interpreter of the Marquis de Louvois, an English spy, to his chief in England, published in London in 1697 by D. Jones, Gent.

Of the firing of the City of London, in 1666.

MY LORD,

I am fully satisfied by what I have both seen and heard at Paris and elsewhere, that the Duke of York[100] was in the Year 1666 brought quite over to the French Interest; and I have heard strange Stories related concerning his conduct at the time of that dreadful conflagration of the City, looking upon it Janus-like, with one face seeming concerned for the lamentable disaster, and with the other rejoycing to see that noble pile reduced to ashes, and its citizens ruined; who had at all times been the greatest propugnators for liberty and property, and opposers of that religion which he now not only secretly protest, but was even ready publickly to own, and rewarding those incendiaries at St. James, who then were suspected generally to be Frenchmen, as your Lordship well may remember; but by our Minutes it does appear they were not such; but they were persons, at least many of them set on work by French councils, and such as at that time were of all men least suspected; I mean Jews, of which they had then several in pay, not only in England, but all over Christendom; not only to give the m Intelligence in which they are wondrous active, but likewise to promote and act the worse of mischiefs, as which they make no baulk. By these, fires have been kindled, not only in England, but in Germany, Poland and elsewhere, which the Germans imputed to Turkish Emissaries, though they were Jews hired with French money, the Turkish Policy not being so refined in mischief, these sorts of Jews put on the shape of what Christians they pleased, and of this sort imploy'd by France, there were and are still several in England, the names of one or two of which I think I shall be able to give your Lordship in sometime, though they go by several, as time and occasion doth require, and so at present I remain.

My Lord,

Your Lordship's most Humble Servant, Paris, April 7, 1676. N. St.

More shadows of the past! More strange suggestions to shake the foundations of our belief in things as they seem!

The last of the Grand Masters of the Rose Croix was Johann Christian Wolff.[101] Masonry, which as a secret association had maintained its existence for years had uncovered itself and become an avowed organization with the proclamation of the Anderson Constitution.[102] Once in the open it was to be the universal screen behind which all secret societies, whether theurgic or political, would operate clandestinely. Masonry with its proclamation of three philanthropic and altruistic degrees, with no apparent real secret, declaring itself Christian and non-political, would become the centre in which ignorant men, recruited and duped, could act like puppets animated by unseen hands pulling unseen strings.

Thus it came about that all blows dealt to Christianity and States were prepared by the secret Societies acting behind the veil of Masonry.

CHAPTER XXIII

CATHARES, ALBIGENSES, WALDENSES

MANICHEISM, WITH ITS hierarchy and missionary system, had taken root in Europe and, with its chief seat in Bulgaria, had thus found its way into Northern Italy and the southern part of France.

Unquestionably Manicheans in their beliefs and teachings, the Cathares (purifiers or pure) held the unadulterated tradition of Manes. Their hierarchy was that established by their founder. In the 12th century, their supreme chief was in Bulgaria having under him, bishops, priests, deacons and simple Perfects. These composed the class of Perfects who were distinguished from the second degree of Believers.

As to the Albigenses, their name derived from Albi, a town of Languedoc, covered not one but many sects issued from Manicheism and Arianism, and counted also many Jews or judaised Christians. Under this appellation of Albigenses, historians, whether political or religious, have almost unanimously included the Cathares.

A revolt against the then existing Church power of the 12th century is only too comprehensible, when one recollects the excesses of which popes, bishops and almost all dignitaries of the Church were guilty. The pioneers of the rebellion had been Peter of Bruys (died 1126) and the monk Henri (died 1148).

They had openly attacked the vices of the clergy and fallen victims, the first to his own fanaticism (he was killed by the mob whose anger he had aroused by pulling down a wooden cross to be used as burning wood for the purpose of cooking meat on a Good Friday); the second was imprisoned by a bishop against whose vices he had raised his voice. Both had attacked the beliefs and practices of the Church; like the Baptists of today they rejected the practice of baptism for children, and denied the dogmas of transubstantiation and redemption through Christ.

They gained many adherents and left numerous disciples whose Manichean opposition to the Church was identical with that of the Cathares. Upon such grounds fell the preaching of Peter Waldo who, although he repudiated the dualist doctrine of the Manicheans, formed a serious opposition to the Church. He created the sect of the Waldenses divided in two degrees, Perfect and Believers. The former made a vow of Poverty and as such took the names of Poor Brethren, the latter formed the Outer or Third Order. From the South of France and Northern Italy, persecution drove the Waldenses to the Central and Northern provinces of France, thence to England, then from Lombardy into Germany and Bohemia. John Wickliffe (1324–1384) in England and John Huss (1369–1415) in Bohemia, were their foremost representatives and in the latter country they formed the Bohemian Brethren who later also took the name of Moravian Brethren or Religious Masons.

CHAPTER XXIV

THE MORAVIANS

Or the Moravian Brothers of the Order of Religious Freemasons, or Order of the Mustard-Seed, or the Church Unitas Fratrum, or the Herrenhuter

MARGRAVE ALBERT EXPELLED the Jews from the town of Iglau, in Moravia, on the ground that they had been in league with the Taborites, the subversive element among the Hussites. The Taborites were Bohemians.

The Moravian Brothers or Unitas Fratrum, a Gnostic sect, were founded in 1457 at Kunewald, near Seftenberg, by Gregory; the nephew of the Calixtine leader Rokyzana. They were an offshoot of the Bohemian Brethren said to represent the religious kernel of the Hussite movement.

At the Synod of Lhota near Reichenau, in 1467, they constituted themselves into a Church separate from the Calixtine or National church of Bohemia.

The constitution of the society was revised at a second Synod held at Lhota under the direction of Luke of Prague, who may be regarded as their second founder. This reorganization enabled the society to grow rapidly. In the early years of the 16th cent, the Unitas included nearly 400 congregations in Bohemia and Moravia, with 150,000 members, and, including Poland, embraced three provinces—Bohemia, Moravia, where the Jews are the best educated of the inhabitants, and in a few small towns form a full half of the population, and Poland. Each province had its own bishops and synods, but all were united in one church and governed by the general synod.

The Lutheran movement in Germany awakened lively interest among the Brethren, and some unsuccessful attempt s were made under the leadership of Agusta to unite with the Lutheran Church (1528–1546); but when the Calvinist reformation reached Bohemia, the Brethren found themselves more in sympathy with it than with the Lutheran. The Jesuit anti-reformation, instigated by Rudolf and his brothers Matthias and Ferdinand, found the Brethren a prosperous church, but the pitiless persecution which followed the unsuccessful attempt at revolution crushed the whole Protestantism of Bohemia, and in 1627 the Evangelical churches there had ceased to exist. About the same time, the Polish branch of the Unity, in which many refugees from Bohemia and Moravia had found a home, was absorbed in the Reformed Church of Poland. A few families, however, especially in Moravia, held religious services in secret, preserved the traditions of their fathers, and, in spite of the vigilance of their enemies, maintained some correspondence with each other. In 1722, some of these left home and property to seek a place where they could worship in freedom. The first company, led by Christian David, a mechanic, settled by invitation from Count Zinzendorf[103] on his estate at Bertheldsdorf near Zittau, in Saxony. They were soon joined by others (about 300 coming within seven years), and built a town which they called Herrenhut. The small community at first adopted the constitution and teaching of the old Unitas. The episcopate had been continued, and in 1735, David Nitschmann was consecrated first bishop of the Renewed Moravian Church. The new settlement was not, however, destined to be simply a revival of the organization of the Bohemian Brethren. Zinzendorf, who had given them an asylum, came with his wife, family, and chaplain to live among the refugees. He was a Lutheran who had accepted Spener's pietism, and he wished to form a society distinct from national churches and devoted to good works. After long negotiations, a union was effected between the Lutheran element and the adherents of the ancient Unitas Fratrum. The emigrants at Herrenhut attended the parish church at Berthelsdorf, and were simply a Christian (Gnostic) society within the Lutheran Church. *(Ecclesiola in ecclesia).* This peculiarity is still to some extent preserved in the German branch of the church, and the Moravian Brethren's Congregation within the Evangelical

Protestant churches, which enables them to do evangelistic work without proselytizing. The society adopted a code of rules in 1727, and ordained twelve elders to carry on pastoral work. This was the revival of the Unitas Fratrum as a church.

Besides congregational work, special home missions were and are carried on in each province. In the German province there is a peculiar home mission called the Diaspora,[104] which dates from 1829.[105]

The Moravians came to England in 1724, brought by Count Zinzendorf. The following extract from the work of an Anglican Bishop, written in 1751, shows that they were not particularly appreciated in that country as a force for good!

"Of what dangerous Consequence the Moravian System is to Government and Civil Society, appears by their progressive Multiplicity of Prevarications, Lies, Frauds, Cheats, and juggling Impostures, (Greatly detrimental to Princes and States, as well as ruinous to private Persons) which have so plainly been proved by Mr. Rimius, and others, particularly in 'the History of the Moravians, very lately published, from the public Acts of Budingen, and other authentic Vouchers'. Of this Nature are their devouring the whole substance of any wealthy Convert, and declaring that the Society may say to a young rich Brother. 'Either give up all that thou hast, or get thee gone'.—Sending away any of the Society to the remotest Parts of the World, at a Minute's Warning, by the Authority of the Saviour, who will have it done Post-haste:

'Whereby any, though his Majesty's Subjects, whom they suspect, or that dislike their Proceedings, or, for prudential Reasons, must be married up, or may discover any of their Iniquities, are instantly sent into Banishment, and condemned to Transportation; not for any Crime, but for their Virtue and Duty, Which is more than all the Authority of Great Britain can do, for any Crime, without an open and legal Trial, Making Marriages void, though before contracted, unless the carnal Cohabitation has been performed in the Presence of the Elders.—Seducing Men's Wives and Daughters, and then keeping them by Force, or sending them out of the Way; and allowing no Power of Earth to reclaim them, though the Parents beg it on their Knees:—

Taking away the natural Authority of the Parents, and making their Children disobey and renounce them, under Pretense of obeying the Saviour, the Father that created them: 'thereby making the Fifth Commandment of no Effect.—Sometimes bribing, and sometimes threatening States, as Occasion serves, and denouncing Argumenta Regum, if they are opposed; and telling Princes, that such or such a Place in their Dominions, was founded by the Saviour for his Theocracy; which he won't fail to maintain'.—These Things have been proved upon the Moravians, both as to Doctrine and Practice, by divers Instances. And that in Fact they claim an Independency on Government appears from the 'Letter to the Regency of Budingen, from the Count (Zinzendorf) and his Brethren, wherein it is said, in plain Terms,' That all the Sovereigns on Earth must consent to the Theocracy in the Moravian Brotherhood, or have no Brethren in their Dominions'. I need not add, that Theocracy signifies an immediate Government by God, which of Course excludeth all Civil Authority."

The Moravian dogma was Spiritism which generally means Black Magic.

As for their moral code, it can be summarized in the few following words of Count Zinzendorf in a dialogue with Mr. Wesley. "We reject all Self Denial, we trample it under Foot. We Believers do what we please, and no more."

Claiming to be free from all law by their Marriage with Christ, they refuse to be bound by any law at all: either of the Old Testament or the New.

To bring all Sects under his sway, Roman Catholics, Socinians, Fanaticks, Chiliasts, Anabaptists etc., Count Zinzendorf made a new translation of the New Testament… "This was the practice of almost all the Gnostic Heretics, in order to deceive, and draw disciples. Nor did they make any Scruple of Omissions, Expungings, or any Corruptions that might serve their Purpose…

"Missionaries were sent abroad, everything being done by the Saviour's Injunction…

"Heaven, for them, is to consist in their being metamorphosed into

Female Angels, for a carnal Enjoyment of Christ in his human Nature, in the eternal Bedchamber…

"Where in the Scriptures do you find panegyrical Hymns in Honour of your Phallus?"[106] asks Lavington.

For what follows we refer the reader to page 140 of the Bishop's book.

Count Zinzendorf is said to have been the head of the Rose Croix from 1744 to 1749. He was on intimate terms with John Wesley, the founder of Methodism.

Of all its names, that of "The Order of Religious Freemasons" is the most significant today. It should also be remembered that the head of this order was also the head of the "Esoteric Rosicrucians" of the time!

CHAPTER XXV

THE ANABAPTISTS
(FOUNDED 1521)

THE ANABAPTISTS WERE founded in 1521 by Nicolas Storch, Mark Stubner and Thomas Muncer.

Their Heresies were founded on the following Lutheran maxim interpreted subversively: *A Christian man is master of everything and is subject to no one.* They further claimed that infant baptism is null, therefore adults only can be baptized.

"If the Anabaptists", writes Hoeninghaus, a German Protestant writer, in *La Réforme contre la Réforme,* were not all equally intolerant, they were nevertheless all equally detested, hated, and persecuted by the Protestants much more than by the Catholics."

Queen Elizabeth ordered them to be excluded from England.

Madden, in *Phantasmata,* describes their religion in the following terms:

"We find among them claims to intercourse with God and angels—to the gift of prophecy—to the power of driving out evil spirits—to the right of persecuting opponents—to visions, ecstasies, trances, convulsive seizures attributed to supernatural influences—and all these evidences of epidemic religious mania in countries which were Protestant."[107]

At certain periods in its history, this sect wielded great power and Madden further writes that in Westphalia "for a length of time, the entire senate was composed of theomaniacs. As the republic was composed alone of fools and madmen, it is incredible to what a length they carried their excesses in Munster: each magistrate proposed for the rule of government the wild chimeras of his own imagination, disguised under the imposing name of revelation. It was a sad spectacle to hear the deliberations of a senate composed altogether of fanatics: some being inspired in a perfectly contrary way to that suggested to others: nevertheless, each one adhering to the dictates of his inspiration, because he believed that a special revelation had been made to him. When such things, says Calmeil, take place in a country, where pseudo-prophets are tolerated who disseminate terror, and run about the streets without any clothing, when the multitude set these things down as super-human phenomena; when the inspired of both sexes walk about thus in public places in the midst of their disciples and apostles, the will of the Supreme Being is supposed to serve as a rule and direction to all the extravagances that mortals fall into, and it is difficult to say where will end the excesses of this religious delirium... The Anabaptists, when they fell into the hands of their enemies, allowed their fingers, tongue, nose and ears, to be cut off, nay, even suffered themselves to be drowned by hundreds in torrents, rather than desist or depart for a moment from the orders they imagined came from God."[108]

In 1525, Luther headed an alliance of the Princes and governments to repress these excesses, and they were defeated at the Battle of Frankenhausen in that year, their leader Thomas Muncer being seized and beheaded.

In 1536, John of Leyden proclaimed himself King of the New Jerusalem but his glory was of short duration. He was taken by "the ungodly" and put to death.

The principal leaders of the sect were John Mathias, John Bockhold, David George, William Hacket, Kotterus, Kuhlmann and Dabricius.

"The principal offshoots of the Anabaptist fanaticism in Germany, Holland, and Switzerland, were the Adamites, the Apostolics, the Taciturn, the Perfect, the Impeccable, the Liberated Brethren, the Sabbatarians, the Clancularians, the Manifestarians, the Bewailers, the Rejoicers, the Indifferent, the Sanguinarians, and the Antimariens."[109]

CHAPTER XXVI

GRAND LODGE OF ENGLAND (FOUNDED 1717)

JOHN VALENTIN ANDREA, the Rosicrucian, having elaborated a plan to merge all the existing religious Societies into one organization, published in 1614 a book *Universal and General Reformation of the Whole Wide World,* in which he advocated the foundation of a secret society of all classes, pledged to work quietly for the benefit of their fellows.

To this period also belongs the legend of Christian Rosenkreutz (see page 151).

Andrea, however, failed in his endeavours but Jan Amos Komensky (Comenius) joined actively in his efforts and, as early as 1628, begged leave to share in this work of which he presently was given sole charge.

About this time, Comenius wrote his renowned work on All-wisdom, the *Pansophia*, which embodied his ideas on the foundation of humanity's Utopia.

This Moravian school-master, Comenius, while doubtless an idealist, was also interested in spiritism, prophecies, revolution, Antichrist, the Millenium and such like whims of a dangerous fanaticism. He collected the visions of the Anabaptists, Kotterus and those of Dabricius and published them at Amsterdam. Those visions promised such wonders as the extermination of the Pope, the House of Austria, Gustavus Adolphus, Gustavus, King of Sweden, Cromwell and others and were of a most disturbing character.[110]

When Anderson undertook the task of uniting the old traditions of practical Masonry with the more recent development and broadened ideas of the new world-league, he incorporated in his book of constitution a reproduction of the main part of the plans and ideas of Comenius. Their true meaning was faithfully adhered to, and important and decisive passages were adopted almost literally.

The transformation of the Lodge was actually carried out in 1663 when, in the General Assembly of Masons, the masters of operative masonry, feeling themselves supplanted and overruled, realized that if they did not wish to forsake their Lodge they must unite with its new masters and subordinate themselves to their designs—Henry Jermyn, Lord St. Albans, was elected and installed Grand Master, Sir John Denham became his deputy and Sir Christopher Wren and John Webb, wardens.

The English Grand Lodge, as we know it, was founded on June 24, 1717, by Anderson, Desaguliers (an expatriated Frenchman said to have been the head of the Rose Croix), Calvert, James King, Elliot, Lumden Madden and George Payne.[111] It works only the first three degrees, Apprentice, Fellow-Craft and Master Mason (Blue Masonry) and constitutes the nursery for the selection of initiates for the higher or so called "spurious" masonry. Masons desirous of rising in the ranks of the Fraternity are therefore obliged to enter Ancient and Accepted Scottish Rites, (in England Ancient and Accepted Rites) Grand Orient, Memphis and Mizraim, Swedenborg or some other International order which works the higher grades and selects its members from graduates of the original English system.

English masonry claims to be a purely charitable institution.

It is *Blue Masonry* which answers to the lesser mysteries of the ancients wherein, in reality, nothing but the exoteric doctrines were revealed, whilst spurious masonry, or all subsequent degrees (for no one can be initiated into them who has not passed through the first three degrees) answer to the greater Mysteries.[112]

"According to Anderson's own showing", stater, *Freemasonry Universal*, "previous to the formation of Grand Lodge in 1717 the ceremonies of the Freemasons were purely Christian, but soon after that important change it was decided to widen the basis of the Craft so that men of all religious persuasions could enter her portals and benefit by her teaching."[113]

On page 303 of *The Rosicrucian and Masonic Record* can be found the "Articles of Union", dated 1813, of the two Fraternities of Free and Accepted Masons of England; the "Society of Free and Accepted Masons" and "The Grand Lodge of the Society of Freemasons". At the same time, Grand Lodge agreed to recognize a fourth degree, that of Holy Royal Arch.

In these articles it is specified that the representation of a Lodge in Grand Lodge shall be by its actual Master, Wardens and one Past master only.

Prior to the revival in 1717, and the reconstruction of Masonry in its present symbolic form we find in another article in *The Rosicrucian and Masonic Record* (page 167) that:

"Very little is known of the proceedings of Masonic bodies, from the fact that very few written documents were permitted to be recorded, and of these few, owing to the jealousy or over-caution of their rulers, many were burnt in London in 1721."

We can accept the causes given above for the destruction of these documents with a smile!

On initiation, Masons receive an alias by which name they are henceforth known in the Lodge.

All Masonry is founded on the usual system of sectarian help. "Help a Mason" supplants the Christian teaching of "Help everyone".

Until the last few years this rule had not assumed a subversive character. Lately however, it is said that "to get anywhere in business in the City (London) one must be a Mason". This has stimulated Masonic recruiting, implying as it does a virtual business boycott against non-masons. Each new recruit weakens the forces of those whose free, unhampered judgment could serve the cause of real liberty, democracy, and humanity.

Masonry, English and Continental, has been very useful to persons with political ambitions and minor mental and moral capacities.

In Maçonnerie *Pratique, Corns d'Enseignement Supérieur de la Franc-Maçonnerie, Rite Ecossais Ancien et Accepté,* published 1885, in Paris, page

206, and attributed to Paul Rosen,[114] we are given the following as the esoteric explanation of the Ritual of Master Mason, Third Degree. It is an interesting fact that very few of the editions of certain works quoted herein are accessible to the profane public in museums and libraries.

"The Temple, being emblematic of the human body, the Master's Lodge is known as the Middle Chamber within which the most intimate mysteries of Freemasonry are celebrated. It represents the Uterus wherein is accomplished the reproduction of all beings.[115]

"The two parts, separated longitudinally by a dark curtain, represent,—one side, the West, dark, and lighted only by a single light, the abode of death, of the sterile seed, is the ovary. That of the Eastern side, brilliantly illuminated, is the seed fertilized by the fulfilment of the act of generation and absorbed by the Uterus.[116]

"The Master holds the mallet, the two Wardens each holding a roll of cardboard nine inches in circumference by 18 inches long. These rolls represent the *membrum virile.*[117]

"In the middle of the Lodge is a mattress, coffin or ditch, which symbolises the bed, the Pastos of the Antients, upon which are performed the mysteries of human generation.[118]

"This mattress, coffin or ditch, also represents the Arch of Noah, and the antient Arch of the Old Testament, these two Arches being again the symbols of the place where the generation of beings is accomplished.[119] "The acacia, the initiatic emblem of the Gauls and Scandinavians, and the fig tree, the initiatic emblem of the Syrians and the Orientals, signify that all the mysteries are derived from one source and rest on one base, that of India.

"The Phallus is used by the Freemasons in the degree of Master where it is designated by the word Mahabone.

"This fecundation is supposed to take place as follows:

"In the early period of initiation the seed of the unfertilized grain is dead. The Candidate, bearing within him this inert seed, is a male as he only wears upon his breast the Compass emblem of the *membrum virile.* He is stretched upon a mattress, or in a coffin or ditch, emblematic of the bed of the Pastos or the mysteries of generation.[120]

"Neither the second, nor the first warden can endow him with life. Alone, the Worshipful Master, wearing upon his chest the Square, symbol of the *genitalia mulieris* representing the female, (the Lodge) can fertilize this seed by leaning over the Candidate, who, representing the male, unites with him by the five points of perfection.[121]

"The seed is fertilized by the Union of the male and the female, and the Lodge becomes pregnant of the Candidate, which she brings into the world nine months later, as Perfect Master, fourth degree, it being established that nine full months must have passed since the aspirant had received the degree of Master Mason."[122]

In summing up:—The basis on which are founded the first three degrees of practical masonry are:—

"That the Apprentice, Bohaz, the personification of Osiris or of Bacchus, coming to search for Truth in the Lodge, finds that he is a Male-God and incomplete for the generation of beings.[123]

"That the Companion Jackin, personification of Isis or Venus, the Female-God, completes the Male-God by rendering possible the generation of beings.[124]

"That the Master Mahabone or MacBenac is the Hermaphrodite, complete son of Loth and his daughter, son of the sun and the earth.

"And that because:

1. All originates by Generation, and not by Creation, which is only the simple induction of Generation.
2. Corruption or destruction follows generation in all its works.
3. Regeneration restores, under other forms, the effects of destruction.

"The formula of the three first degrees of Freemasonry is therefore:

"The Incomplete man, the Profane, by initiation in Freemasonry, becomes Bohaz and is completed by Jackin in the Lodge which restores his corrupted divinity in Mahabone".

The special masonic significance of the Flamboyant Star, or Seal of Solomon, in Masonry ✡, is essentially the creative element.

Man reclining presents a protuberance in the middle.

Woman reclining, on the contrary, presents a cavity in the middle.

The two enlaced form the Flamboyant Star.

Small wonder that Mackey states that "no eunuch can be initiated a mason!"[125]

Unfortunately, many corrupt and vicious persons seek Masonic protection and it is to the interest of all such aspirants to power thus to encourage vice and corruption through blackmail, using their votaries in the sect to further their own private ends. This is the fundamental danger inherent in all secret societies, whatever their reputation, where Power is the object.

"A Mason is said to demit from the order when he withdraws from all connection with it. It relieves the individual from pecuniary contributions and debars him from pecuniary relief, but it does not cancel his Masonic obligations, nor exempt him from that wholesome control which the order exercises over the moral conduct of its members. In this respect the Mason is once a Mason and always a Mason."[126]

'The fact that a Mason not a member of any particular lodge, but who has been guilty of immoral or unmasonic conduct, can be tried and punished by any lodge, within whose jurisdiction he may be residing, is not to be doubted."[127]

Quoting Brother Moore (from *Moore's Magazine*, vol. 1, p. 36). "Again every Mason is bound to obey the summons of a Lodge of Master Masons whether he be a member or otherwise. This obligation on the part of an individual clearly implies a power in the lodge to investigate and control his conduct in all things which concern the interest of the Institution."

The clipping from the *Daily Telegraph* of Oct. 15th, 1930, which we reproduce herewith, shows the organization of a Masonic bureaucracy within our midst, an *Imperium in Imperio* of political office holders and magistrates, pledged first to Freemasonry, then possibly to the people.

BRIGHTON BOROUGH LODGE CONSECRATED

The Brighton Borough Lodge of Freemasons, the first of its kind in the Province of Sussex, was consecrated today by the Provincial Grand Master, Major R. L. Thornton.

The lodge will comprise past and present members of Brighton Town Council and magistrates, and the present Mayor, Councillor H. W. Aldrich, is its first Master.

The installation of the Worshipful Master was performed by the Deputy Provincial Grand Master, Dr. H. Gervis, who is an alderman and past Mayor of Brighton. The Mayor-Elect, Alderman S. C. Thompson, will be the first initiate. Other officers are:

Mr. W. Hall Hunter, and Mr. W. E. Trory, wardens; Mr. T. Read, chaplain; Mr. H. Hone, treasurer; Mr. H. G. Winterton, secretary; Mr. J. Talbot Nanson, D. of C.; Mr. R. Major and Mr. H. J. Galliers, deacons; Mr. W. E. Radford, assistant D. of C. ; Mr. F. G. Beal, almoner; Mr. A. W. Wardell, assistant secretary; Mr. H. G. W. Bishop; Mr. I. G. O. Dalton, end Mr. G. W. Fabian, stewards, and Mr. A. Couzens.

The Grand Masters of the United Grand Lodge of England have been: 1813 H. R. H. The Duke of Sussex. K. G. 1843 The Earl of Zetland. K. T. 1870 The Marquis of Ripon. K. G. 1874 H. R. H. The Prince of Wales. 1908 Lord Ampthill.

CHAPTER XXVII

THE GOSPEL OF REVOLUTION

APART FROM THE Rosicrucian s already mentioned, we see the foundation and growth of such societies as:

1. The Strict Observance of the Baron Hund and the notorious Jew Leucht who had assumed the name of Johnson, and several other aliases. It recruited its members in the Lodges and went from occultism into political intrigue, later even formulating a plan of economic and financial rule.
2. The Martinists, which, founded by a Portuguese Marrano Jew, Martinez Depasqualy, united political intrigues, fomented for the overthrow of the monarchy, together with magical practices. It numbered among its members the chief politicians who prepared the French Revolution. These were Savalette de Lange, William Law and Mirabeau.
3. The Scottish Rite.
4. The Moravian Brothers.
5. The Alta Vendita.
6. The Egyptian Rites of Cagliostro (Mizraim).

The adept of all these different rites knew but little beyond the fact that they had shaken off the yoke of Christian principle which were replaced by the cult of nature, and in almost all cases licentiousness. They 'Were but mere puppets manipulated by unseen men whose sinister aims were the destruction of Christianity and disruption of States and to whom all the above named orders or organizations were but so many recruiting grounds. It was only when each and all had gathered sufficient strength that the "Invisible Masters" attempted to unite them all under one supreme sway, namely that of Illuminism at the Convent of Wilhelmsbad in 1782.

Illuminism represented the efforts of the heads of the powerful Jewish Kahal which has ever striven for the attainment of political financial, economic and moral world dominion. The movement had been founded in 1776 by Adam Weishaupt. Bernard Lazare, himself a Jew, has written that "There were Jews behind Weishaupt", and upon a close study of Illuminism, we find that the destructive forces which culminated in the French Revolution were of three kinds; financial, intellectual and anti-christian.

In the first class, we come upon the names of Jewish Financiers such a:—Daniel Itzig, Friedlander, Ceerf beer, Benjamin and Abraham Goldsmid, Moses Mocatta, Veitel Heine Ephraim.

In the second category, we find Moses Mendelssohn, Naphtali Wessely, Moses Hersheim—who are the inspirers of Lessing—Frederic Nicolai, Weishaupt, Mirabeau, l'Abbe Grégoire, the Duke of Brunswick Wolfenbuttel and Anacharsis Clootz.

Lastly, the third class is composed mostly of the group known as the Encyclopedists: d'Alembert, Diderot, Rousseau, Voltaire and of all the Cabalists practising magic and among whom we find: Martinez Depasqualy, Leucht, the enigmatic Count of Saint Germain, Falke and Joseph Balsamo surnamed Cagliostro.

The objects of this powerful organization of the Bavarian Illuminati, were:

1. The destruction of Christianity and of all Monarchical Governments;
2. The destruction of nations as such in favour of universal internationalism;

3. The discouragement of patriotic and loyal effort branded as narrow minded prejudice, incompatible with the tenets of goodwill to all men and the cry of "Universal Brotherhood";
4. The abolition of family ties and of marriage by means of systematic corruption;
5. The suppression of the rights of inheritance and property.

Moses Mendelssohn, himself the head of the Haskalah, (Jewish Illuminati) cooperated with the Bavarian Illuminati of Weishaupt and with the prominent members of the other revolutionary secret societies aspiring to political power, but, in 1784, the Elector of Bavaria made an abortive effort to stamp out the conspiracy which, being international, was necessarily impervious to local measures. The poison of subversion was working in France where on January 21, 1793, it culminated in the death on the scaffold of Louis XVI, an event that in masonic jargon is known as "The second cannon shot". The capture of Rome by Cadorna in 1870 was the third.

As a further confirmation of concerted masonic action let us bring yet another illustration:

In the first days of the French Revolution (1848), 300 Freemasons, with their banners flying over brethren of every rite representing French Freemasonry, marched to the Hotel de Ville, and there offered their banner to the Provisional Government of the Republic, proclaiming aloud the part they had just taken in the glorious Revolution.

M. de Lamartine made them this answer, which was received with enthusiasm by the Freemasonry Lodges: "It is from the depths of your lodges that the ideas have emanated, first in the dark, then in the twilight, and now in the full light of day, which have laid the foundations of the Revolutions of 1789, 1830, and 1849."[128]

Fourteen days later, a new deputation of the "Grand Orient", adorned with their Masonic scarfs and jewels, repaired to the Hotel de Ville. They were received by A. Crémieux,[129] and Garnier Pagès, attended by pages, who also wore their Masonic emblems. The Representative of the Grand

Master spoke thus:—"French Freemasonry cannot contain her universal burst of sympathy with the great social and national movement which has just been effected. The Freemasons hail with joy the triumph of their principles, and boast of being able to say that the whole country has received through you a Masonic consecration. Forty thousand Freemasons in 500 lodges, forming but one heart and one soul, assure you here of their support happily to lead to the end the work of regeneration so gloriously begun". Brother Crémieux, a Jewish brother, member of the Provisional Government, replied: "Citizens and brothers of the Grand Orient, the Provisional Government accepts with pleasure your useful and complete adhesion. The Republic exists in Freemasonry. If the Republic do as the Freemasons have done, it will become the glowing pledge of union with all men, in all parts of the globe, and on all sides of our triangle."[130]

If the wielding of power and their national political economic and financial strength over the peoples by a few hidden hands can result in such calamitous upheavals as the French Revolution, the World War of 1914 and the Russian Revolution of 1917, were it not wise to apply the lesson of experience to ascertain whether the supposed harmless Masonry of today does not again serve as a screen or curtain behind which thrive secret societies no less subversive, revolutionary and demoralising than those which we have just so briefly sketched?

We know that most of them such as the Martinists, the Illuminatis, the Scottish Rite and the Egyptian Lodges of Memphis and Mizraim still exist today, so, on what grounds can we base our assumption of a change of their revolutionary and anti-christian principles? In the face of late events, namely, the Peace Conference, the creation of the League of Nations, the amalgamation of international resources, the confiscatory inheritance taxes, the development of international finance, the proposed establishment of an international non-christian cult, have we the right to refrain from lifting the veil of Masonry behind which subversive movements are so conveniently hidden?

CHAPTER XXVIII

THE PREPARATION

THIS CHAPTER IS compiled largely of extracts, some transcribed verbatim and others elaborated to include information necessary to the reader from:—

History of Freemasonry and Concordant Orders by H. L. Stillson & W. J. Hughan.

Adriano Lemmi by Domenico Margiotta 33°.

Ex-Secretaire de la Loge Savonarola, de Florence;

Ex-Venerable de la Loge Giordano Bruno, de Palmi;

Ex-Souverain Grand Inspecteur General 33° degré, du Rite Ecossais Ancien et Accepté;

Ex-Souverain Prince de l'Ordre (33° 90° 95°) du Rile de Memphis et Misraim de Naples; etc. etc.

Ex-Inspecteur permanent et Souverain Délégué DU GRAND DIRECTOIRE CENTRAL DE NAPLES, POUR L'EUROPE (Haute-Maçonnerie Universelle).

It is necessary to give a brief review of the history of Ancient and Accepted Scottish Rites. This society originates from the rite called Scottish of Perfection or of Heredom, in twenty-five degrees, worked in the eighteenth century in Europe by Masons devoting themselves to occultism. The following statement with regard to the introduction of this rite in America is made in a report by Albert Pike:

"We can soon learn how it was that the Council degrees came, about 1766, from France, and not from Prussia. In 1761, the Lodges and Councils of the superior degrees being extended throughout Europe, Frederic II (Frederic the Great), King of Prussia, as Grand Commander of the, Order of Princes of the Royal Secret, or 32 degrees, was by general consent acknowledged and recognized as Sovereign and Supreme Head of the Scotch Rite."[131]

"On the 25th Oct. 1762, the Grand Masonic Constitutions were finally ratified in Berlin and proclaimed for the government of all Masonic bodies working in the Scotch Rite over the two hemispheres; and in the same year they were transmitted to the Jew, Stephen Morin, who had been appointed, at the request of Lacorne, in August, 1761, Inspector General for the New World by the Grand Consistory of Princes of the Royal Secret, convened at Paris, under the presidency of Chaillon de Joinville, representative of Frederic (the Great) and Substitute General of the Order.[132]

It will be remembered that the 33rd degree was not then created; and under Frederic the Great, there was no rank higher than the 32nd degree nor anybody superior to a Consistory."[133]

Morin went to Santo Domingo where he was joined by Moses M. Hays and Henry Andrew Francken. The latter founded a branch of the rite in Jamaica, while to the former was entrusted the task of founding lodges in North America. The Jew Hays established a Sublime Lodge of Perfection in Boston, of which he constituted himself Grand Master and charged one of his co-religionists, and brother Mason, Isaac Dacosta, who, in 1758 had founded the St. Andrew Lodge in Boston, with the mission of introducing Masonry into South Carolina.

Though on August 27, in 1766, Bro. Morin's patent was revoked by the Grand Body in Paris for "propagating strange and monstrous doctrines" exercising bad faith etc., etc.,[134] and given to Bro. Martin, Morin continued constituting chapters and councils and, with Sovereign Grand Inspector General, The 33rd and ultimate degree of the Ancient and Accepted Scottish Rite. It is not known when or where this grade originated. The theory which ascribes it to the King of Prussia has long since been discarded by intelligent Masons. The number of Inspectors in a kingdom or republic must not exceed nine. These, organized in a body, constitute the Supreme Council, which claims jurisdiction over all the Ineffable and Sublime degrees. The presiding officer is styled Sovereign Grand Commander.

See also Blanchard 33, *Scottish Rite Masonry*, vol. II, p. 484. "And though made within the memory of men now living, we read, in the same Note by Macoy: It is not certainly known, when or where this degree originated; that is to say, its origin is concealed. This is the most infamous Masonic act, next to burning their records of fifty-nine years before the war, (American Civil War) to hide treason. But slavery then ruled the country, and this 33rd Charleston degree ruled the lodge. And the Southern lodge-rooms worked up the most unjustifiable and infamous war on record. The Southern people "were dragooned into it, by leaders secretly sworn to obey Masonic leaders, or have their throats cut."

Dacosta, in 1783, seventeen years after his patent had been annulled, he erected in Charleston "The Grand Lodge of Perfection". Dacosta was its Grand Master. Joseph M. Meyers was his eventual successor, and "when the Grand Council of Princes of Jerusalem was established in Charleston, February 20, 1788, he, as one of the Deputy-Inspectors who established it, deposited in the archives certified copies of the degree of Royal and Select Masters from guidance and government of that new body."[135]

The two Masonic powers of Boston and Charleston created numerous lodges and inner shrines in the United States and gave themselves the title of Mother Lodges of the United States.

In view of the historical fact that the American War of Independence broke out in 1773, it is interesting to find that the Lodge of Perfection, at Albany (NewYork), was directed as early as 1770 to transmit reports to Berlin.[136] This indeed becomes significant when considered with the circumstances surrounding the "Boston Tea Party", which are so ably described in *The History of Freemasonry and Concordant Orders* by Stillson and Hughan, that we take the liberty of here transcribing some lines from this remarkable publication:[137]

"Grand Master (Joseph) Warren was appointed on March 3, 1772, by the Grand Master of Scotland, Grand Master of Masons for the Continent of America." Tradition says that the 'Mohawks', the 'High Sons of Liberty', met at the lodge at the 'Green Dragon Tavern' which was denounced by the Tories as 'a nest of traitors'. General Joseph Warren and other leading Masons made it the headquarters of the Revolution. On November 30, 1773, the Lodge of St. Andrew's (that founded by Dacosta and of which Warren was a member) was closed without the transaction of any business, in consequence of the fewness of the brethren present, the consignees of tea having broken up the brethren's nerve. On the 16th of December following, it is said the line of march was taken from the lodge-room to destroy the tea on the then arriving ships.

"On April 8, 1776, the Grand Lodge was convened for the performance of a sad and solemn duty, that of attending the funeral of Grand Master Warren, who was killed at Bunker Hill."

In 1738, Pope Clement XI I had excommunicated the Freemasons.

We extract the following instructive points from *Adriano Lemmi* by Margiotta:[138]

"Sovereign Princes of Jerusalem was the title born by the deputies of the Grand Master when they received missions to found lodges and visit regions where they had high jurisdiction. The name was that of a function and not a degree of initiation and there was one deputy only for each region. On May 15, 1781, at a convention of Deputy Inspectors convoked by Hays and Meyers at Philadelphia, Moses Cohen was named deputy inspector of Jamaica, as Francken, originally appointed by Stephen Morin to found lodges there, had neglected his mandate. Soon another Jewish Freemason came to Jamaica. This was Hyman Isaac Long who derived his powers from Morin, through Francken, Hays, Spitzer and Moses Cohen, and who was to play a great role in the sect.

"The convention of Philadelphia had decided that, in the future, there might be several Sovereign Princes of Jerusalem per region. By virtue of this decision, Moses Cohen conferred this title on Isaac Long who, finding his sphere of action too restricted at Jamaica soon went to Charleston. He was an active man who had formed great plans. Not only did he create other Lodges, but he brought other rites (such as that of Royal Arch) under the obedience of the Mother Lodge at Charleston. The Mother Lodge at Boston however did not prosper." Nevertheless, when one thinks of the immense territory of the United States, one understands that the Lodges, at the start, could only be very few and far between, so masonry vegetated for a long time in North America. In 1795, Isaac Long went to Europe, leaving Colonel John Mitchell the direction of the Mother Lodge of Charleston.

"When he returned to the United States, six years later, he brought the plan of his great idea, which was the creation of a rite of 33 degrees destined to become universal. With Colonel John Mitchell, Doctor Frederic Dalcho, Abraham Alexander, Isaac Auld and Emanuel de la Motta, all Sovereign Princes of Jerusalem, he constituted this rite, taking twenty-five degrees of the system of Heredom, six Templar grades in which were merged four degrees borrowed from the German Illuminism[139] of Adam Weishaupt, and two grades called grades of administration, the last of which supplanted the function of Deputy Inspector (Sovereign Prince of Jerusalem) and took the title of Sovereign Grand Inspector General 33rd and last degree. This was his crowning achievement. Isaac Long gave the institution the name of Ancient and Accepted Scottish Rites, and the first great constitutions were signed at Charleston, on May 31st 1801."

It was Isaac Long who created de Grasse and his father-in-law, de la Hogue, Deputy Grand Inspectors General.

"In order to insure great popularity for the rite, he linked it directly with the Templars by a mysterious legend. The high grades of other rites had already thought of pretending to avenge the Templars, condemned in the Middle Ages by the Papacy and the Monarchy. In the ceremonial of certain initiations, a pretext was thus contrived for swearing hatred and death to royalty and the church.

But Isaac Long had found better than that. According to the tradition, the Knights Templar, convicted of secret conspiracy and maleficent occultism, had taken refuge in Scotland where they succeeded in eluding their pursuers. It was said that they had succeeded in buying the head of the Grand Master Jacques Bourgignon de Molay from the executioner, after it had been severed from the body and that they had contrived to place in safety the monstrous idol called Baphomet which they worshipped in their secret assemblies.

When Long arrived in Charleston in 1801, he brought with him this Baphomet which he claimed to have recovered as well as a skull which he declared to be that of the Grand Master Molay. They were signal relics, holy things! Long affirmed that he had been assured by the Good God in person that victory over the Church was contingent on these precious relics, and that the Templar Baphomet was the Palladium which would lead Freemasonry to victory".

To this other authors have added that this skull is known as the relic of Saint Jacques and is placed upon a high pedestal in the Hall of the Supreme Council of Scottish Rites, in the temple at Charleston, where annually, on the 11th of March, it talks and vomits flames.

Its conversational propensities were however not revealed until Gallatin Mackey, who claimed to be the reincarnation of Jacques de Molay, developed the proclivity for going into an annual trance on the 11th of March. This trance lasted about one hour, during which the skull conversed volubly about itself and all sorts of other things."

Pursuing the subject further, Margiotta states that:

"The Mother Lodge of Boston had ceased functioning for some years but that of Charleston, reconstituted according to the new Scottish System in 33 degrees, became the root of the tree which was to spread its branches over the entire world. The Superior Lodge of the Grand Sovereign Inspectors General, in each country, was to be called the Supreme Council, and it is from the Supreme Council of Charleston that all the others were to emanate. It is thus the first Supreme Council of the Globe.

"Such is the history of the origin of this rite which attracted Mazzini's attention for, during the years which preceded the taking of Rome by the army of Piedmont, he could see that the previsions of Isaac Long had been realized. So it was in Pike, the successor of Long, himself the Sovereign Commander Grand Master, that the great revolutionary conspirator sought an ally in his work the object of which was the total destruction of the church."[140]

The following address,[141] issued from Paris by Giuseppe Mazzini[142] to his friends in Italy, October 1846, fully sets forth the deep laid plans by which Freemasonry sought to engage all classes.

"In great countries, it is by the people we must go to regeneration; in yours, by the princes. We must absolutely make them of our side. It is easy. The Pope will march in reform through principle and of necessity; the King of Piedmont through the idea of the crown of Italy; the Grand Duke of Tuscany through inclination and irritation; the King of Naples through force; and the little princes will have to think of other things besides reform. The people yet in servitude can only sing its wants. Profit by the least concession to assemble the masses, were it only to testify gratitude.... Fetes, songs, assemblies, numerous relations established among men of all opinions, suffice to make ideas gush out, to give the people a feeling of its strength and render it exacting... Italy is still what France was before the Revolution; she wants, then, Mirabeau, Lafayette, and others. A great lord may be held back by his material interests, but he may be taken by vanity. Leave him the chief place whilst he will go with you. There are few who would go to the end.

"The essential thing is, that the goal of the great revolution be unknown to them; let us never permit them to see more than the first step. In Italy, the clergy are rich in money and the faith of the people. You must manage them in both those interests, and as much as possible make their influence of use.

"Learned discussions are neither necessary nor opportune. There are regenerative words which contain all that need be often repeated to the people. Liberty, rights of man, progress, equality, fraternity, are what the people will understand above all when opposed to the words, despotism, privileges, tyranny, etc., etc.

"Nearly two thousand years ago, a great philosopher, called Christ, preached the fraternity which the world yet seeks. Accept, then, all the help offered you. Whoever will make one step towards you must be yours till he quits you. A king gives a more liberal law; applaud him, and ask for the one that must follow. A minister shows intention of progress; give him out as a model. A lord affects to pout at his privileges; put yourself under his direction if he will stop, you will have time to let him go: he will remain isolated, and without strength against you, and you will have a thousand ways to make unpopular all who oppose your projects. All personal discontent, all deceptions, all bruised ambition, may serve the cause of progress by giving them a. new direction. The army is the greatest enemy to the progress of socialism. It must be paralysed by the education of the people. Clerical power is personified in the Jesuits. The odium of that name is already a power for the socialists. Make use of it. Associate! Associate! everything is in that word. The secret societies give irresistible strength to the party that can call upon them. Do not fear to see them split: the more the better. All go to the same end by different ways. The secret will be often violated; so much the better; the secret is necessary to give security to the members, but a certain transparency is needed to inspire fire to the stationary.

Courage, then and persevere!"

That Freemasonry has not always enjoyed immunity the following quotation will serve to show.

"In the year 1735, the States General of Holland proscribed the secret Masonic League, and the French government imitated the example in 1735. In 1757, in Scotland, the Synod of Stirling adopted a resolution debarring all adhering Freemasons from the ordinances of religion.

"The Great Council of Berne proscribed Freemasonry in 1748, Bavaria followed in 1799, and its total suppression took place in 1845, The Regency of Milan and the Governor of Venice acted in a similar manner by it in 1814. John VI, King of Portugal, prohibited Freemasonry in the strictest manner in 1816, and renewed it in 1824. In 1820 several lodges were closed in Prussia for political intrigues; and in the same year Alexander I banished the order from the whole Russian Empire. A similar occurrence took place four years later in Modena and Spain... Yet today, some men boast of belonging to a secret society, the members of which were declared, by an Act of George III , felons, and liable to transportation for life !"[143]

Speaking of Masons, in 1876, Richard Carlile wrote: "Let them not wait to be disbanded by the Legislature, as a useless and mischievous association: but let them anticipate the spirit of a coming age... The deluge of mystery has not only overwhelmed Babylon but Egypt, Greece, Rome, and will, if we do not light up the spirit of revelation in time, most assuredly overthrow this British nation. It is even now in danger, from the dissension of its internal mysteries, of becoming an easy prey to some more barbarously mysterious power. Thus fell Babylon, Egypt, Jerusalem, Greece, "Rome, and why not Britain, if Britain retain those seeds of disease and weakness? Tell me not that the safety of a country is in its superstition, or in its secret and mysterious bands."[144]

This warning however passed unheeded. During the time that has elapsed between the publication of Carlile's book and the present day, we see England honeycombed with societies, subversive of law, order and morals.

Numerous are the homes which have become resorts where, today, the shameful orgies of Medmenham are enacted anew. They are the secret haunts of social cliques and associations, and behind such screens as art, antiques and dressmaking thrive, as though they were highly protected, the white slave traffic, the dope traffic and gambling which serve as a dragnet and decoy for the service of the Great God Pan.

CHAPTER XXIX

GENERAL PEPE AND THE "ONE BIG UNION"

AT THE PRESENT moment, when we are surfeited with the words unions and mergers, to say nothing of cartels, a new interest is awakened by the perusal of Thomas Frost's book on Secret Societies, from which we extract the following:

"Two results of great importance in the progress of the European revolution proceeded from the events that occurred at Naples in 1820–21. One was the reorganization of the Carbonari, consequent upon the publicity given to the system when it had brought about the revolution, and the secrecy in which it had hitherto been enveloped was no longer deemed necessary; the other was the extension of the system beyond the Alps. When the Neapolitan revolution had been effected, the Carbonari emerged from their mystery, published their constitution and statutes, and ceased to conceal their patents and their cards of membership. In the Papal States, in Lombardy, and in Piedmont, the veil of secrecy was maintained for a little time longer, partly through the adoption by the Carbonari in those portions of the peninsula of symbols and pass-words different from those of the Neapolitan lodges, partly by the formation of the various societies of the Adelphi, the Guelphs, the Brother Protectors, and the Italian Federati, which were similar, and yet not the same, though all holding the same principles, and having a common object. But after the collapse of the Piedmontese revolution, so much doubt and fear existed among the leaders as to the extent to which the secrets of the system were known that they were all effaced, and consigned to oblivion. The scattered directors of the movement drew together the broken threads of the conspiracy as soon as they were able, but with a new nomenclature and a new symbolism.[145]

"The dispersion of the Carbonaro leaders had, at the same time, the effect of extending the system in France, where it had been introduced towards the end of 1820 and creating centres of revolutionary agitation in the foreign cities in which they temporarily located themselves.

General Pepe proceeded to Barcelona when the counter-revolution was imminent at Naples, and his life was no longer safe there; and to the same city went several of the Piedmontese revolutionists when their country was Austrianized after the same lawless fashion.

Scalvini and Ugoni took refuge at Geneva; others of the proscribed proceeded to London. This dispersion, and the progress which Carbonarism was making in France, suggested to General Pepe the idea of an international secret society, which should combine for a common purpose the advanced political reformers of all the European States.

Shortly after his arrival at Madrid, to which city he proceeded from Barcelona, he propounded to two or three ultra-Liberal deputies the plan of this society, the object of which, he says, 'was to enable the members to correspond and by these means preclude the possibility of a renewal of that want of union which had been experienced amongst the most noted patriots of Spain and Portugal, Naples and Piedmont. Several deputies of the Cortes were inclined to regard such an association as extremely beneficial to the public cause, more especially in their own peninsula, where a great want of concord existed between the Portuguese and the Spaniards. The society was accordingly founded; several members of the Cortes formed part of it, as well as General Ballesteros, Councillor of State. I still preserve the regulations of this society, the great object of which was to open a communication between the most enlightened patriots of the different cities in Europe. It was decided that I should exert myself to give it extension in Lisbon, London and Paris; and that, in the event of my success, other members should proceed to propagate it over Italy and Germany'.

"Having organized in Madrid the first circle of the Constitutional Society of European Patriots, Pepe proceeded to Lisbon, where he was even more successful in his efforts than in the Spanish capital. Two of the Ministers, and several Councillors of State and members of the Cortes signified their adhesion, and, before Pepe left, a flourishing circle was formed, under the direction of Almeida-Moraes, the president of the Cortes. From Lisbon the general proceeded by sea to London, where, as he says, he soon found that 'a secret society in England among men of mind is a thing quite out of the order of probability'. He mentioned the society to a few, but met with no encouragement. The Duke of Sussex and Sir Robert "Wilson read the statutes and regulations of the society, but only as a matter of curiosity."

This curiosity is doubtless responsible for the creation of what was later known as The International Committee of London. The particular Duke of Sussex, here referred to was Grand Master of the Grand Lodge of England from 1813–1843, and this interview with the Italian revolutionary is of great significance showing as it does the effort, at this date, to subvert English Freemasonry to the aims of The International. According to the system which worked out later, English Freemasonry retained, to all appearances, its original autonomy.

But to proceed with the statement of Frost:

"Pepe next opened a correspondence with Lafayette, who hailed the proposed international organization of the secret societies as 'a Holy Alliance opposed to that of despotism,' and at once associated himself with it. He, with Manuel and Argenson, the triumvirate that was supposed to have directed the Associated Patriots of 1816, were earnestly engaged at that time in the reorganisation of the Carbonari of France, upon a new system, which promised more perfect impenetrability; and Buonarotti was similarly engaged at Geneva, with a view to renewed operations in Italy."

"It has been doubted whether Lafayette, Manuel,[146] and Argenson,[147] with others who were supposed to be the leaders of the Carbonari in France, were actually the chiefs of the society; and, with regard to Manuel at least, the point is not susceptible of positive demonstration. There are, in all countries, men of superior station who, when a collision between the people and the Government is impending, are aware of what is going on, and hold themselves prepared to step to the front when the movement has advanced to a point at which they can do so with advantage to the cause and safety to themselves; but who take care not to commit themselves to it prematurely, or to allow any trace to exist of their connexion with it. This has been thought by some to have been the real position of the individuals whom others have asserted to have been the actual leaders of the Carbonari, as they had previously been held to be of the Associated Patriots; but though there is no absolute proof that they were the Grand Elect there can be very little, if any, moral doubt upon the point."

The Author of *Secret Societies of the European Revolution* writes the foregoing paragraph but fails to explain it.

Who and what are the men he refers to?

Such indeed are the political principles adopted by the leaders of Freemasonry. Therein lies its power. As soon as any political movement becomes inevitable, as soon as public pressure on an existing government becomes too strong, this sect, in the name of Liberty, Equality and Fraternity, takes the secret leadership of the opposing faction. Through the new government which becomes the subservient tool of its capricious master, who, at any moment, may suppress its fledgling, by creating and backing a new opposition, it holds, not the balance of power but all the power.

Thus: *Those who rule Freemasonry today, rule the world.*

And Frost further adds:

"In 1831, the French Government had not only proclaimed a policy of non-intervention, but had expressly declared that France would not permit intervention on the part of any other Power in the affairs of any nation in Europe. Lafayette was deceived by these professions, and assured Misley (the agent of the Masonic Revolutionary Committee) that the Italians had nothing to fear."

In that year Masonry made an attempt to cast off the Austrian yoke in Italy by using France as its base of operations. Owing however to French non-cooperation the revolution failed.

"A few days afterwards, Misley and Linati arrived at Marseilles and chartered a vessel, aboard which they put a couple of cannon and twelve hundred muskets. They were joined by General Pepe, Count Grilenzoni, the advocate Mantovani, Dr. Franceschini, and Lieutenant Mori; but, at the last moment, the Prefect received a telegraphic order from Paris to prevent their embarkation and lay an embargo on the vessel. General Pepe evaded the vigilance of the police, however, and contrived to reach Hyères, where he heard of the entrance of the Austrians into Bologna, and thereupon abandoned his intention of giving the aid of his reputation and experience to the revolutionary cause."

In connexion with the agitation provoked in Piedmont, during the reign of Charles Albert, by Mazzini's "Young Italy" movement in 1848, the veteran General Pepe again comes into prominence. On March 29, 1848, he arrived at Naples, and was sent for by King Ferdinand who invited him "to form a Ministry, of which he should have the Presidency, with the Ministries of War and Marine." Every difficulty however was thrown in the way of Pepe's projected military operations, "the Naval Department insisting that the fleet could not convey troops, the King interposing various delays and the Pope refusing permission for more than one battalion or squadron to pass daily. Seventeen thousand troops at last started, but with orders not to cross the Po until the King commanded the passage!"[148]

There was much marching and countermarching but the secret societies had not yet won.

The tangled history of the "Young Italy" movement in its early stages is well explained by Thomas Frost in *Secret Societies of the European Revolution*, and anyone particularly interested in that phase of political history would do well to refer to this book. Due allowance must however be made for certain omissions and inaccurate deductions on the part of the author who, in 1876, could not have access to information which is now available to anyone seeking it.

CHAPTER XXX

ALBERT PIKE AND GIUSEPPE MAZZINI

THIS CHAPTER IS compiled largely of extracts, some transcribed verbatim and others elaborated to include information necessary to the reader, from:

Adriano Lemmi by Domenico Margiotta 33°
Maçonnerie Pratique by Paul Rosen 33°
Initiation Human and Solar by Alice A. Bailey
Le Diable au XIXe Siècle by Dr. Bataille.

Adriano Lemmi wrote: "The anniversary of Sept. 20, the day on which Rome became the capital of Italy, when the temporal power of the Pope was overthrown, concerns Freemasonry exclusively. It is an anniversary, a purely masonic festival, which marks the date of the arrival of Italian Freemasonry in Rome, the aim for which it had for many years been striving." The date of Sept. 20, 1870, is not only an Italian date, it is above all a great masonic date, for it marks the organization of a supreme rite, introduced into Freemasonry, to lend a satanic character to the vague divinity more or less well known by the name of "The Great Architect of the Universe".

During the last years preceding the capture of Rome, Mazzini had established relations with the Masonic chief of Scottish Rites, Albert Pike, President of the Supreme Council of Charleston, United States.

Pike was a great student of the Cabala and the occult.

Mazzini had understood that Freemasonry was a powerful lever with which to revolutionize the world, but he saw it divided into numerous rites, often rivals, and even hostile to one another. Aspiring to Italian Unity as a means of breaking the temporal power of the Holy See, he dreamt of a union of masonry throughout the world to destroy the church itself as a spiritual power.

He addressed himself to Pike in preference to another Grand Orient or Supreme Council chief because of the many international ramifications of Ancient and Accepted Scottish Rites, as Pike, its recognised chief, had succeeded in gaining considerable influence over all the Supreme National Councils of this rite which had hitherto been of a purely dogmatic and liturgic character.

Mazzini, who was very practical, said that it would be inadvisable to favour one rite only to the exclusion of all the others. In a letter to Albert Pike, dated Jan. 22, 1870, he writes. "We must allow all the federations to continue just as they are, with their systems, their central authorities and their divers modes of correspondence between high grades of the same rite, organized as they are at present, but we must create a supreme rite, which will remain unknown, to which we will call those Masons of high degree whom we shall select. With regard to their brothers in masonry, these men must be pledged to the strictest secrecy. Through this supreme rite, we will govern all Freemasonry which will become the one international centre, the more powerful because its direction will be unknown."

Thus at the time when Mazzini formed the scheme of unifying Freemasonry by creating one central universal direction reserved to a small number of high masons chosen with the greatest care, he selected Albert Pike as an ally.

Pike was born in Boston on Dec. 29, 1809.

His parents, in modest circumstances, succeeded in giving him a course at Harvard College. He then went to join his family at Newbury port. There, for a while, he taught in a primary school till he moved to Fairhaven where he continued his career of pedagogue.

In 1833 he went to Little Rock.

From 1830 to 1840, Masonry in the United States had fallen into disrepute and almost ceased to exist. After the torture and death of William Morgan in 1826, many lodges faded into oblivion to resuscitate only after the storm of public censure had abated.

During the Civil War, Pike served as brigadier-general in the Confederate army. The Confederate government named him Indian Commissioner and charged him with the conduct of negotiations with the most powerful savage tribes, to raise an army of their warriors. To facilitate his organization of this army he was made Governor of Indian Territory, and once these hordes were united, they were placed under his command. What followed can be easily understood as his troops were composed of Chickasaws, Comanches, Creeks, Cherokees, Miamis, Osages, Kansas and Chocaws, with all of whom he personally was on the best of terms. Among them, he was known as "the faithful pale-face friend and protector". It was no longer war—it was an orgy of murder and atrocities so terrible that the foreign powers interfered. Representations made by England, threatening intervention in the name of humanity, finally compelled Jefferson Davis to disband his auxiliary Indian troops.

Mrs. Liliana Pike Room gives us the following chronological history of her father's early Masonic career. She says that he became an Oddfellow, sometime in the forties, and in 1850 entered the Masonic Fraternity. After that he gradually ceased to be active as an Oddfellow. Soon becoming prominent in Masonry he advanced rapidly to the highest honours. His Masonic record is as follows:

"He was initiated in Western Star Lodge at Little Rock, Arkansas, in 1850.

"Raised to the degree of Worshipful Master, in Western Star Lodge No. 1, Little Rock, Arkansas, in July 1850.

"He became Charter Member of Magnolia Lodge, No. 60, Little Rock, Arkansas, and was Worshipful Master *ad vitam* of that lodge in 1853.

"Exalted in Union Chapter No. 2 R. A. M. Little Rock, Arkansas, in 1850.

"Greeted as Royal and Select Master at Washington, D. C, 1852.

"Created Knight Templar 1858 Washington Commandary No. 1. K. T. in Washington.

"Elected Grand High Priest of the Grand Chapter of Arkansas, in 1853.

"In 1856, met Brother Theodor S. Parvin of Connecticut and received degrees of A. A. (Ancient and Accepted Scottish Rite) from 4° to 32° inclusive, on March 20th, 1853.

"Coroneted Honorary Inspector General, April 25th, 1857. Crowned Active Member of Supreme Council, Southern Jurisdiction March 20th, 1858, at Charleston, South Carolina, and on the resignation of Brother John Honour as Grand Commander, was elected M. P. Sovereign Grand Commander of the Supreme Council for the Southern Jurisdiction of the United States, January 2nd, 1859."

Mrs. Room further adds "I will state here what he told me himself, that Sovereign Grand Commander Honour, his predecessor, resigned that office expressly that he might be elected Sovereign Grand Commander." The secretary of the Supreme Council at Charleston, at this time, and its ruling power was Pike's great friend, Gallatin Mackey.

On the other hand, Margiotta gives the following particulars:

"Towards this epoch, Pike and Mackey received the visit of Longfellow. This Longfellow was a Scottish Rites Mason who, in 1837, had taken up his residence in the United States, becoming the intimate friend and private secretary of Moses Holbrook, then Sovereign Commander of the Supreme Council of Charleston. The intimacy between Longfellow and Holbrook became quickly serious as both had thoroughly studied the occult sciences and enjoyed discussing the mysteries of the Cabala.

'When Longfellow asked his Grand Master's permission to join the order of the Oddfellows for the purpose of studying its organization, his request was granted.[149]

"Oddfellow is the name adopted by the members of a society founded in London towards 1788. Their meeting places were called Lodges, as in Masonry, and many were dissolved under the suspicion that their character was subversive, though the visible aims of the fraternity were simply mutual help and diversion. But the society, changing its location and its name, continued a precarious existence till, in 1809, several members founded a new lodge at Manchester. Then some of them separated in 1813 and formed the independent Order of Oddfellows (I. 0. 0. F.) the members of the general council of which were all to reside at Manchester. The order was introduced in America, in 1819, by the blacksmith (Thomas) Wildey, who founded Washington Lodge No. 1, at Baltimore. This town became the headquarters of the American and Canadian Oddfellows and, thanks to the energy of Wildey, the order made great headway and spread with rapidity.

"Longfellow and Holbrook, while exchanging views on the Cabala, had formed the project of creating a Satanic rite in which the adepts would be instructed in Black Magic, but Holbrook, the Grand Master of the Supreme Council of Charleston, who had already composed a suitable ritual and sacrilegious mass called *Adonaicide Mass*, died, retarding the fulfilment of the project." He was succeeded by John Honour, after whose death the dream of the Jew, Moses Holbrook, to subvert Masonry, was fulfilled by Albert Pike on a gigantic scale.

"Longfellow left Charleston after the death of his patron and, in 1854, went to Hamilton, Canada. There, with the authorisation of Wildey, he submitted the rituals of Holbrook to this flourishing society and it was decided to graft a second and separate class of adepts, practising secret Satanism, on to the original body. But Wildey, becoming suddenly jealous, refused the use of his premises."

"Undiscouraged by obstacles placed in his way by Wildey, Longfellow returned to Charleston in 1857, where he had interviews with Pike and Mackey to whom he revealed his plan. The innovation of Longfellow was declared to be marvellous, but Pike, who had himself already thought of introducing Luciferianism into the inner shrines of Scottish Rites Freemasonry, would not take a definite stand, so Longfellow addressed himself directly to the Grand Master John Honour. He seemed indifferent to the subject on the grounds that one could not introduce Satanism into the Supreme Council of Scottish Rites without the knowledge of his lieutenant-commander, Charles Furman, who was opposed to changes of this kind. Finally Longfellow obtained from Wildey the authorisation secretly to use the Order of the Oddfellows for the initiations of the second class, which was to form an absolutely secret rite and to have its centre at Hamilton. The adepts of the second class Oddfellows, practising Satanism, then took the name of Re-Theurgist-Optimates[150] (used by the Palladists also) and Longfellow became the Grand Priest of the 'New Evocative Magic'.

As a consequence of the intrigues and manoeuvres of some members of the Masonic organization, the office of Grand Master had become an elective position which was now destined to be filled by the particular member of the Fraternity selected by the conspirators. Among these was Gallatin Mackey, a Luciferian, who proposed Albert Pike, another Luciferian, for the post of Grand Master of the Supreme Council of Charleston to which he was duly elected on January 6th 1859, his candidacy being unopposed.

Margiotta adds:

"Once Grand Master, Pike reestablished the supremacy of his Supreme Council and succeeded gradually in becoming an important Masonic personage and the real chief of Scottish Rites".

In 1806, a jeweller, Joseph Cerneau, founded a rival rite in New York composed of the same 33 degrees of initiation as the order of which he himself was chief. This rite, which was later worked by F. Foulhouze, an American, excited the ire of the Sovereign Pontiff of Universal Freemasonry who waged a ceaseless warfare of excommunication against it.

From letters scattered through different masonic archives, it is evident that Mazzini formed his great project after 1866. The grand patriarch of the sect in Europe, Lord Palmerston, had died. Convinced that the power he had wielded was purely the result of personal influence with the different chiefs and that, not being based on an efficient organization it was unlikely to endure, Mazzini set himself to study the problem of the international organization of Freemasonry, and in 1870 reached an agreement with Pike for the creation of the Supreme Rite.

The Franco-Prussian war, which, enabled the King of Piedmont, already called King of Italy, to take Rome, favoured the abolition of the temporal power of the Pope, and at this time the constitution of central high masonry was decreed and signed between Albert Pike and Giuseppe Mazzini. The act of creation is dated Sept. 20, 1870, the day upon which the army of invasion, commanded by the Freemason, General Cadorna, entered the Eternal City.

The two founders divided their powers according to the following plan. To Pike was given dogmatic authority and the title of Sovereign Pontiff of Universal Freemasonry, while Mazzini held the executive authority with the title of Sovereign Chief of Political Action. Mazzini evinced great deference towards the views of the Patriarch of Charleston and begged him to draw up the statutes of the grades of the Supreme Secret Rite which would thus be the liturgic bonds of the members of centralized high masonry.

Albert Pike, in honour of his Templar Baphomet, which was in the keeping of his first and historic Supreme Council, named the order the *New and Reformed Palladian Rite or New and Reformed Palladium.*[151]

"It was agreed", continues Margiotta, "that the existence of this rite would be kept strictly secret and that no mention of it would ever be made in the assemblies of the Lodges and Inner Shrines of other rites, even when by accident, the meeting might happen to be composed exclusively of brothers having the perfect initiation, for the secret of the new institution was only to be divulged with the greatest caution to a chosen few belonging to the ordinary high grades.[152]

"To recruit adepts, they planned to use some members of the other rites, but in the beginning they meant to rely principally on those among the initiates of Ancient and Accepted Scottish Rites who were already addicted to occultism.

"Everyone knows that in masonry from the degree of Master, a mason may, without being a member of a lodge, assist at sessions as a visitor, at Lodges not belonging to his own rite or even to his own national federation, provided he is a regular active mason and presents himself at a lodge working at a degree equal to, or below the highest degree of which he is possessed. Thus a Rose Croix (18th degree Scottish Rites), travelling in any country, may, if he frequents assiduously his lodge and chapter, present himself at any lodge of a degree equal, to or inferior to his own and assist at a seance, but he cannot enter an areopagus of Knights Kadosch (30th degree), even one of his own rite. A 33rd would be well received everywhere, in any country, in any rite the existence of which is acknowledged. Thus it was particularly the initiates of the thirty-third degree Scottish Rites, who, owing to their extensive international ramifications, were privileged to recruit adepts for Palladism. That is why the supreme rite created its Triangles (the name given to Palladian Lodges) by degrees, but these were established on a firm base, the lowliest of its initiates being brothers long tested in ordinary masonry.

"One will better understand these precautions knowing that Palladism is essentially a Luciferian rite. Its religion is Manichean neo-gnosticism, teaching that the divinity is dual and that Lucifer is the equal of Adonay, with Lucifer, the God of Light and Goodness struggling for humanity against Adonay the God of Darkness and Evil. In stating this principle of the secret cult of the triangles, Albert Pike had only specified and unveiled the dogmas of the high grades of all other masonries, for in no matter what rite, the Great Architect of the Universe is not the God worshipped by the Christians.

"For other reasons these precautions were still necessary, in order to render possible the exercise of a supreme central directing power, reaching all the rites through the personal influence of the Elects and Perfect Initiates, these being invested with privileges, and giving the impulse, which emanated from the source of the highest universal authority. If Brothers, not fully initiated, had suspected the existence of this supreme organization, it is evident that, in the ordinary Lodges there would always have been a tendency to resist the motions of such privileged persons.

"To insure the creation and good working of this formidable machine of Palladism, Mazzini had reserved for himself the office of Chief of Political Action nor had he hesitated in bowing to the will of the Patriarch of Charleston who, by his preponderance in Scottish Rites, could easily penetrate all countries of the globe with" the new institution. That is the reason for Mazzini giving supremacy to the dogmatic over the political authority in International Freemasonry.

'The Holy See of the Dogma for the whole masonic world was set up at Charleston, the sacred city of the Palladium. Pike, the Sovereign Pontiff of Lucifer, was the president of the Supreme Dogmatic Directory, composed of ten brothers of the highest grades who formed his Supreme Grand College of Emeritus Masons. The Sovereign Executive Directory of High Masonry was established at Rome under Mazzini himself who, knowing the rivalry between the different Supreme Councils in Italy, seldom appeared at the official meetings of the Grand Orient of Rome, and, so as not to awaken suspicion in the minds of ordinary high grade Italian Masons in whom he had not confided the secret of the new institution, pretended to be occupied with socialism only".

Rut was this interest, plan or pretence?

In the following paragraph on the International in *World Revolution* by N. Webster, page 179, we find a link, if not the link, between Mazzini and Karl Marx. Mazzini and his International Masons are already preparing the subversion of the Socialist Labour movement.

"At the meeting in St. Martin's Hall, on September 28, 1864, when the 'International' was definitely founded, Marx played no part at all. 'I was present', he wrote Engels, 'only as a dumb personage on the platform'. Rut he was named nevertheless a member of the sub-committee, the other members being Mazzini's secretary—a Polish Jew named Wolff—Le Lubez, a French Freemason, Cremer, the secretary of the English Masons' Union, and Weston, the Owenite. At the first meeting of this committee, Wolff placed before it the statutes of Mazzini's Working-men's Association, proposing them as the basis of the new association; Le Lubez suggested amendments described by Marx as 'perfectly childish'. 'I was firmly resolved', he wrote, 'not to leave a single line if possible of all their balderdash'. In a few weeks he had succeeded in establishing his authority. 'My propositions were all accepted by the commission'."

As to whether Marx thus manoeuvred himself into a dominant position in the movement, or Mazzini's agents manoeuvred Marx into this position to suit their own ends, is left to our imagination, but the fact of someone, not an outstanding personality, being elected or nominated on a committee for no particular reason, generally means, to anyone versed in the technique of political tricks, that the nomination or election was something arranged "behind the scenes".

On page 46 in *La Theologie Politique de Mazzini et l'Internationale*, Bakounine, the celebrated Russian anarchist, refutes certain statements said to have been current in London about himself at the time, in the following terms:

"But in 1864, while on my way through London, he (Karl Marx) came to see me, and assured me that he (Mazzini) had never taken any part direct or indirect in these calumnies against me which he himself had considered most infamous. I had to believe."

It is a fact that for a certain length of time Mazzini and Marx were closely associated.

An eminent Mason, the atheist leader of the Italian Socialists, Alberto Mario, husband of Miss Jessie White, an ardent Mazzinian and the authoress of a history of her hero—*Delia vita di Giuseppe Mazzini*—was moreover a tool of Pike whom he generally consulted on all important matters. Thus, in order to divert the attention of the imperfect initiates, Mazzini organized a congress of working men in Rome, in October 1871. A close examination of the work of this congress shows however that it was only pretence for nothing practical was attempted or accomplished. On the other hand, he busied himself with grouping all the political elements of the sect in which occult manoeuvre his agent, Adriano Lemmi, helped him more than anyone else.

"When Pike sent him a copy of his Luciferian rituals, Mazzini was full of an enthusiastic praise for his colleague's work which he expressed in his articles in *La Roma del Popolo*. The public however failed to understand the sentiment that inspired him to proclaim the existence of a divinity and denounce materialism and atheism. One was puzzled to find this man a mystic. He showed himself extremely religious yet he declared himself the sworn enemy of the Church!"[153]

Pike's literary achievements were numerous. These were, *Ariel, Morals and Dogma, The Sacred Hymns, The Sephar H. Debarim, Book of the Word,*[154] *Legenda Magistralia, Ritual of the New and Reformed Palladium (4 grades out of 5)* The Book of Revelations, The Supreme Verb, The Ritual of Elect Magus, and The Book of Apadno, which latter contains the prophecies concerning the reign of the Anti-Christ from the Satanic point of view.

The theological dogma of Albert Pike is explained in the 'Instructions' issued by him, on July 14, 1889, to the 23 Supreme Councils of the world and have been recorded by A. C. De La Rive in *La Femme et l'Enfant dans la Franc-Maçonnerie Universelle* (page 588) from which book we translate and quote as follows:

"That which we must say to the crowd is—We worship a God, but it is the God that one adores without superstition.

"To you, Sovereign Grand Inspectors General, we say this, that you may repeat it to the Brethren of the 32nd, 31st and 30th degrees—The Masonic religion should be, by all of us initiates of the high degrees, maintained in the purity of the Luciferian doctrine.

"If Lucifer were not God, would Adonay (The God of the Christians) whose deeds prove his cruelty, perfidy, and hatred of man, barbarism and repulsion for science, would Adonay and his priests, calumniate him ?

"Yes, Lucifer is God, and unfortunately Adonay is also God. For the eternal law is that there is no light without shade, no beauty without ugliness, no white without black, for the absolute can only exist as two Gods: darkness being necessary to light to serve as its foil as the pedestal is necessary to the statue, and the brake to the locomotive.

"In analogical and universal dynamics one can only lean on that which will resist. Thus the universe is balanced by two forces which maintain its equilibrium: the force of attraction and that of repulsion. These two forces exist in physics, philosophy and religion. And the scientific reality of the divine dualism is demonstrated by the phenomena of polarity and by the universal law of sympathies and antipathies. That is why the intelligent disciples of Zoroaster, as well as, after them, the Gnostics, the Manicheans and the Templars have admitted, as the only logical metaphysical conception, the system of the two divine principles fighting eternally, and one cannot believe the one inferior in power to the other.

"Thus, the doctrine of Satanism is a heresy; and the true and pure philosophic religion is the belief in Lucifer, the equal of Adonay; but

Lucifer, God of Light and God of Good, is struggling for humanity against Adonay, the God of Darkness and Evil."

One must not lose sight of the fact that Pike occupied simultaneously the positions of Grand Master of the Central Directory of Washington, that of Grand Commander of the Supreme Council of Charleston and that of Sovereign Pontiff of Universal Freemasonry.

In 1880, a charter was granted him by the Royal Order of Scotland for the foundation of Lodges in America appointing him Provincial Grand Master of the order of H. R. M. He was indeed a great organizer.

Margiotta further writes:

"The two secret chiefs, Pike and Mazzini, finally completed the organization of high masonry, establishing four Grand Central Directories for the world, functioning thenceforth to gather information for the benefit of their political policy and dogmatic propaganda. These were, The Grand Central Directories for North America at Washington, for South America at Montevideo, for Europe at Naples, and for Asia and Oceania at Calcutta. Later, a central Sub-Directory for Africa was founded at Port Louis, Island of Mauritius, and after the death of Mazzini, the supreme chief constituted a Universal Sovereign Administrative Directory at Berlin which ranked in the hierarchy after the Sovereign Executive Directories and before the four Great Central Directories."

Gallatin Mackey, the confidant of Albert Pike, died in Charleston on June 20, 1881. He was the author of many works on masonry, namely *The Lexicon of Freemasonry*, published in New York in 1845, *The History of Freemasonry in South Carolina, The Manual of the Lodge, The Masonic Ritualist, The Symbolism of Freemasonry and The Encyclopedia of Freemasonry*, the authorship of which is generally now attributed to Albert George Mackey.

According to the fundamental constitution of the Palladium, the nomination of the Chief of Political Action, the President of the Sovereign Executive Directory, was not an elective office. Its incumbent was an appointee of the Sovereign Pontiff of Universal Freemasonry.

When Mazzini felt himself to be dying, he designated Adriano Lemmi as his successor. He died on March 11 1872, at Pisa, and Albert Pike, deferring to his wishes, named Adriano Lemmi as his successor.

Pike was not only an organizer and a politician, he was also, in his religious capacity, as Cabalist and spiritist, a mystic on whose personality the following anecdote sheds a flood of light.

"Speaking before the Supreme Council of Charlesion, on October 20, 1884, he gave an account of his recent travels through the United States and some incidental experiences. One of these, he described as follows:—'At Saint Louis, we operated the grand rites, and through Sister Ingersoll, who is a first class medium, received astonishing revelations during a solemn Palladian session at which I presided, assisted by Brother Friedman and Sister Warhnburn. Without putting Sister Ingersoll to sleep, we saturated her with the spirit of Ariel himself, but Ariel took possession of her with 329 more spirits of fire and the seance from then on was marvellous. Sister Ingersoll, lifted into space, floated over the assembly and her garments were suddenly devoured by a flame which enfolded, without burning her. We saw her thus in a state of nudity for over ten minutes. Flitting above our heads, as though borne by an invisible cloud, or upheld by beneficent spirits, she answered all questions put to her. We thus soon had the latest news of our very illustrious brother Adriano Lemmi. Then, Astaroth, in person, revealed himself, flying beside our medium and holding her hand. He breathed upon her and her clothes, returning from nowhere, clothed her again. Finally Astaroth vanished and our sister fell gently on to a chair where, with her head thrown back she gave up Ariel and the 329 spirits who had accompanied him.

We counted 330 exhalations in all at the end of this most successful experiment."[155]

A number of books of this period refer to what must have been a wireless telephone in the possession of the heads of the Masonic organization. A translation of the detailed description of this instrument, given in Bataille's book, is quoted herewith as being of interest in these days when magic sometimes becomes experimental science. At the date on which this description was first printed (1894) wireless was unknown.

"In his house, Gallatin Mackey once showed me that Arcula Mystica (the Mystic Box), of which there are only seven examples in existence, at Charleston, Borne, Berlin, Washington, Monte Video, Naples and

Calcutta.[156] "The exterior of this small box resembles a liqueurs receptacle. A spring catch opens simultaneously its two doors and lid. Inside, in the middle, stands a telephone mouthpiece in silver, which, at first sight, one would take for a very small trumpet or hunting horn. At the left is a little rope made of twisted silver threads, one end of which is attached to the machine while the other extremity ends in a, kind of little bell which one holds to one's ear to hear the voice of the person with whom one is speaking, just like the telephone of today. At the right is a toad, in silver, with its mouth open. Placed around the opening of the mouth-piece, stand seven statuettes in gold, each on a small separate silver pedestal representing symbolically the seven cardinal virtues of the Palladian Ladder.

"Each of these seven statuettes designates one of the Directories. The statuette Ignis (sacred fire) divine endeavour, stands for the Supreme Dogmatic Directory of Charleston; Ratio (Reason, triumphant over superstition), the Sovereign Executive Directory of Rome; Labor (Labour) the Sovereign Administrative Directory of Berlin; Ubertas (fecundity), Caritas (Masonic Charity), Emancipatio (the emancipation of humanity shedding the yoke of all despotisms) and Felicitas (Happiness derived from virtuous practices) representing the four Grand Central Directories of Washington, Naples, Monte Video and Calcutta.

"When the Supreme Dogmatical chief wishes to communicate, for example, with the head of political action, he presses his finger on the Statuette Ignis and on the Statuette Ratio: these sink into their sockets and at the same instant, a strong whistling is heard in Rome, in the office where Lemmi keeps his Arcula Mystica; Lemmi opens his box and sees the statuette of Ignis sunk, while tiny, harmless flames issue from the throat of the silver toad. Then he knows that the Sovereign Pontiff of Charleston wishes to speak to him. He presses down the statuette of Ratio in his box and from then on, the conversation between the two chiefs proceeds, each one speaking directly into the mouthpiece described above, while at the same time holding to his ear the small silver bell.

"At the end of the conversation, each chief replaces the golden statuettes by pulling them up by the head.

"Every Sovereign Grand Master of a Directory travels with his Arcula

Mystica. This box is personally confided to him. That of the Administrative Directory of Berlin is kept by the Sovereign Finance Delegate... who is actually Bleichroeder (1893).

"It is evidently necessary to detach the memory of Albert Pike from the great number of exaggerated legends which cling to his name, but with a man of this type one never knows just what to think. His reputation as an Occultist had overstepped the doors of the lodges and inner shrines. Everyone knew from hearsay that he gave himself up to Luciferian practices."

Owing to the discredit cast upon Bataille's writings, we now quote in corroboration of the existence of such rites as described above from the well-known theosophist Mrs. Alice A. Bailey's book, *Initiation Human and Solar*, (published 1922 by the Lucifer Publishing Co., New York), which has never been challenged:—Such quotations touch upon the following subjects:

Description of the Deity.
Description of Initiation and fire.
Description, of Sex and fire.
Description of the Seven Rays.

1. "The Lord of the World, the One Initiator, He Who is called in the Bible 'The Ancient of Days', and in the Hindu Scriptures the First Kumara, He, Sanat Kumara it is, Who from His throne at Shamballa in the Gobi desert, presides over the Lodge of Masters, and holds in His hands the reins of government in all the three departments. Called in some Scriptures 'the Great Sacrifice', He has chosen to watch over the evolution of men and devas until all have been occultly 'saved'. He it is Who, four times a year, meets in conference with all the Chohans and Masters, and authorises what shall be done to further the ends of evolution."[157]

Call it Lucifer, Satan or the Devil, it is always the same old manifestation revamped now as Sanat Kumara and, while he may indeed seem to be a very good god, his presence alone is our only concern at the moment.

2. As to initiation,—"The Hierophant utters the word, and the force is literally thrown into the initiate's bodies and centres, passing down through the centres on the mental plane, via the astral centres, to the centres on etheric levels, which finally absorb it. This is the stupendous moment for the initiate, and brings to him a realisation of the literal absolute truth of the phrase that 'God is a consuming fire'. He knows past all gainsaying that fiery energy and electric force constitute the sum-total of all that is. He is literally bathed in the fires of purification; he sees fire on all sides, pouring out through the Rod (of initiation) circulating around the Triangle, and passing through the bodies of the two sponsoring adepts. For a brief second, the entire Lodge of Masters and initiates, standing in their ceremonial places without the Triangle, are hidden from view by a wall of fire. The initiate sees no one, save the Hierophant, and is aware of nothing but a fiery blaze of pure, blue-white flame, which burns, but destroys not, which intensifies the activity of every atom in his body without disintegrating, and which purifies his entire nature. The fire tries his work, of what sort it is, and he passes through the Flame.[158]

"At the fifth initiation the great secret which concerns the fire or spirit aspect is revealed to the wondering and amazed Master, and He realises in a sense incomprehensible to man the fact that all is fire and fire is all."[159]

3. "Let the disciple transfer the fire from the lower triangle to the higher, and preserve that which is created through the fire of the midway point.[160]

"This means, literally, the control by the initiate of the sex impulse, as usually understood, and the transference of the fire which now normally vitalises the generative organs to the throat centre, thus leading to creation upon the mental plane through the agency of mind..."

4. As to the seven rays:

Groups of Egos are formed:

1. According to their ray.
2. According to their sub-ray.
3. According to their rat e of vibration.

They are also grouped for purposes of classification:

1. As Egos, according to the egoic ray.
2. As personalities, according to the subray which is governing the personality.[161]

"All are graded and charted. The Masters have Their Halls of Records, with a system of tabulation incomprehensible to us owing to its magnitude and its necessary intricacies wherein these charts are kept. They are under the care of a Chohan of a Ray, each Ray having its own collection of charts... These Halls of Records are mostly on the lowest levels of the mental plane and the highest of the astral, as they can be there most fully utilised and are most easily accessible." "While the ray business may be an excellent scientific, though little known, method of keeping in touch with the adepts it has one very serious disadvantage, namely, that whoever is attuned to a ray is, in case of revenge or evil intent on the part of a superior, (shall we say scientist?) vulnerable on this ray!"

One is almost astonished at the frankness displayed by Mrs. Bailey in her revelations concerning the secrets of Initiation, when one remembers the tragic fate of William Morgan, the secret condemnation, kidnapping and sequestration, torture and final assassination of this New York Journalist who had published for the profane public the principal masonic rituals of the period.

Carlile, in his *Manual of Freemasonry*, gives the following particulars:— "My exposure of Freemasonry, in 1825, led to its exposure in the United States of America; and a Mason there, of the name of William Morgan, having announced his intention of assisting in the work of exposure, was kidnapped, under pretended forms and warrants of law, by his brother

Masons, removed from the State of New York to the borders of Canada, near the falls of Niagara, and there most barbarously murdered. This happened in 1826. The States have been for many years much excited upon the subject; a regular warfare has arisen between Masons and anti-Masons. Societies of anti-Masons have been formed, newspapers and magazines started, and many pamphlets and volumes, with much correspondence, published; so that before the slavery question was passed amongst them, all parties had merged themselves into Masons and anti-Masons. Several persons were punished for the abduction of Morgan: but the murderers were sheltered by Masonic Lodges, and rescued from justice."

"The story of the murder of William Morgan for the crime of violating Masonic secrecy has long been a well-known historical fact; but in August, 1875, the full particulars were brought to light by the publication of two letters from the Venerable Thurlow Weed. The facts were as follows:[162]

"In the year 1826, Morgan, who had passed through all the degrees of Masonry and held a very high position in the Order, conceived the idea of publishing a book disclosing all the secrets of the sect. What his motive may have been is only conjectural. Mr. Weed was living at that time in the town of Rochester, New York, and Morgan requested him to publish the projected book. Mr. Weed declined, and Morgan went to the adjoining town of Batavia, where he arranged with another person for the publication.

"He had written a portion of the book, and was engaged in completing it when he was arrested on a false charge of larceny, on the 10th Sept., and conveyed to the jail of Ontario county. The sheriff and officers of this prison were Masons. His house was searched, and his manuscripts were seized and destroyed.

"On the evening of the 12th Sept, he was discharged by the interference of some of the conspirators, and, as he passed out of the door of the jail, was seized by them, taken a short distance, and then forcibly put into a carriage. He was carried, in the course of that night, on to the ridge-road about two miles beyond the village of Rochester. During the next day, he was taken to Lewiston, a distance of seventy or eighty miles, and from thence to Fort Niagara, at the mouth of the Niagara River. His benevolent captors had decided on bringing him here in the hope that their brother Masons of Canada would aid them in disposing of him. His murder was not then contemplated; but it was hoped that the Canadian Masons would take charge of him and send him to end his days among the Indian tribes, in the north-west of Canada. Placing their prisoner in Fort Niagara, his captors crossed the river into Canada to attend a meeting of a lodge there; but the Canadian Masons, after much deliberation, refused to become parties to the business. The American Masons returned to Fort Niagara, and in a few days afterwards a large number of men, high in the order, assembled a short distance off to open an Encampment of Knight Templars, the additional power of the 'sealed obligation' being necessary for such a case. At night they dined together, and, after dinner, the chaplain gave a sentiment so significant that all thoughts were turned towards Fort Niagara. The 'sentiment' was, in fact, 'death to all traitors' and immediately afterwards one of the company, Colonel King, arose from the table and called four of the others to accompany him. These were Whitney, a stonemason; Chubbuch, a farmer; Garside, a butcher; and Howard, a bookbinder. 'They were all' says Mr. Weed, 'men of correct habits and good character, and all, I doubt not, were moved by an enthusiastic but most misguided sense of duty'. King told them that he had an order from the Grand Master, the execution of which required their assistance, and they replied that they would obey it. The five murderers were then driven in a carriage to the fort where Morgan was confined. It was just midnight. They told the doomed man that his friends had completed their arrangements for his removal to Canada, where his life would be safe. He consented to go with them, and they walked to the wharf where a boat was waiting for them; they embarked and rowed away into the darkness. When the boat reached the point where Niagara River empties itself into Lake Ontario, the murderers threw off all pretence, and with some horrible mummeries ordered Morgan to prepare for death. They wound a rope around him, attaching to each end of it a heavy weight, and threw him overboard. He sank like a stone, and the murderers returned to tell their comrades that the traitor had met a traitor's doom. One of the murderers,

Whitney, told all these particulars to Mr. Weed a few months afterwards, but it is only now, when all the criminals are dead, that he makes the fact public. The body of Morgan was found a year afterwards, identified by his wife and friends, and buried; and although the Masons tried to dispute the identification, their efforts were futile. None of the murderers was ever brought to justice."[163]

So much for the oath of secrecy and brotherhood I Nowadays, greater precautions are observed in getting rid of the enemies of the sect. Some little study and the cooperation of a few culpable doctors, its auxiliaries and affiliates, enable the terrible sect to dispose easily of their enemies. The victim of their vengeance, swallowing some disease germ, meets a fate that none can prove to have been artificially contrived. This is the secret of secrets, denied again and again! And yet the charge remains! For plague, cholera and all epidemics can be let loose on the world at a word from the Hidden Masters!

But to return to the organization of Freemasonry. It is necessary here to say that in many instances, where a masculine lodge has a feminine annex, its existence is frequently completely ignored by the majority of the brothers. No mutual visiting is allowed among the female members of the lower masonic degrees, for a sister may enter lodges other than her own, only after she has herself attained the fifth degree. As well as masculine General Inspectors on permanent missions, in direct communication with Charleston, there are General Inspectresses, high grade women masons belonging to ordinary Masonry who, while not necessarily affiliated to palladism, serve the purpose of its leaders, their good offices being much appreciated when they furnish useful information to headquarters. These women are privileged to enter the lodges and inner shrines of masonry only, but are not admitted to Palladian triangles. As for men belonging to an adoptive lodge where brothers and sisters work together they must have at least attained the 32nd (Prince of the Royal Secret) or a corresponding grade in another rote before they can enter an Areopagus of Sublime Ecossaise.

As regards the position of women in Masonry, we think that this cannot be better explained than in the words of Albert Pike himself. In *La*

Femme et l'Enfant dans la Franc-Maçonnerie Universelle page 578, A. C. De La Rive states that on July 14, 1889, Albert Pike, Sovereign Pontiff of Universal Freemasonry, addressed to the 23 Supreme Confederated Councils of the world the following instructions, which we quote herewith in part.

"To the science of Faust, the real Mason will join the impassibility of Job. He will eradicate superstition from his heart and cultivate decision of character. He will accept pleasure only when he wishes it and will wish it only when he should do so.

"We earnestly recommend the creation of Lodges of Adoption. They are indispensable to the formation of Masons who are indeed Masters of themselves. The pnest tries to subdue his flesh by enforced celibacy... The real Mason, on the contrary, reaches perfection, that is to say achieves self-mastery, by using his zeal in the Lodges of Adoption in submitting to all natural ordeals. Commerce with women, belonging to all brethren, forms for him an armour against those passions which lead hearts astray. He alone can really possess voluptuousness. To be able, at will, to use or to abstain, is a twofold power. Woman fetters thee by thy desires, we say to the adept, well, use women often and without passion; thou wilt thus become master of thy desires, and thou wilt enchain woman. From which it must perforce result that the real Mason will succeed in easily solving the problem of the flesh.

"It is evidently not absolutely necessary that the man whom you are leading towards the high grades be immediately perfect and have understood our secret on his entrance into Masonry. That which we ask you is first to observe him with the greatest care during his apprenticeship and afterwards, when he enters the Lodge of Adoption as Companion to use that as your criterion, your instrument of infallible control." The Lodge of Brothers which has failed to annex a Lodge of Sisters is incomplete and destined inevitably never to produce anything but Brethren, with whom politics are the chief concern, men who will be chiefly preoccupied with intrigue and rivalry, who will do bad work and whose politics will be incoherent." Dr. Bataille elucidates this point in the following terms:

"Concerning androgynous lodges, Masons generally give the same answer. They either say 'Yes, once upon a time there were sister masons but there are none any longer' or, if forced to make a concession say, 'Lodges admitting women are irregular and function entirely outside of Masonry proper, unrecognized by Grand Orients and Supreme Councils'".

"Having referred to the great care exercised to hide the existence of the sister masons, it is now opportune to expose the ruse employed in stifling further investigation. From time to time, one of the semi initiates is urged to bring a resolution suggesting the establishment of feminine lodges, and a petition is drawn up and sent in to the Grand Orient or Supreme Council, whereupon the chiefs gravely insert a decree in the official bulletin rejecting the petition, and emphasising the point that 'the constitution is opposed to the creation of regular female lodges'. Then, whenever the question of sister masons is raised in the profane press,—quick! The Grand Orients and Supreme Councils publish these famous decrees."[164]

In certain cities where masonic secrecy is less carefully guarded, a part of the masonic premises is available for the use of the profane public and daily lectures or instructions of the brother professors. In these rooms, every evening, accounting, stenography, foreign languages and other popular professional accomplishments are taught, a great activity is thus created around masonic headquarters and the entrance of a woman more or less attracts no attention. The sister masons, however, know to which room they must go and, once past the threshold of the building, it is not to the professorial lecture room that they wend their way.

In connection with Eastern occultism and its organization Dr. Bataille made the following statement and curious deduction: "A number of Satanic monasteries are concealed today under the guise of Musulman harems or annexes to Lama, or Brahmin monasteries, but it is possible that someday these institutions might take root in Europe where, under a deceptive exterior, one of these communities might be established. When one knows the true mission of the 'Pink Serpents' one wonders if Christianity will not presently assist at this crowning abomination—a convent of so called Christians practising luciferianism.

"The 'Pink Serpents' are sister masons. They are the luciferian missionaries and operate as individuals and under conditions of the greatest secrecy. No records of the money appropriated for these religious spies are shown."

But let us resume the subject of Palladism as explained by Dr. Bataille.

"This super-rite, which is masonic luciferian spiritism, must not be confused with the machinery of high masonry. Palladism is the cult of Satan in the inner shrines of a rite superposed to ail the rites. It is a cult, a religion. High masonry is a supreme administration involving an organization much more highly developed than Palladism whose secret leaders, some of whom are not luciferian, act in concert and accept a superior central authority in order that their work may be the more effective.[165]

"In founding the New and Reformed Palladian rite, General Pike did not create masonic occultism. Anderson, Desaguliers, Weishaupt, Swedenborg, Lessing, Frederic II of Prussia, Mesmer, Pernety, Cagliostro, Martinez Pasqualis and his disciple Saint-Martin,. Francia (the dictator of Paraguay) Lord Palmerston, General Contreras, Mazzini, and many other distinguished Freemasons practised occultism and worked at the Great Work of the Cabala,[166] but before the year 1870, the inner shrines all operated without other direction than that of the theurgic rituals of Swedenborg, Saint-Martin, Laffon, Landebat, and the Vicomte de la Jonquière, etc. and the Masonic initiates of Hermeticism were widely dispersed in different schools which were local and not international.

"While Pike laid the foundation of Palladism at Charleston, Mazzini organized the centralization of Political action in Rome, and two years after the founding of the Sovereign Executive and the Supreme Dogmatic Directories, a third, the Sovereign Administrative Directory, was instituted in Berlin. This latter functioned by means of a constantly renewed committee of seven taken from the Supreme Councils, Grand Encampments, Grand Orients, and Grand Lodges of the world. By means of an ingeniously contrived system of rotation, these representatives act by virtue of their mandate for three months only. Each of the existing rites, with the exception of the Palladian, send annually to Berlin two of its members of the Superior degrees, drawn from any country except Germany, which alone, of all those represented, is entitled to one permanent member whose quarterly term of office expires at the end of the time allotted to the particular lodge of which he is a delegate... The members of the Sovereign Administrative Directory are always given 120 days notice of their appointments in order to enable them to plan what would appear to be a pleasure trip or a holiday, when, in fact, they are going on the business of the association.

"Two special delegates are permanently attached to the Directory of Berlin, one for finance and one for propaganda. At the present date, (1894) Bleichroeder fills the first mentioned position and Findel, a non-luciferian, the second. These officers are obliged to live in Germany and to be in a sufficiently independent position to be able to go to the seat of the Directory at a moment's notice.

"The business of the Propaganda agent is to furnish information to the chiefs at Rome and Charleston... He receives monthly, by secret messenger from Berlin, the report of all measures formulated at the Sovereign Administrative Directory relating to means and methods judged useful in spreading the principles of the association.

"After a meeting he examines, coordinates and frames a report of the decisions upon which, three months later, the seven members of the Berlin Directory will vote. Of these seven members, thanks to the system of rotation explained above, there are always at least two who, having belonged to the Directory at the time of the submission of the resolution under consideration, are able to furnish commentaries and explanations to the new comers. Only resolutions having obtained a favourable vote of five or seven voices can be registered by the delegate recorder, and these can be finally adopted only on the second following month, if they pass unanimously.[167] In the event of one or more persons opposing a measure, the matter is referred to the Chief at Rome after which, failing his approval, it is settled arbitrarily by the chief at Charleston from whose decision there is no appeal.

"The business of the financial agent is not a matter of funds, it consists in drawing up a general balance sheet of all rites, in all countries with the brother accountant working under his orders as a sworn expert." As above said, the Palladian rite has no share in the functioning of the Sovereign Administrative Directory. This should again prove that Palladism is superposed to all the other rites. It is the luciferian religion and only need concern itself with the triangles which have a separate budget. Being the real hidden power, known only to the perfect initiates, it need not unveil itself even to this permanent committee which constitutes the highest expression of the administrative power of the great international association. One must also not lose sight of the fact that among the masonic powers, there are several countries where the Symbolic Grand Lodges recognize only three grades of which that of Master is the third and highest degree.

These lodges, like the others, are entitled to send two delegates from time to time to Berlin, and, as a consequence of having suppressed the high grades for their adepts, these Federations are necessarily kept in complete ignorance of the existence of Palladism. The Supreme chiefs of Charleston and Rome appear to them solely as earnest, active brothers who should be consulted because of their great personal experience—but that is all."

"Finally the Palladists have no need to be officially represented in Berlin, as most of the members of the Supreme Councils, Grand Encampments and Grand Orients are their men and any important proposition is immediately communicated to them.

"Under the Sovereign Directory, the Executive at Rome and the Administrative at Berlin, come the Grand Central Directories which are bureaus of registration in the different parts of the world. These are located in North America, South America, Europe, Asia and Oceania. There is as well a sub-Directory for Africa. At their heads are the high grade trusted brothers by whom everything that emanates from the Supreme Councils, Grand Encampments, Grand Orients and Grand Lodges of their jurisdiction is centralized. Independent of the Sovereign Administrative Directory of Berlin, they operate directly under the chiefs of Rome and Charleston and it is by these central Directories that these two great intriguers are kept informed of the trend of world affairs.

"As everything comes to the Grand Central Directories so everything emanates from them. Five messengers to Washington, Montevideo, Naples, Calcutta, and Port Louis will put in motion the formidable machinery of Freemasonry the world over."

If the organization described in the foregoing pages which were written by Bataille forty years ago has progressed along the lines above indicated, one can easily conjecture the degree of perfection which has doubtless been attained today.

CHAPTER XXXI

PRACTICAL POLITICS

THE GAME OF politics is the pursuit of power. In all democracies, there are two separate organizations playing the political game. The open and *visible* one, the members of which hold office as members of a government, and the *invisible* one composed of individuals who control this visible organization and in whom is vested the real power, the essence of which is *finance*, controlling the publicity which makes or unmakes its tools.

This financial power may be used to promote truth or fallacies, good or evil, national prosperity or national ruin, but so long as human nature is what it is, so long as jealousy, greed, personal ambition and expediency can sway the lives of men, so long will the rule of the invisible power prevail by methods inimical to the best interests of a nation. The strength of a democracy thus lies at the mercy of invisible leaders who, being nationally irresponsible, cannot be called to account for the consequences of the acts of the governments they control. This at the same time constitutes the inherent weakness of any form of government, the apotheosis of which is the control of both parties in the state, right and left, radical and conservative, by the same forces. Then, only the puppets change while the rule of the individuals controlling the machine continues unhindered. Voters who wonder why their efforts have failed, wonder in vain. As the dupes of a controlled publicity their privilege of the vote is a farce.

If all factions in a state can be controlled from one source, why should

International Control be impracticable? Italy, if one follows its history for the last hundred years, gives a sequence of good illustrations of such possibilities and affords us a chance to follow the progressive stages of masonic centralization and imposition of Internationalism upon nations, as conceived by Mazzini, Pike, Palmerston and Bismarck.

International control was Mazzini's dream. His cynical remark "We aspire to corrupt in order to rule" leaves one little faith in the idealism of this Patriarch of International Freemasonry. That he applied his motto is shown by the use he made of Francesco Crispi.

As Palamenghi-Crispi writes:[168]

"Crispi became personally acquainted with Mazzini in London, in January, 1855, but they had corresponded since 1850, when, their golden dream of liberty and independence banished by the return of all the tyranny of the past, the bravest of the patriots had once more begun to conspire.

"While pondering the idea of founding a National Committee in which the various regions of Italy should be represented, Mazzini also determined to form a fund for the carrying out of great enterprises. And 'as it is impossible to obtain large sums secretly and from a few people' he wrote, he worked out a plan for a National Loan, to be raised by the issue of bonds to be redeemed by a liberated Italy.

"The first act of the National Committee was to authorise the issue of such bonds to the amount of ten million lire."

In his youth, Francesco Crispi made a mistake, and blackmail made him a ruler of men. As the tool of Mazzini, he ruled Italy for many years, and as the ruler of Italy, he wielded the secret power of International Masonry in accordance with the policy of his masters.

According to *Crispi* 33° by D. Vaughan, "Crispi, in Palladism, Brother v Serafino-Chiocciola, was born at Ribera, in Sicily, on Oct. 4, 1819. His father, Tommaso Crispi, a lawyer, destined him to the church, but in 1837, he married Felicita Valle, a pretty young girl with whom he was infatuated. In 1856, he abandoned her for Rosalia Montmasson, deserting the latter in 1878 to marry Lina Barbagallo, widow Capellani. At this period, he was openly accused of bigamy and though challenged to do so, he never produced the documents necessary to prove the death of his first wife, Felicita Valle.

"After his marriage in 1837, he practised law and in 1838 joined one of the numerous secret societies which in those days infested Sicily. Presently he started his career as a political intriguer and conspirator travelling over the world on his sinister business under different aliases and false passports provided for him by Mazzini, who, in view of his confidential position as friend of the King of Naples, had bought his services as a spy."

Domenico Margiotta states in *Francesco Crispi, son Œuvre Néfaste*, that he found among the papers of his grandfather—a member of Young Italy who had been condemned to death as the head of the conspiracy, which penalty he however successfully escaped—a telegram from Mazzini, instructing the organization to "give Crispi promptly thirty thousand ducats to begin with on the account of the Neapolitan Committee of Young Italy and let him get to work."

"While at Malta in 1855, he joined the masonic lodge, "Zetland", under English jurisdiction from which he was shortly expelled for the theft of 800 francs from one of its members. He went to London shortly afterwards. There, Lord Palmerston had returned to power. By becoming an ardent admirer and fanatical follower of Mazzini, Crispi simultaneously entered the good graces of Palmerston who was on the very best of terms with the Italian leader.

In 1856, believing that Napoleon III, in cooperation with Cavour, was the secret arbiter of the destinies of Italy, and the greatest obstacle to the realization of his own republican schemes, Mazzini induced Crispi to go to Paris.

While he was there, a number of attempts were made on the life of the Emperor, among others that of Orsini on Jan. 14, 1858, but, though strongly suspected of participation in these conspiracies by the police or Paris, no evidence for a direct charge of complicity against Crispi was ever obtained. However, it is known that he and Orsini had previously met in London where the latter had shown him how to make the famous bombs, the use and manufacture of which Crispi afterwards taught his followers in Sicily.

By August 3, 1858, he was back in London, the Paris police having developed too great a zeal on his behalf during his sojourn in the French capital.

At last by 1860, the various Italian conspiracies crystallized into one. Everything was ready for the fulfilment of Mazzini's dream of United Italy. Bertani, Bixio and Crispi decided to go to Turin themselves to see General Garibaldi and, after the British Minister, Sir James Hudson, had confirmed certain information on conditions in Palermo, which had been furnished by the Genoese deputies, the General seemed at last inclined to take action. He ordered Bixio to Genoa to charter a ship and Crispi to Milan to receive from Enrico Besana the arms and the money already subscribed. This subscription was begun by General Garibaldi himself and, in view of later developments, it is a significant fact that one of the contributions he received for the famous expedition of the One Thousand, was the sum of fifty thousand francs from the Jew, Cornelius Herz.

Twelve thousand guns were in the hands of Massimo d'Azeglio, then governor of Milan who, by order of the government, surrendered them to the rebels.

Finally, General Garibaldi arrived in Genoa on April 14. On the 16th, Crispi returned to Turin where he saw the Minister of the Interior, Farini, who, having by that time changed his mind concerning the Italian expedition, had ceased to be a dictator and had assumed the attitude of a diplomatic satellite of Cavour. He proved quite intractable. Back in Genoa, Crispi found La Farina again, this time with orders to report all developments to Cavour. Cavour, warned not to interfere with Garibaldi, raised no obstacles to the progress of the plot. He only advised waiting for better news from the Island of Sicily, and promised to cooperate with a million guns, as soon as the time for the expedition seemed propitious.

Still Garibaldi hesitated. The Sicilian news was contradictory. On April 26, Crispi received from Niccola Fabrizzi a message from Malta reading "Failure in the provinces and in the town of Palermo. Many exiles arriving at Malta on English ships." Luckily a few days later, a communication from Palermo, published by the Gazette of Turin, told of the great proportions assumed by the insurrection in Sicily, This communication had been invented and written at Genoa by Crispi for the purposes of overcoming the last scruples of Garibaldi!

One day, the second of May, Crispi and Garibaldi were alone in a room looking seaward, in the Villa Spinola Quarti. They were talking about the expedition. Crispi as usual, was fighting the vacillations of Garibaldi. Suddenly, the General interrupted him saying, "You are the only one to encourage me in this enterprise, Everyone else tries to dissuade me. Why?" "Because I am profoundly convinced that it will be helpful to the fatherland and that it will cover you with glory. I fear only one thing: The uncertainty of the sea."

"I answer for the sea" said Garibaldi.

"And I answer for the land" said Crispi. Garibaldi was persuaded and the die was cast.

After the victorious expedition of the One Thousand had placed the group of conspirators in power in Sicily, each was rewarded according to his merits, Crispi becoming Minister of Foreign Affairs. Cavour had died on June 6, 1861, poisoned, it is said, on May 28, by order of Mazzini.

Until 1861, Crispi had cooperated whole heartedly with the revolutionaries but, as time wore on, he began to think that it might be more to his personal advantage to serve the King than Mazzini.

His plan was discovered by Mazzini's spies and in 1862, the deputy of Castelvetrano found himself facing death for treason at the hands of his former friends and accomplices, under conditions that enslaved him body and soul forever after, to the International Sect.

Early in April 1862, he attended a Freemasonic dinner of the *Associations Emancipatrice* at Turin. Suddenly he felt ill, very ill, fire seemed to be burning within him. He was in the throes of the most appalling agony. Instead of offering assistance, the other guests began to laugh, then, one of them rising, spoke to him severely in the following terms:

"Francesco, you went to visit King Victor Emmanuel, without telling us of your intention and you offered him your secret services. You let him know that you were ready to go over at the first opportunity. Till then your opinions had been republican. Well, that is treason. We have condemned you. You are poisoned. You are a dead man."

The poison had indeed been administered in the bread. Among the organizers of the banquet was the baker Dolfi, who had formerly contributed to the expulsion of the Grand Duke of Tuscany and who had become one of the members of the Radical Directing Committee. On this occasion, Dolfi had kneaded the bread himself, and each guest had found his place at the table marked by a small roll bearing his name, traced on its golden crust by a fillet of whitish dough. All the guests, agreeably surprised, had congratulated the baker for his delicate attention, but the piece of bread marked Crispi had been separately kneaded and contained the poison.

Crispi realized full well that he was lost. He knew there was no escape and that all the exits to the banquet hall were closed, moreover, he was too weak to tight. Without recrimination and in the throes of acute pain, he dropped into a chair upon which, writhing in agony, he awaited a lingering death.

The others surrounded him, watching him in silence with profound contempt. Suddenly, a door opened, a curtain was raised and a man appeared. He advanced slowly. It was Mazzini.

"Poor wretch!" said he to the dying man. "I pity you."

At these words, Crispi looked up. His dim eyes gleamed suddenly and he murmured feebly.

"Yes, ambition made me betray... It is true ... I was going to sell myself... But I die... Do not insult my agony... Do not mock me... 1 suffer too much!"

"I do not speak to you in derision," answered the grand master, "Francesco Crispi, I forgive you... Drink this and you are saved. You will be reborn..."

So saying, he forced his teeth apart and pressing a small vial to the lips of the dying man poured the counter-poison down his parched throat.

After his last words, Crispi had collapsed. Some time passed. Was he still alive? He seemed a corpse. Little by little, sweat gathered on his face and hands then, slowly, his livid countenance regained some colour.

For a long time he seemed inert. Then his eyelids opened and, looking around with a stunned expression of incomprehension, he asked.

"Where am I?"

"You have returned from the realm of the dead" murmured Mazzini gravely.

"Oh! Yes, I remember now, Mercy! Mercy!" he added suddenly, recalling realities and clinging desperately to life. "I live indeed, Master. Is it not a dream?"

"You live, yes, Francesco; but henceforth you are more completely enslaved than the last of the negroes for whose freedom they are fighting over there in America... You live again and your ambition will be gratified... You will be minister, minister of the Monarchy;

You will hold in your hands the reins of government but, without betraying us, without selling yourself! ... You will part from us, not privately but publicly... We will denounce you, and while denouncing you, we will push you to power. It is the monarchy that you will betray by executing our orders, when we shall have made you minister of the crown... And you will obey us in all things, even should the orders we give you seem contradictory, even should their execution cause you to pass for a madman in the eyes of Europe! Yes, Francesco Crispi, from this day forward, you belong to us, for you must never forget that , should you place us in a position where it might be expedient to cut short your own existence a second time, no power in the world could save you from the death, the sufferings of which you have known today. Live then for Masonry. Fight Royalty and the Church. You will be the gravedigger of this house of Savoy. It is only an instrument for us and we have condemned it to disappear after it has served our purpose."

This plan of action was carried out. In 1864, Crispi, on orders from his master, became a Royalist and duly denounced Mazzini. That is the explanation of his often incoherent and erratic policies in after life. Mazzini's promise was fulfilled and Crispi became Minister of the Interior in 1878.

In 1877, he had been on a tour to Paris, Berlin, London and Vienna. In Paris, he had seen Thiers, Jules Favre and Gambetta; in Germany, Prince Bismarck, with whom he already had an acquaintance of some years standing, and who shared his aversion for France and the Roman Catholic

Church; in England, Lord Derby and Mr. Gladstone; but the true purpose of his mission in these lands is still unknown. As a consequence of his interview with Bismarck, at Salzbourg, Italy, fearing France, threw herself into the hands of the Iron Chancellor. Germany henceforth was to hold her as a dog ready to be set at either against Austria or France when it suited her purpose. The Triple Alliance was formed on May 20, 1882.

Crispi's accession to the ministry was therefore a victory of prime importance to the sect.

After the death of Mazzini, in 1872, Adriano Lemmi took over his masonic heritage and, along with the rest, his slave Francesco Crispi, who, with the Jew Barozilai, became his right hand man.

King Victor Emmanuel died on Jan 9, 1878, and was succeeded by Humbert I. That same year saw the death of Pope Pius IX and the accession to the papacy of Leo XIII.

In 1884, Humbert I was initiated into masonry as Knight Kadosch, under conditions of the greatest secrecy and a lodge, that of Savoia Illuminata, was founded in his honour.

In spite of his exalted masonic position the monarch's political information was always strictly censored by his masonic superiors.

From 1887 to 1891, and again from 1893 to 1896, Crispi acted the part of Prime Minister.

In order to enable him to curry favour with the common people, Lemmi occasionally authorized him to execute political turnovers. The Grand Master Lemmi once said to Humbert "Fear not; the socialism of Crispi will not last; it will provoke no riots, it is simply an electoral manoeuvre" and the king was much gratified at being so well informed. There at least, the 33° King was not deceived. If now and again Crispi resumed his revolutionary complexion, it was only to obtain the votes of those whom he persecuted mercilessly once he had obtained power. To him, a change of opinion was as easy as a change of shirt.[169]

In 1889, came the scandal of the Banca Romana, revealed as such through the efforts of Giovanni Giolitti[170] and in 1892, that of Panama involving another, namely the Grand Cordon of Cornelius Herz, any one of which would have swamped the political career of any unprotected individual. Crispi, though seriously implicated, was supported through an impossible situation by the masonic brotherhood.

The Abyssinian War, itself the result of masonic intrigue, was the terrible manoeuvre calculated to ruin the House of Savoy in the eyes of the Italian people.

It was known that, at the time of the disaster of Adowa, the succession of Adriano Lemmi to the Grand Mastership of the Grand Orient of Italy was open, and that competition for the position was keen. Some favoured the candidacy of Bovio, others that of Nathan, later Mayor of Rome. But Crispi had promised General Baratieri,[171] a masonic dignitary, that he should have the preference above all others, on condition that he win a victory over the Negus. Such an achievement would give Italy another Garibaldi, a popular hero, while simultaneously providing Crispi himself with a useful tool and the position of "top dog" which had never been his before.

But the disastrous defeat of his candidate by Menelek, at the Battle of Adowa on March 2, 1896, resulted in the fall of Crispi, not that of the king.

The agent of Lemmi had played his part but the great game of the Federated Secret Societies had only suffered a temporary setback.

In 1900, King Humbert I was assassinated at Monza. Crispi died in 1901.

The fate of Italy is the fate of all nations governed by political rings. Italy in the 19th century seems to have been the vortex of the intrigue directed against Christianity which today ravages the world, carrying in its wake a general disregard of all ideals, decency, duty and loyalty.

Liberty is corrupted into licentiousness, marital fidelity into perversion, equality into equality of low standards and fraternity into a brotherhood based on mutual slavery under the yoke of International Finance.

And the monster grows apace! Today it bestrides the world under the name of Bolshevism, but it is the same old monster, the heresy of the first centuries of the Christian era and the Middle Ages, namely—Gnosticism.

CHAPTER XXXII

ADRIANO LEMMI

This chapter is compiled largely of extracts, some transcribed verbatim and others elaborated to include information necessary to the reader, from: Adriano Lemmi by Domenico Margiotta 33°

ADRIANO LEMMI WAS born of Roman Catholic parents, at Leghorn, Tuscany, on April 30, 1822. He was the son of Fortunato Lemmi and Teresa Merlino, his lawful wife.

At an early age, he became the despair of his parents. He was dissolute, frequented evil haunts and formed undesirable friendships.

Running away from home on December 29, 1843, he forged a letter stating, under the letterhead of Falconet and Co., that a credit for his account was to be opened on Pastre Bros., Bankers, at Marseilles, where, shortly after his arrival, he scraped acquaintance with Monsieur and Madame Grand Boubagne whom he was soon accused of having robbed of 300 francs. The evidence against him was overwhelming, and he was condemned to a year in prison for that and other minor offences, and also sentenced to five years on probation.

He served his term and bolted to Constantinople, Arriving there early in April 1845, he eked out a precarious existence, first as a kitchen hand, then as the assistant in the shop of an old apothecary, whose preparations he peddled in the streets of Galata.

His employer had a friend, a Polish rabbi who, having been condemned for conspiracy in Russia, had taken refuge in Constantinople. This man took a fancy to him and in an effort to curry favour with the Jews, Lemmi presently asked if he might be received into the religion of Moses. As a diplomatic move, the suggestion was a great success for the apothecary and the rabbi, proud and jubilant to have secured a neophyte, taught him the Talmud, while another rabbi, Abraham Maggioro, instructed him in the mysteries of the Cabala. Together, they initiated him into the secrets of magic, in which he proved an apt pupil and his lot was much improved, but the old apothecary died in 1847, and Lemmi found himself without employment. The Polish rabbi having left Constantinople, he stayed on a while under the protection of his friend Maggioro.

In those days, the few Freemasons coming to Pera were English. Freemasonry had been introduced into Turkey in 1738, but until the Crimean war it suffered many vicissitudes. The English saw their lodges fade away for want of active members, for the government did not favour them. Adriano Lemmi was supposed to have been initiated into Freemasonry in 1848 by an English Mason, but this ceremony seems to have somehow been irregular as it had to be repeated at a later date.

Finally, the era of his trials seemed to end. In 1849, some of his English masonic friends gave him a letter of introduction to the great Magyar, Kossuth, who had come to Constantinople, a fugitive from public opprobrium in his own country.

To save him from starvation, Kossuth took him as his servant at low wages, but he gradually succeeded in ingratiating himself with his patron till finally he became his secretary on the recommendation of Mazzini with whom he was already in correspondence.

When Kossuth went to the United States in 1851, he was accompanied by Lemmi. They were forced to travel via Gibraltar and London as the French authorities refused Kossuth permission to land in France, and Lemmi, knowing that he was wanted by the French police, knew better than to try to do so. In Lodge No. 133 in Cincinnati, U. S. A., Kossuth received the masonic initiation.

On the 2nd of December 1851, Prince Louis Napoleon, then President of the French Republic, announced to the people and the army his intention of submitting to a referendum the plan of a constitution founded on the system favoured by his uncle. It was a Coup d'Etat. At this news Lemmi left Kossuth in America and went to join Mazzini and Ledru Rollin in London.

By this time, Mazzini had already established his reputation as an international intriguer. The "Youth Movement" of the day was already organized:

The societies composing it were:

Young Italy—founded by Mazzini	1831
Young Poland—founded by Simon Konarski	1834
Young England—founded by Benjamin Disraeli	1834
Young Europe—founded by Mazzini	1834
Young Switzerland—founded by Melegari (Emery)	1835
Young Ireland—founded by Smith O'Brien	1843
Young Germany—founded by Hecker & Struve	1848

The oath taken by the members of Young Italy reads as follows:[172]

"In the name of God and of Italy—in the name of all the martyrs of the holy Italian cause, who have fallen beneath foreign and domestic tyranny—by the duties which bind me to the land wherein God has placed me, and to the brothers whom God has given me—by the love, innate in all men, I bear to the country that gave my mother birth, and will be the home of my children—by the hatred, innate in all men, I bear to evil, injustice, usurpation, and arbitrary rule—by the blush that rises to my brow when I stand before the citizens of other lands, to know that I have no rights of citizenship, no country, and no national flag—by the aspiration that thrills my soul towards that liberty for which it was created, and is impotent to exert; towards the good it was created to strive after, and is impotent to achieve in the silence and isolation of slavery—by the memory of our former greatness and the sense of our present degradation—by the tears of Italian mothers for their sons dead on the scaffold, in prison, or in exile—by the sufferings of the millions—

"I ________, believing in the mission entrusted by God to Italy, and the duty of every Italian to strive to attempt its fulfilment—convinced that where God has ordained that a nation shall be, he has given the requisite power to create it; that the people are the depositaries of that power, and that in its right direction, for the people, and by the people, lies the secret of victory—convinced that virtue consists in action and sacrifice, and strength in union and constancy of purpose—I give my name to Young Italy, an association of men holding the same faith, and swear—

"To dedicate myself wholly and forever to the endeavour with them to constitute Italy *one free, independent, Republican nation*—to promote, by every means in my power, whether by written or spoken word, or by action, the education of my Italian brothers towards the aim of Young Italy; towards association, the sole means of its accomplishment; and to virtue, which alone can render the conquest lasting

—to abstain from enrolling myself in any other association from this time forth—to obey all the instructions, in conformity with the spirit of Young Italy, given me by those who represent with me the union of my Italian brothers, and to keep the secret of these instructions, even at the cost of my life—to assist my brothers of the Association both by action and counsel—

"NOW AND FOR EVER!

"This do I swear, invoking upon my head the wrath of God, the abhorrence of man, and the infamy of the perjurer, if I ever betray the whole or a part of this my oath."

The fusion of Young Italy and Carbonarism evidently did not take place till after April 8, 1839, for in a letter of that date, Mazzini writes to L. A. Melegari at Lausanne "It is a mixture of Young Italy and Carbonarism. They have had me approached indirectly to know if I accept the fusion."[173]

After 1851, Lemmi began playing an important part in all politico-masonic assassinations and in all the popular insurrections of which Italy was the scene. On behalf of Mazzini, he kept up relations with the revolutionaries of Tuscany and it was he who inspired the attempt to assassinate the councillor of the Grand Duke's minister, Baldasseroni, in broad daylight, on Oct. 21, 1852.

A letter from which we quote, written from Malta by Francesco Crispi to Mazzini, dated Nov. 13, 1853,[174] gives a most interesting sidelight on the relations then existing between the Great Italian Revolutionary, his ally Crispi and Adriano Lemmi whom Crispi already recognizes as the agent of an organization inimical to his ideals.

"Brother,—the die is cast! At the present moment, an uprising in Sicily is imminent, if, indeed, it has not already taken place. God grant it may not prove a second sixth of February!

"Knowing that I was here you should have forewarned me. Those to whom you have seen fit to entrust the initiative will not be able to exert any influence whatsoever in the provinces of Palermo and Messina! Their names, indeed, may even be greeted there with hostility, and bring about a reaction. Now without Palermo and Messina every attempt in Sicily will prove vain. But what is done is done, and our plain duty now is to work together in helping on the undertaking, and, as far as is possible, in warding off evil consequences. Let me know the plan of action and what orders you have issued to the leaders. Although I have little regard for them, I intend to do my duty, and this for the good of our country and party, upon whose already tarnished reputation another failure would bring utter ruin. You will remember that ever since 1850, I have been ready to hasten to Sicily. At that time we were working to form the National Committee and raise the loan that should provide funds for any great emergency. Then the Sicilian Committee was formed and speedily dissolved, while you worked to prepare an uprising in northern and central Italy, forgetting Sicily entirely. But not so my friends and I, who were convinced that the greatest possibility of success lav in this island. Nor was this all. After your misfortunes in Lombardy you forgot your old friends, and flung yourself into the arms of men who, up to that very moment, had held you and your theories up to ridicule, but who had been clever enough to deceive you through Signor Lemmi, to whom they had declared their intention to act.

"I am no more their enemy than are any of the friends who belong to the party opposed to Calvi."

On February 6, 1853, an incipient insurrection broke out in Milan, then under Austrian dominion, as the result of a proclamation signed by Mazzini and Kossuth. That it was sent by Lemmi from Switzerland to the revolutionary Lombards is a fact well known in Italian masonry.

Though implicated, the Swiss and Piedmontese governments tried to appear unconcerned. Numerous refugees from Northern Italy went to Switzerland or Piedmont following the instructions transmitted by Lemmi.

Piedmont, assisted by England, (who was secretly helping Mazzini's masonry) tried to induce the Emperor of Austria to issue a decree confiscating the properties of the revolutionary refugees, but a bloody protest was made against the measure on the 18th of February when, by order of Kossuth and Mazzini a revolutionary fanatic made an attempt against the life of the Emperor. Lemmi was chosen to arm the assassin who was a Hungarian and a mutual friend of both Kossuth and himself.

Switzerland, under threat of severance of diplomatic relations, was then obliged to banish indiscriminately all political refugees.

Then came the Crimean war, the real causes of which were known only to the chiefs of Freemasonry.

England and Piedmont worked up a quarrel with Russia about Turkey, over the respective spheres of influence of the Christian Greek and Catholic churches at Jerusalem. This rivalry was of little real consequence either to England or Piedmont but it served to turn France against Russia on the pretext of protecting Turkey.

The truth was that for a long time, long before the Hungarian insurrection of Kossuth, the secret chiefs of masonry, headed by Lord Palmerston, had made a plan according to which Prussia was to be exalted at the expense of Austria, German unity was to be achieved to the advantage of the Prussian monarchy, as well as that of Italy to the benefit of the house of Savoy, and a Polish Magyar state was to be created.[175]

Fearing that the Hungarian insurrection might spread to his Polish provinces, a community of monarchic interests had impelled the Tsar to reach an understanding with the Austrian Emperor which had helped to hinder the success of the Magyar revolutionaries. Until this "Entente" could be broken up, the masonic chiefs knew that German and Italian Unity would remain a dream.

Austria was the dupe in this war. As for France, she had to fight with the army of Piedmont so as to prepare public opinion in both countries for the next move against Austria.

All this had been combined by Lord Palmerston who knew how to get his way with all the other secret chiefs, not excepting Mazzini. Kossuth naturally favoured the masonic programme. He wished death to the Tsar for having caused him to lose his position in Hungary. It is also easy to understand how Napoleon II I was drawn into the affair. The chiefs of the sect only had to remind him of his oath as Carbonaro and show him the laurels to be won.

"Mazzini and Kossuth urged on the Crimean war, and English diplomacy prevented Austria from joining Russia. From then on, that power, being opposed by France, England, Piedmont and Turkey, faced inevitable defeat, which happened after a war lasting two years. Austria was separated for ever from Russia and was punished for her ingratitude, for, without even waiting for the end of hostilities, the Mason chiefs, who had used her so successfully, started the work of revolution on her territory.[176]

This war served a great purpose for Adriano Lemmi. It enabled him to get rich.

Through his relations with Mazzini and Kossuth, he obtained contracts for Italian ambulances for the Crimea. These he sent from Geneva. Pocketing a large part of the money, he paid the rest with bad chequees and fled to Malta. This was his first big theft, but his flight did not prevent him and his two accomplices from being condemned by default by the Swiss judge. "On Jan. 4, 1855, Mazzini, chief of the Central European Committee,—the title Mazzini assumed as leader of 'Young Europe'—called a meeting of his accomplices in London at which Félix Pyat, the president of the branch group known as the Communist Revolutionaries, was present. These two committees were in correspondence with one in Brussels, one in Jersey and one in Geneva. At this meeting, the death of Charles III, Duke of Parma, was unanimously voted, and Mazzini sent Lemmi a passport in the name of 'Lewis Broom' under the protection of which he immediately left Malta for the Duchy of Parma. During the one day he spent there, he organized a secret meeting at Castel-Guelfo for March 25, during which lots were drawn and a man called Antonio Carra was thus duly selected by fate to do the deed. Lessons in stabbing were then given on a dummy and Adriano, who presided at the assembly, addressing the assassin-elect said "This day is the feast of the Jesuits and nuns when they celebrate the apparition to their Madonna of an angel announcing the advent of the Messiah as her son. Brother, I announce to thee that thou wilt be the Messiah of the Revolution of Parma. I consecrate thee liberator of the oppressed, saviour of tyrannized men. Strike the despot! Let not thy hand falter. Our God, who is not the God of the priests, will protect thee!"

Two days later, Charles II I fell under the attack of an alleged fanatic who made good his escape. The circumstances of the plot are known because Lemmi often boasted of the part he played in it to Frapolli and others who repeated the story.

Mazzini often acknowledged that his "little Jew "was worth ten good men, so clever was he at choosing the right men for important jobs, and so able at inspiring them with the energy necessary for doing their duty.

The Parma business greatly enhanced the value of Lemmi in the eyes of the principal chiefs. He remained incognito for several days at Sant'Ilario, but the revolution did not come off, for the crime was received by the people with horror, and the widow of Charles III, the daughter of the Duc de Berry, was proclaimed regent for her son Robert, a child of six.

Still under the false name of Lewis Broom, Lemmi went to Reggio, then to Modena, returning to the duchy of Parma in the last days of June, where he prepared the abortive insurrection of July 22, which was quickly suppressed.

In January, 1855, the Piedmontese government suppressed 334 religious institutions at the instigation of the revolutionary societies which, thanks to complicity under the guise of tolerance, were unhindered in the development of their criminal resources.

Lemmi, who had at his disposal as many false papers as might be necessary for his secret missions, again changed his name. Armed with a Hungarian passport, belonging to one of the henchmen of Kossuth, he went to Rome under the name of "Ulrick Putsch", professional cook, and on June 12 there was an attempt to kill Cardinal Antonelli! He immediately reappeared at Genoa where, on the thirteenth of the month, a manifesto was published by Mazzini, inciting the people to insurrection. This was spread by Lemmi in several towns, notably even in Rome where, by a curious coincidence, on July 9, the same day on which he returned to the city of the popes, an attempt was made on the life of Father Beckx, the General of the Jesuits.

In all these movements, in all these crimes where Lemmi's hand is not visible, those of his associates always were.

Lemmi and Orsini—the latter also an agent of Mazzini, had transmitted to the revolutionary committee of Milan their chief's instructions in view of an imminent uprising. Having received their instructions, Lemmi went to Switzerland with his Hungarian passport, and Orsini, under the name of George Hernash, went to Austria where an insurrection, timed to occur simultaneously with that in Lombardy, was to be fomented. Orsini was arrested at Hermanstadt, in Transylvania, brought back to Vienna and transferred to Mantua where he was judged and condemned to death for high treason on August 20, 1855.

Locked up in the castle of San Giorgio, he succeeded in escaping on the night of March 29th, 1856.

On November 13 of the same year, two other agents of Mazzini were taken at Rome.

Under the pretext that the King of Naples was not observing strict neutrality towards Russia, Lord Palmerston obtained the disgrace of Mazza, the Neapolitan Director of Police. In this move, he was aided by Mazzini, who, having caused certain confidential papers to be stolen, knew some things that were none of his business. Mazza, devoted to the King, had been his protector against the machinations of the secret societies.

Napoleon III, too, allowed himself to be influenced by Palmerston who, as patriarch of European Freemasonry, favoured one of his pet projects. This involved the appointment of Prince Murat, Grand Master of the Grand Orient of France, to the throne of Naples and the two Sicilies, and the elimination of the house of Bourbon. England and

France presently threatened to send a squadron to Naples but owing to the protest of Russia, the threat was never carried out.

In September, 1856, the European Committee decided that the King of Naples should be assassinated and that at the same time there should be an insurrection in Sicily. A man named Baron de Bentivegna, who had been introduced by an English high mason, Henri Misley, to Mazzini in London, was entrusted with the task of fomenting the trouble, while Lemmi took charge of the murder. According to the plan, Ferdinand II was to be blown up by a bomb thrown under his carriage by some fanatic selected by Lemmi.

Armed with two bombs, Lemmi went to Sicily. He now travelled under a French passport, provided for him by a friend through Ledru-Rollin, and made out under the name of "Jacques Lathuile", merchant.

Everything was ready both in Palermo and Naples. The dates of the assassination of the king and the outbreak of the revolution were fixed for November 22, but the individual chosen to perform the deed, Filippo Carabi, suddenly lost interest in the project when he realized that the bomb destined for the king would also inevitably prove fatal to himself.

Lemmi was angry over this unexpected check. It was then too late to recruit another executioner but the disobedient Sicilian was eventually punished, for, five years later he was murdered in a Neapolitan lodge where he had gone without apprehension. The archives of the Directory of Naples contain the details of the affair, the sequestration of Carabi in 1861, his accusation before a secret tribunal, the terrible tortures to which he was subjected and his last horrible agony, shrouded in mystery.

Lemmi, now unable to have the assassination and the plot coincide, stayed on nevertheless in Naples, as he hoped to find a substitute for the defaulting murderer.

On the appointed day, November 22, Bentivegna raised the banner of revolt at Cefalú, near Palermo.

"Jacques Lathuile", finding himself obliged to substitute another for the bomb method of assassination, induced a soldier called Agesilas Milano to attempt the life of the king, so, while Ferdinand II was reviewing his troops, Milano stepped forward and struck him twice in the chest with his bayonet. Luckily for the king, the instrument bent, failing even to wound him. Milano was arrested, judged and shot, but Mazzini, qualifying him as a martyr, had a commemoration medal struck in his honour.

As for the insurrection in Sicily, it was suppressed, Bentivegna was captured and shot on December 20, but Lemmi-Lathuile left the country as soon as he realized that things were not going well. His identity was never revealed and can today only be definitely established by the records of the secret masonic trial of Filippo Carabi in the archives of the Directory of Naples.

In 1857, a splendid farce was enacted by Piedmont. It has since been repeatedly proved that Cavour and Rattazzi were in agreement with the Mazzinians and the Garibaldians with regard to the scheme for a United Italy, under the house of Savoy—that is to say, they favoured the dispossession of the legitimate sovereigns of the duchies of Tuscany, Parma, Modena, the Papal States and the Kingdom of the two Sicilies, and the wresting of Lombardy and Venice from Austria. In the eyes of the European monarchs who were not in the secret, Piedmont wished to appear innocent of any connivance in the plot, and to have been forced only reluctantly to acquiesce. The secretary and faithful friend of Count Cavour was the Piedmontese Isaac Artom,[177] while l'Olper, later rabbi of Turin and also the friend and counsellor of Mazzini, was one of the most open advocates of Italian Independence.

A few Freemasons in English, French and Prussian diplomacy alone knew what was being plotted, so the International Committee of London decreed an up-heaval in Tuscany for the year 1857 and, in order that Piedmont might not be suspected of complicity, it was arranged that an insurrection should be staged in that kingdom at the same time as the one in Tuscany. That was the comedy!

The insurrection occurred but failed in its object. In London, the same year, Mazzini hatched a plot against Napoleon III. It was not the first.

As the French Emperor did not seem sufficiently active on behalf of Italian Unity, it was decided to stimulate him by terror. Mazzini, Kossuth and Ledru-Rollin were reinforced in the committee of London by Herzen, Bakunin, Turr and Klapka and, early in the year 1857, Paolo

Tibaldi, Giuseppe Bartolotti and Paolo Grilli were chosen by Mazzini and Ledru-Rollin to kill Napoleon. Massarenti, another tool of Mazzini's, gave the m fifty golden Napoleons when they left for Paris to perpetrate the crime and, addressing them before their departure, Mazzini said "You will study the habits of the Emperor and you will strike when you find the opportunity favorable." Massarenti, Campanella, Tibaldi, Grilli and Bartolotti, the active tools of the plot, were all personal friends of Lemmi. To quote the words of the Imperial Attorney at the hearing of the Court of Assizes at Paris, August 7, 1857, when Grilli was sentenced to deportation, Mazzini and Ledru-Rollin were the chiefs of all plots the object of which was assassination.

On January 14, 1858, at the door of the Opera House in Paris, another attempt was made on the life of the French Emperor. Three bombs killed eight and wounded 156 persons. Some of the guilty were arrested but others, among whom was our hero, Adriano Lemmi, now masquerading under the name of James MacGregor, escaped. Lemmi had come to Paris ostensibly to visit Giuseppe Mazzoni, his Tuscan compatriot, then professor of languages in the French capital. Orsini, who had taken the pseudonym of Alsop on reaching Paris, Pierri, and Rudio the principal actors in the drama were caught and condemned to death. The first two were executed, Rudio's sentence being commuted to hard labour for life. Orsini was not unknown to Napoleon III. Together, they had belonged to the Lodge of Cesna as members of the Carbonari. In 1874 the *Giornale di Firenze* published the account of Napoleon's visit to his imprisoned assassin who warned him that, unless he showed a disposition to help the Unity of Italy, other bombs were reserved for him. Napoleon acquiesced, and one saw the famous will of Felice Orsini published by the Imperial official journal which enabled the French deputy Monsieur Keller to remark before the legislative body on March 13, 1861, that "the Italian war was the execution of the will of Orsini."

We must here be permitted a somewhat lengthy digression unfolding the progress of political corruption and its affinity with secret societies.

As a result of the Orsini conspiracy, Palmerston sponsored "The Conspiracy to Murder" Bill, a measure framed to hamper International Assassins in the free use of English territory for hatching plots against foreign potentates. The Bill passed its first reading in Parliament, Disraeli voting for it, but at the second reading, Milner Gibson, a Radical, moved an amendment which was in effect a vote of censure on Palmerston and a challenge to the French. This was eventually carried by 19 votes, Disraeli's support being, of course, the decisive factor. An explanation of this change of front is afforded in Ashley's *Life of Lord Palmerston*. Seated in the Peers' Gallery, Lord Derby listened to the debate, and watched the tide rising against the Prime Minister. Convinced that he could be overthrown, he "sent hasty word to his lieutenant that they should take it at the flood which led to office," and thereupon Disraeli "plunged into the stream."[178]

Lord Palmerston fell and was succeeded by Lord Darby.

Where does Disraeli—Lord Beaconsfield—come into the scheme? We know him as the author of many novels that, while not being evidential, serve to show the knowledge of their author on subjects of International significance: He knew how things were done and, like a naughty boy, told tales out of school.

Young Italy, Young Ireland, lastly Young England with Disraeli as its founder. What do we really know of Young England beyond what the Primrose League would have us think?

We know that Disraeli was always in debt, always short of money and we know that people under such conditions are seldom their own masters. Who were his masters?

Disraeli's father, Isaac d'lsraeli, was offered the leadership of their sect by the Jews of London. He refused. Was it also offered to his son?

Writing of Lord Beaconsfield, A. A. B. passes a casual remark in the (London) *Evening Standard* of Monday, October 29, 1928—"The name of the heroine of *Lothair*, the work of his meridian, is that of his wife. Mary Anne ruled *the underworld of secret societies*." Are we to search there for the invisible masters?

A further light is thrown upon this epoch of English history by no less an authority than the *Encyclopaedia Britannica*, 9th Edition. In an article on Prince Metternich it says:—Metternich "in one of his most earnest writings places side by side, as instances of evil sought for its own sake, the action of the secret societies in Germany, the Carbonaria of Italy and the attempt s of the English to carry the Reform Bill!"

We do know that the Reform Bill was one of Disraeli's victories!

Again one wonders at Metternich. That great reactionary might well have disliked the Reform Bill but this remark does not just indicate dislike—it is a positive indictment when read with the knowledge available to the historians of today.

Therein lies a singular coincidence of facts. On the one hand, we have one of two statesmen, Metternich, decrying the English Reform Bill and on the other, Disraeli getting it passed in the English Parliament. Yet, both men, ever impecunious, were ruled by money coming from the same source, namely, the Rothschilds who, in Austria as well as in London, were actively becoming the masters of the national finances of both countries.[179]

In 1862, the First International came into being and the part played in it by such Freemasons as Karl Marx, Tolain, Fribourg, Varlin, Camelinat, Beslay, Malon and Corbon is well known.

But to return to the programme of Young Italy. The Piedmontese were not quite satisfied with the results of the hasty treaty of Villafranca (1859), but the revolutionaries had attained their object as far as Tuscany, the Duchies of Parm a and Modena and the Pontifical States were concerned, though they did not dare to dispossess the Pope without some preliminary political manoeuvres. The revolution in the kingdom of the two Sicilies had failed again but it was soon to succeed.

By way of retaliation, the International Committee of London began a propaganda in Lombardy among the students in the colleges as a result of which the University of Pavia was forced to close. This movement which started in December was the precursor of the coming war. Lord Palmerston's plan was in process of realization.

To Francesco Crispi, a tool of Lemmi, was now assigned the task in which he and Bentivegna had failed. He was in London when the news of the death by poison of Ferdinand II reached the International Masonic Committee. Mazzini's tool in the poison plot was Monsignor Caputo, a priest who had succeeded in winning the confidence of the king as his confessor. He was a Freemason, and a Sublime Maître Parfait, belonging to one of the most evil branches of the sect. The poison was administered in a slice of melon and. the king died in agony, on May 22, 1857.

Freemasonry had won, for Francis II, who now succeeded his father, was too young and inexperienced to be able to cope with any serious political situation alone.

At this period, the states of Tuscany, Parma and. Modena were trying to form a coalition but Dr. Farini, a Freemason, had become dictator, and dictated regardless of popular sentiment. Lemmi was continually running back and forth from England with instructions from the London Committee to the local revolutionary chiefs and, in his secret capacity, was very active through the different assemblies where the votes of the sold or terrorized members went for annexation to Piedmont, regardless of the wishes of the majorities in their constituencies.

Travelling under the assumed names of Emmanuel Pareda and Toby Glivan, Crispi spent much of his time during the next two years in Sicily as an agitator fomenting trouble. A great uprising was planned for Oct. 12, but, though Lemmi was there to help, their combined efforts on that date were futile.

Still they persisted, and by propaganda and underground work, they prepared for the great event of 1860. When Garibaldi, Grand Master *ad vitam* of Ancient and Accepted Scottish Rites, at Palermo, landed at Marsala with his famous "thousand" on the 11th May, he found everything ready. His expedition would, however, have failed had it not been for the Piedmontese gold which bought the chief functionaries of the King of Naples, one of whose ministers, Liborio Romano, was chief of Sicilian Masonry and presided at the Scottish Consistory at Naples. Francis' friend and confidant, General Nunziante, Duc of Mignano, was bought by Cavour for four millions!

Organized at Genoa by Dr. Bertani, this supposedly spontaneous act of the famous general which the government of Victor Emmanuel publicly disavowed, was organized by Cavour who furnished the money by drafts on Mr. Bombrini, director of the bank, as proved by a letter, written by the King himself to the American Commodore, William de Rohan.

June 27th 1860.

Commander;

I enclose herewith Medici's [one of Garibaldi's generals] two letters which you will put into other envelopes and give to Cavour.

I have already given three millions to Bertani.

Return immediately to Palermo to tell Garibaldi that I will send him Valerio instead of La Farina, and that he is to advance at once on Messina, as Francesco [the King of Naples] is on the point of giving the Neapolitans a constitution.

Your friend,

VICTOR EMMANUEL.

This letter which was published in Rome, in 1881, by the son of Victor Emmanuel in the *Fanfulla* with an article by Commodore William de Rohan was never challenged. Margiotta then adds—"there is little more to be said concerning the connivance of Cavour and Garibaldi. Victor Emmanuel did nothing against his wish as the official newspapers allege, for everything that happened in 1860 was settled in advance. It was necessary to save appearances and to deceive Russian and Austrian diplomacy which was not in the secret, so that was Cavour's reason for allowing Garibaldi to play the part of an undisciplined revolutionary, taking on himself alone the responsibility of his adventures."

The policies of the Grand Master Cavour and the Grand Master Mazzini, each representing two different Masonic currents emanating from different sources, met on the issue of the destruction of the Papacy which it was hoped to submerge through the unification of Italy.

Cavour aimed at unity in the form of a constitutional monarchy under the house of Savoy and Mazzini, aiming at a republic, found himself forced into a compromise which obliged him to accept, temporarily at least, a Piedmontese monarchy for United Italy.

The captain of Freemasonry was Garibaldi, the tool of Palmerston, Cavour and Mazzini.

While working thus together and helping one another, Mazzini and Cavour each followed an occult personal and distinct line of action, the secrets of which they did not share. Each in his mysterious work had his chief agent, the man he trusted. The chief agents of Cavour were his Jewish secretary Isaac Artom and Carletti and the chief agents of Mazzini were his Jewish secretaries, Wolf, Lemmi and L'Olper.

After the flight of the Grand Duke of Tuscany, Lemmi went to Florence where, to better mask his play, he became a banker. His patrons Mazzini and Kossuth were never in want of money furnished either by England or Masonry. He made money, practising usury as a good Jew, charging it is said up to 200 and 300 per cent, but, in politics, he continued as a valuable auxiliary to Mazzini.

Garibaldi and Mazzini wished to push on to Rome but Victor Emmanuel thought it more prudent to leave well enough alone for the time being, and the Piedmontese government finally overruled the revolutionaries. Mazzini and Crispi were even asked to leave Naples by the authorities though Lemmi was not molested.

Cavour knew him to be the secret agent of Mazzini and had him watched and his record investigated but, though he did not trouble himself much about him, he wanted to insure himself against all anti-monarchist action on his part.

During this inquiry, he came across the records of Lemmi's youthful exploits at Marseilles in 1844, so he asked the government of Napoleon II I for an official copy of this document which lay in the archives of the Ministry of the Interior of the Italian government for 31 years and proved a powerful weapon in the hands of Victor Emmanuel, and Humbert I. Chafing under the menace of the existence of this document however, Lemmi induced Crispi in 1893 to arrange for its disappearance, but this move was forestalled by an implacable enemy of Lemmi who succeeded in getting possession of the famous paper.[180]

In 1867, Lemmi entered into negotiations with the Freemason Graf von Bismarck and the first projects of alliance between Prussia and Italy date thenceforth. Lemmi hated France as much as did Mazzini, so it is not surprising to find the m both intriguing with Bismarck to bring about a Franco-Italian estrangement.

Napoleon III, by the convention of Sept. 15, 1864, had established

Rome and its surrounding territory as distinct from the Kingdom of Italy, so that till 1870, the church still retained this last fragment of its temporal possessions but, towards 1865, Mazzini organized an association for Italian Unity, the object of which was the Union of these States with the rest of Italy, with Rome for the capital, according to Garibaldi's programme. Mazzini however was afraid to go to Rome without the consent of France, thinking that the destruction of the temporal power of the Pope, in the face of French opposition, could only be obtained by means of a revolution.

No one is ignorant of the negotiations between France, Austria and Italy in 1867, fruitless, because of Napoleon's refusal to accede to the proposal of the Austrian minister de Beust to allow "United" Italy freedom to march on Rome. France, subsequently abandoned by Italy, met her fate at Sedan in 1870 and Bismarck used Mazzini and Italian Freemasonry to break the Franco-Italian alliance and to force Victor Emmanuel to take Rome in spite of the wishes of the French people.

When the Franco-Prussian war broke out in 1870, the time for revolution was ripe. In July, shortly after the declaration of hostilities, the Italian revolutionaries held a mass meeting in the theatre at Milan, organized by the most notorious and dreaded agitators in Italy. After this public meeting, there was a secret political one attended by 15 high masons. Those present, according to Oreste Cucchi, who was told of it by Fabrizi himself, were: Doctor Timoteo Riboli, Francesco Crispi, Colonel Cucchi, Asproni, Bertani, Fabrizi, Frapolli, Cairoli, Rattazzi, Seismit Doda, Morelli, Sineo, Cosentini, Mancini and General Raffaelo Cadorna. The object of this conference was to determine the line of conduct to be adopted in the event of the defeat of Napoleon's army, and it was decided to send Cucchi to Bismarck to obtain from the Prussian government the necessary arms to go to Rome should Victor Emmanuel persist in his attitude of vacillation. Cucchi accomplished his mysterious mission, and Bismarck concluded a deal whereby Prussia was to furnish guns and money to the Italian revolutionaries, in return for which they were to keep up agitation to prevent an Italian alliance with the French nation.

Everything was ready. Still, Victor Emmanuel hesitated.

Public opinion was rapidly being manufactured with the assistance of Bismarck's money, so the deputies of the Left who signed a petition for the occupation of Rome, on being asked what they would do if the ministry refused their demand answered "We will make barricades and with the people we will go to Rome without you!"

The government then decided to act, and General Cadorna, who had already been selected by Freemasonry to lead a popular army should the government not wish to send him there in an official capacity, marched on Rome.

The operations of war began on September 15, 1870, and on September 20, at five o'clock in the morning, the cannon of Cadorna settled the Roman question. The Porta Pia was forced. The sacrifice was accomplished. Freemasonry had triumphed.

But Freemasonry had won again when, according to Mr. George d'Heylli, writing in February 1871,[181] "Mr. Gambetta, who was the arbitrary master of that country's (France) destiny during the three months that his dictatorship lasted, was able, without anyone daring to oppose his conduct, to misuse his power in order to unsettle the country and satisfy his own ambitions. He trampled the country's laws under foot, by slighting the most elementary rules of civilised society, by hunting from their benches magistrates immovibles, and from the council chambers those who had been elected by suffrage, by taking the war into his own hands, by promoting and depriving officers of their rank, by suddenly changing, according to his own whims and fancies or those of his advisers, his opinions, schemes and plans."

Such indeed is the example given by all the demagogues who act in the name of "The People"!

In the discussion concerning the fate of the fomenters of the Commune, Gambetta made one of his most eloquent speeches, the result of which was that a vote of amnesty was passed in their favour.

In 1871, he further consolidated his power by issuing a decree declaring that the former servitors of the Empire would be ineligible to membership in the National Assembly which was convened to ratify the treaty with Prussia.

By this time, Adriano Lemmi had attained prosperity and become the owner of vast estates near Florence.

Mazzini died on March 11, 1872, and, at his request, Lemmi was appointed by Albert Pike to succeed him as chief of the Sovereign Executive Directory.

In 1870, the Marquis of Ripon, who had succeeded the Earl of Zetland as Grand Master of the Grand Lodge of England, resigned his office and became a Roman Catholic. He was succeeded by the Prince of Wales, later to be Edward VII, King of England, received Knight Kadosch in 1882 on Jan. 28, and Affilié Supérieur, Grand Orient, in 1883.[182]

Adriano Lemmi, a Palladist, though not yet a member of the Supreme Council of Rome, soon concluded that the secret superior authority conferred on him could best be enhanced in Italy by smashing the various Supreme Councils for the benefit of one. Unity of Italian Masonry was then his aim. Success in this project depended on slow, deliberate manoeuvring, secrecy concerning his palladist affiliation, temporary restriction of the number of triangles in the peninsula and, above all, forbearance in dealing with the rival powers established in the ordinary rites.

In 1875, the scene of Masonic intrigue had shifted to England. The Khedive of Egypt, being at the time financially embarrassed offered his shares in the Suez Canal Co. for sale.

"The Duc Decazes, French Minister of Foreign Affairs, failed to inform the French authorities of the Khedive's predicament, while the Rothschilds", (on the information of their Egyptian agent, Ambroise Cinadino) "secretly advanced to Disraeli, then Prime Minister of England, the necessary funds to deliver the controlling interest of the canal to Britain, thus striking an International Coup d'etat, the significance of which was only dimly appreciated when, in the following year, Disraeli had Queen Victoria proclaimed Empress of India."[183]

Thus the controlling interest of the great waterway to the East was vested in England to have and to hold, till the British Empire, about to be created, should cease to serve the purpose of its makers.

In June 1877, Adriano Lemmi[184] became an ordinary member of the Grand Orient of Italy at Rome, of which Giuseppe Mazzoni was Grand

Master, keeping this affiliation secret till 1883, when he let it be known that he was joint Grand Master with Giuseppe Petroni.

"At this date, the rivalry for supremacy in Scottish Rites had become acute, for the Roman Grand Orient wished to dominate over the Supreme Council of Italy at Turin, of which Timoteo Riboli was Grand Master. The Grand Commander of the Roman Supreme Council was Senator Colonel George Tamajo, though its real chief was Luigi Castellazzo. With the secret aid of the latter and the further assistance of Count Piancini, Tamajo was induced to abdicate his rights for 50,000 francs, and on January 21, 1885, the Supreme Council of Rome was absorbed by the Grand Orient of Italy.

All Lemmi now required to complete his victory was to absorb the Supreme Council of Turin, but Riboli, the only real and legitimate representative of Italian Freemasonry, recognized by the Convention of Universal Scottish Rites at Lausanne, in 1875, and by all the Masonic powers of the world, had no wish to part with a source of revenue or to defer to the little Jew at Rome who was invested with no recognized superior authority.

Lemmi, who well knew that his secret title of Palladist chief assured him eventual supremacy, addressed himself to the Sovereign Pontiff at Charleston, Albert Pike, to whom he explained the danger to Italian Masonry of such intense dissensions and the necessity for fusion in the great struggle against the Vatican, stating further that the authority of Rome, the capital of Italy since 1870, must be recognized by the foreign Masonic powers.

His reasons appealed to the Sovereign Pontiff of Universal Freemasonry who, in November 1886, entirely disarmed Riboli by promising him an indemnity of 30,000 francs. Riboli acquiesced and the money was handed out from the central fund of the order.

In the Supreme Administrative Directory of Berlin, the payment of this sum is recorded in the balance sheet of 1887 under the heading of exceptional expenses in the following terms:[185]

"Suppression of the Supr. Cons. of Italy sitting at Turin. Extraordinary indemnity allowed to F. T. R. on the proposal of the F.A. L. and approved by the secret committee of Feb. 28th, 30,000 francs.

Before pocketing his 30,000 francs, Riboli raised a great row, abusing Lemmi and objecting to the fusion of the Supreme Council of Turin with that of Rome. Ignoring the fact that in 1885 Tamajo had received 50, 000 francs for the same reason, he sent protests broadcast in the shape of balustres demonstrating the legality of the supreme Council of Turin and the illegality of that of the Roman Centre.

Many Freemasons rallied to his assistance. A great movement was started to do away with the despotism of Lemmi, and numerous Lodges were founded under the "obedience of Turin."

Lemmi however, being Chief of Political Action in high masonry, had a great advantage over his opponents, but he could not make good his title before the lodges, nine-tenths of whose members ignored the very existence of Universal Central Masonry, the secret of which was to be kept under penalty of death. On the other hand, this was solely a matter concerning Scottish Rites for the protection of which the Supreme Council of Switzerland existed as the Executive power of the Scottish Confederation. This council is distinctly separate from the secret executive of Central high masonry whose one concern is international politics, so no confusion was possible.

During a nine months' campaign, Lemmi's opponents gained many adherents for Riboli, who, suddenly reversing his position, capitulated on the intervention of Albert Pike. Thirty thousand francs had done the trick.

For the benefit of his dupes, Pike had deceitfully declared in the fundamental constitution of high masonry that the Constitution, Statutes and Regulations of each rite would always be respected by Charleston. In order to propitiate Lemmi, he tore up that rite of which Riboli believed him to be the Patriarch and President!

The Supreme Council of Lausanne was much embarrassed inasmuch as, where Scottish Rites was concerned, it was obliged to admit that Lemmi's opponents were in the right, and that as a Scottish Rites Mason he, as Petroni's successor, the Chief of Political Action of secret high masonry, was a rebel.

In an effort to beat the devil around the bush, Riboli and Tamajo, pretending to take Lemmi as their temporary delegate, accepted for themselves the empty honorary title of Sovereign Grand Commander *ad vitam*, while Lemmi became Sovereign Grand Commander delegate invested with the real power.

Italian Freemasonry was united. A meeting was convened at Florence in January 1887, by Tamajo and Riboli at which seven brothers from Rome and seven from Turin, under orders from Charleston, ratified this agreement.

Lemmi misappropriated masonic funds and profited by his position to exploit everyone, during which period of frenzied finance, he pocketed over four hundred thousand francs. Many complaints of his conduct were sent to the Supreme Directory at Charleston but while passing through the hands of Phileas Walder who shared in the loot, anything to Lemmi's discredit was suppressed, never reaching Pike who trusted him till the end.

It was in 1881 that Lemmi had embarked on his campaign for the de-christianization of Italy, giving, under his invisible direction, an organization to the scattered forces of anticlericalism. Mazzini had made no mistake for Lemmi persecuted the church with a savage hatred.

During a Masonic congress held at Milan in 1881, the following resolutions were adopted:—

1

Measures are to be taken to counteract the work of the institutions known as "Œuvres Pies" (Charitable Works) which were founded by Clericalism to corrupt the people under the misnomer of Charity. The morals of the country thus endangered need reforming as well as the laws.

2

Women are henceforth to be eligible for Freemasonry and feminine lodges are to be founded as soon as possible.

3

It is deemed necessary by the congress to establish workmen's lodges in the city as well as in the country. These lodges to be free, except for a nominal fee to cover unavoidable expenses.

4

It is decided to institute a corps of secret masonic messengers whose mission is to transmit to all lodges the orders and instructions of the chief. These messengers are to be chosen from among Masons having no personal encumbrances and whose devotion to the order has been of long standing. They are to be registered at no particular lodge deriving their powers directly from the central authority of Italian masonry.

5

A corps of brother propagandists, themselves unknown as Masons, is to be created. They are to travel from town to town as peddlers and merchants of all kinds, spreading everywhere, notably among the rural populations, opinions favourable to masonry. In the course of their peregrinations hey are to abstain from visiting local masonic lodges and are to be known as "Travelling Brothers."

6

Should the order wish to initiate a personage of very high social rank or one who, in the opinion of the Grand Master should happen to be in a position demanding the strictest secrecy, his initiation need be known only to the Assistant Grand Master or the Grand Secretary and the Grand Treasurer.

7

The congress declares the solution of the social questions and the winning for the legitimate workers of their rights to be its chief concern. The Lodges are authorized to hold debates on the most practical means of obtaining governmental support for all measures tending to abolish pauperism and the improvement of the lot of the working classes.

This, the seventh resolution of the Congress, to be made public.

8

The liberal forces of Italy are to be secretly organized and the lodges are to act in such a way as to gain for Freemasonry a majority of the national representation in Parliament.

The Congress adopts for Italy the rule passed by the Grand Orient of France in 1848, under the title "Masonic rules to be followed with regard to elections."

9

The Congress declares the chief object of the efforts of Italian Freemasonry to be, for the present, to obtain from the government:—

a—The regulation of the ecclesiastical patrimony, the property of which belongs to the state and the administration of which belongs to the civil powers:

b—The strenuous application of all existing laws guaranteeing to the civil society its independence with regard to clerical influence:

c—The enforcement of existing laws by virtue of which religious congregations are to be suppressed, and the suggestion of measures calculated to prevent these laws from being evaded:

d—The promulgation of the law relating to the property of religious bodies (confiscation):

e—The suppression of all religious instruction in the schools:

f—The creation of schools for young girls where the pupils can be protected from any kind of clerical influence.

10

Finally the Congress decided to create by masonic initiative one great, politically non-partisan, anti-clerical party whose object would be to fight and destroy clericalism by any and all means.

Adriano Lemmi promptly obeyed Pike's orders and the resolutions of the Congress which he himself had dictated, by establishing in Rome on July 13, 1881, ten anticlerical auxiliary lodges, the foundation expenses of which were paid by the Supreme Directory of Rome. By his order, similar lodges were founded in almost every important town of the peninsula.

Lemmi is a Satanist and he organized the anti-clerical movement as a Satanist.[186] Besides his effort to destroy the church, he led a movement to spread "The Nature cult "well knowing that the secret protection of this sect would always be afforded him in the event of that of the anti-catholic government of Italy being withdrawn. This sect does not as yet dare to reveal its supreme aim as, say the chiefs, "the world is not yet ready to receive enlightenment by the true light."

So Lemmi first preached Lucifer and then fought Christianity by combating the idea of the supernatural!

All his discourses and manifests were composed either by Ulisse Bacci, an atheist, or Umberto dal Medico, a Luciferian.

His instructions to the Italian anti-clericals were also put into operation by the Freemasons of other countries, for the supreme object of the sect is the suppression, by a terrible social upheaval, of the religion of God, and its substitution by that of Satan, known to the dupes of Masonry as "The Great Architect of the Universe."

On November 21, 1888, Lemmi wrote Pike a letter appealing for help in his fight against the Vatican. The letter closed with the following paragraph:—

"Help us in our struggle against the Vatican, thou whose authority is supreme, and under thy impulse all the lodges of Europe and America will rally to our cause."

Pike needed little urging and immediately fell in with Lemmi's plans.

On March 30th, 1889, the Mother Lodge Archimede took the initiative in an effort to shake off Lemmi's tyrannical yoke by announcing the formation of "The Masonic Federation of the Independent Lodges of Italy." Lemmi was much perturbed by this effort at secession which he finally succeeded in crushing by the use of the power of gold. After the Federation had called a second congress, he sent one of his secret agents to Palermo with ten thousand francs to buy off the Scelsi brothers. Discord was thus sown in the ranks of the Federation. Soon, the disintegration was complete, the centre of Palermo vanished and opposition was crushed.

Towards this period, Lemmi got control of the Italian tobacco monopoly through which he succeeded, by swindling methods, in acquiring several millions. The whole affair was aired in Parliament but the intimidated deputies voted to save the reputation of the sect and in order to suppress the scandal, although Colonel Achille Bizzoni, Depute Matteo Renato, Impriani Poerio and several newspapers took up the matter and made a great row which ended in the usual way when the public gets tired of a subject.

As a result of Lemmi's politics in the elections of 1890, no decent honest and independent candidate for political position had a chance of being elected against one of his hand-picked nominees. Italian politics became a Freemasonic monopoly and the people were mercilessly exploited by the dregs of society backed by Lemmi and his money, much of which was extorted from the Banca Romana.

On April 2, 1891, Albert Pike died and was succeeded in the supreme Grand College of Masons by Albert George Mackey, who held the post for two years and five months. There were great rivalries between the members of Pike's staff, and Albert George Mackey was chosen as a compromise candidate who was unlikely to interfere seriously with any of the others.

With neither strength of character, energy nor activity, he was no match for Lemmi who aspired to the supreme Masonic power as well as to the handling of the Masonic central funds for the expenditure of a large part of which no account was required by the Supreme Directory at Berlin.

The International organization was now a formidable machine composed of 77 triangular provinces, the archdiocese of high masonry and 33 Lotus Mother Lodges, the founder lodges and generators of Palladism.

With Phileas Walder as accomplice, Lemmi lost no time in starting to undermine the power of Charleston, but to realize this project it was first necessary to create a movement in the triangular provinces. To this end, he employed his secret political agents of the Executive Directory of Rome, practically all of whom were Jews. These agents were registered in the central directory only by a number and a special Masonic name and were unknown even to the Grand Masters of the provincial lodges as well as to the brothers and sisters at the head of a Lotus Mother Lodge.

His particular agent in London in 1893 was supposed to be an old Piccadilly Jew called Daniel Mold. The came under which he was registered for this Triangular province, in the Grand Central Directory at Naples, was Adam-Kadzmoun, the magical value of the letters of which, when added, give the total of 244 exactly as do the letters of his real name.

Lemmi was not forced to rely solely upon his special agents, for he also had the unanimous support of the powerful secret Jewish lodges.

By the decree of Sept. 12, 1874, which confirmed a treaty signed by Armand Levi for the Jewish B'nai B'rith (brothers of the Alliance) of America, Germany and England and the supreme authority of Charleston, Albert Pike authorized the Jewish Freemasons to form a secret federation functioning side by side with the ordinary lodges. This secret society was to bear the title of Sovereign Patriarchal Council and its Universal centre was to be at Hamburg, Valentinskamp Strasse. In subscriptions alone, it collected one million four hundred thousand francs a year which were used for general Jewish propaganda.[187]

Under the terms of this document (given in full on p. 225 of *Adriano Lemmi* by D. Margiotta), Jewish Masonry, unlike Gentile Masonry, was not to be graded, its members were exempt from belonging to any other official rite and "the secret of its existence" was to be most strictly kept by those members of High Masonry who had been informed by the Supreme Dogmatic Directory of its existence.[188]

The latter clause in the agreement is. undoubtedly responsible for the equivocal attitude of all High Masons with regard to the past and present, national and international, secret political activities of the B'nai B'rith. In the interests of humanity, the conspiracy of secrecy should be revealed, for the control of the international balance of power and the possibilities of the international spy system thus established, are a menace to the welfare and peace of the peoples of the world.

"A Jew of French descent, this Armand Levi, above referred to, had attached himself to the Napoleons at an early time and was employed by them in various ways... As a member of the "International" he represented the possibilities of an Imperial Socialism... and when the barricades were built, his name was in the Commune and his voice was raised for the extremist counsels. He it was who rose in the Hotel de Ville, to ask that all the deputies of Paris should be summoned from Versailles, and if they would not come should be deposed, convicted, and condemned to death."[189]

It was indeed in the heart of the Jewish lodges that the plans to manufacture the public opinion necessary to the success of Lemmi's ambitious project were made, and what actually happened was the result of a plot of the Sovereign Patriarchal Council of Hamburg against the Supreme Dogmatic Directory of Charleston.

Hamburg won in the end and the secret Jewish control of the powerful machine of International Masonry was assured.

The Jewish Lodges were Lemmi's willing tools, and fifty thousand Masons, simultaneously Palladists and members of the Hamburg federation, under orders given by the Jewish agents in the pay of the Chief of Political action, made over a period of three months, in the triangles and secret Jewish lodges, a splendid propaganda calculated to induce discussion and approval of the transfer of the Supreme Dogmatic Directory of Charleston to Rome. Everywhere, by every means, the agents of Lemmi worked indefatigably to create a demand for the removal of the headquarters of the order from Charleston to Rome, on the pretext that the power of the Vatican could be better fought at close quarters. These reclamations of a noisy minority were then magnified for the benefit of the Grand Council of Masons at Charleston into a threat of imminent secession and, after much manoeuvring, Phileas Walder succeeded in inducing George Mackey and the American Masons to sign the decree convening the Sovereign Convention. Walder, having remarked that Lemmi was not to be a candidate for the Supreme Grand Mastership in case of the passage of a vote of transfer of which he maintained there was no danger, seeing that the majority of the triangles favoured Charleston as the seat of High Masonry, the American Masons, over confident of the outcome of the convention, overlooked the importance of the choice of the town in which it was to meet.

On May 20, 1893, after all the delegates had been elected, Lemmi suddenly launched his decree of chief organizer appointing Rome as the convention city.

Had everything been straight, Charleston would have come out of the trial of the secret Convention with a majority of 52 votes, for only 25 provinces favoured the move to Rome, but to Lemmi, all ways, including bribery and crime, were good.

On the eve of the opening of the Convention, fourteen of the delegates favouring Charleston were suddenly taken ill, and elections for substitute delegates were held in five of the Grand Triangles but in the remaining nine, the provincial Grand Masters, owing to lack of time or some other reason, referred the matter by telegram to Charleston. George Mackey answered "Send Bovio proxy to provide a European substitute."

It was suicide. Bovio, Grand Master General of the Grand Central Directory of Naples, and his lieutenants were entirely devoted to Lemmi in whom George Mackey continued blindly to confide. The nine sudden illnesses of the American delegates (the only ones he knew of) had failed to open his eyes and he continued counting 52 votes against the transfer!

Apart from two or three American delegates, all those who landed in England in August and were entertained by the Mother Lodge of the Lotus of England in the secret temple at 32, Oxford Street (Frascati's) were oblivious of the imminent crisis.

When the Grand Central Directory of Naples received these proxies, nine Italian delegates were named to represent Cleveland, Memphis, Guatemala, Havana, Caracas, Lima, La Paz, Treinta-y-Tres and Port Louis, one of whom abstained from voting while the rest cynically voted against the wishes of the province they represented.

The count of the ballots gave the following result out of 77 delegates:

48 delegates for the transfer to Rome,

25 delegates against the transfer to Rome,

4 delegates not voting the transfer to Rome. After this essentially fraudulent transfer of the real masonic power from Charleston to Rome, the rest was easy.

The ten Masons of Charleston retained their empty titles in an honorary capacity while Lemmi, now self-styled Sovereign Pontiff, named ten other active Masons, but owing to the difficulties attendant on the meetings of these widely dispersed magnates, he created a Supreme Triangle, with two assistants Carducci and Ferrari, the members of which were:—

- Patriarch Emeritus Mason, Germany, Findel (Kether-368) at Leipzig.
- Patriarch Emeritus Mason, of India, Hobbs (Khokhma-926) at Calcutta.

- Patriarch Emeritus Mason, Hungary, Antal de Berecz (Binah-721) at Budapest.
- Patriarch Emeritus Mason, Australia, W. J. Clarke (Khesed-409) at Melbourne.
- Patriarch Emeritus Mason, England, David Sandeman (Din-476) at London.[190]
- Patriarch Emeritus Mason, France, Floquet, (Tiphereth-1255) at Paris.
- Patriarch Emeritus Mason, Egypt, Gerasimos Poggio (Netzakh-1165) at Alexandria.
- Patriarch Emeritus Mason, Spain, Miguel Morayta (Hod-816) at Madrid.
- Patriarch Emeritus Mason, Chili, B. Alamos-Gonzales (Iesod-1152) at Valparaiso.
- Patriarch Emeritus Mason, Belgium, Goblet d'Alviella (Malkhuth-697).

International Masonry under Lemmi becomes Satanic and Jewish, International Jewry has much to explain!

Lemmi died in 1896 and was succeeded by Ernesto Nathan, an English Jew, who, in view of the intimacy which had existed between his mother, Sarah Nathan and Mazzini, was said to have been the latter's natural son.

Lemmi left a son called Silvano Lemmi.

In 1895, a schismatic masonic group calling itself the Grand Orient of Italy was founded. On March 5, 1899, it held a meeting at which it adopted a constitution of its own after which Lemmi' s Grand Orient and the new one settled down to a state of secret civil war.

Secrecy was imperative for, prior to 1895, the row between the various Masonic factions had become so acute that the profane public had begun to get seriously interested in the Political Masonic affairs of the contending factions.

The outcome of this dispute was the exposures made in the following books:

- *Mémoires d'une Ex-Palladiste* and *Le 33° Crispi*, by Diana Vaughan.
- *Le Palladisme andy a-t-il des femmes dans la franc Maçonnerie*, by Leo Taxil.
- *Adriano Lemmi*, by Domenico Margiotta.
- *Le Diable au XIXe Siècle*, by Dr. Bataille.
- *La Femme et l'Enfant dans la Franc-Maçonnerie* and *La Franc-Maçonnerie Universelle*, by A. de la Rive.
- *L'Ennemie Sociale*, by Paul Rosen.
- *Satan et Cie*, by Paul Rosen.

To inaugurate a policy of suppression these revelations were shown to have been a hoax, a mystification. The manoeuvre was successful. On the 19t h of April, 1897, the author, writing under the pseudonym of Diana Vaughan, mysteriously disappeared and Leo Taxil publicly repudiated his own allegations against Freemasonry.

Once again the public heard, believed and forgot. What happened to Palladism, the super rite?[191]

At the foot of page 76 of Mrs. Nesta Webster's *Secret Societies*, we find the following note: "Thus Hastings, *Encyclopaedia of Religion and Ethics*, omits all reference to Satanism before 1880 and observes:

'The evidence of the existence of either Satanists or Palladists consists entirely of the writings of a group of men in Paris'.

"It then proceeds to devote five columns out of the six and a half which compose the article to describing the works of two notorious romancers, Leo Taxil and Bataille. There is not a word of real information to be found there."

Indeed we owe Mrs. Webster a debt of gratitude for thus drawing our attention to this curious effort in an otherwise presumably reliable work, to eliminate certain phases of religious history. Those phases are the personal histories of Albert Pike, the Great Freemason and Giuseppe Mazzini, the Great Revolutionist.

The photostats and documents here appended show the re-organization of the super-rite under the general name of Illuminism, linked as we know with "Societas Rosicruciana in Anglia". Patents of the Ancient

Order of Oriental Templars, then in its embryonic stages (1902) are also shown.

In 1917, this organization unobtrusively declared itself the super rite.

The history of the Ancient Order of Oriental Templars is given on a subsequent page.

CHAPTER XXXIII

THE INTERLOCKING DIRECTORATE

FREEMASONRY, AS THE average mason sees it, teaches brotherhood and many worthy and exalted principles. It is primarily a charity organization and only good men are eligible to its ranks. To them the G in the Pentagon means God, but needless to say, if it's teaching were not of a noble idealistic character it would make few proselytes.

Within the lodges, and among the members thereof, are members of other rites which the British Mason is deliberately taught contemptuously to refuse to acknowledge as Masonic. Many of these are the recruiting sergeants for the secret societies who make their selection at leisure, choosing only such initiates as seem to them likely to serve their ends.

Once in the higher grades, a man who has, too late, been found to be intractable, can continue to the highest visible point of initiation along the track prepared by those who mean him to know nothing. All is beautiful, all is noble, he sees only the best, and forever advertises the goodness of Freemasonry.

Though in this capacity he may do nothing else, he becomes an important factor in recruiting.

It is frequently alleged that no English Mason is permitted to attend a Lodge meeting of the Grand Orient or of any other so called irregular masonry.

This is nonsense!

If such a statement is to be considered, how are we to reconcile the fact that Wm. Wynn Westcott, an English Mason, appointed Junior Grand Deacon to the Grand Lodge of England in 1902 and the head of the "Societas Rosicruciana in Anglia" and "Golden Dawn," was also the Secretary of the Rite of Swedenborg, Knight Kadosch in Ancient and Accepted Scottish Rites, Grand Standard Bearer, Royal Arch, Grand Lodge of England, and Regent of the Illuminati and on intimate terms with one of its founders, the German, Theodore Reuss 33° 90° 96°.

Among his other titles, Theodore Reuss included the following:—Magus Supremus in Mundo of the Esoteric Rosicrucians, Fra. Superior and Outer Head in Mundo of the Ancient Order of Oriental Templars (O. T. O.); Sovereign Grand Master General *ad vitam* of the Ancient Rites of Masonry, Memphis and Mizraim Rites of Masonry for the German Empire and its dependencies: Terniasimus Regens of the I O; S. I. 33°, etc., etc.

To further emphasize the interlocking character of this organization, we print herewith a partial list of the Masonic offices held by John Yarker, quoted from an article published in *The Equinox* Volume X, 1913 under the title: "In Memoriam".

May this end forever the oft repeated fable of British Masonic isolation!

Royal Grand Commander of the Rose Croix and Kadosch, 1868 to 1874.

Scottish Rite of 33° (and received certificate dating from 1811), January 27th, 1871.

Admitted 33° of Cerneau Rite and Honorary Member in New York, August 21st, 1871.

Installed Grand Master, 96° of Ancient and Primitive Rite at Freemasons Hall, London, October 8th, 1872. Absolute Sovereign Grand Master, Rite of Mizraim, 90°, from 1871 down to the present time.

Received over twelve patents of 33° of the Supreme Council in various parts of the world.

Past Senior Grand Warden of Greece by Patent, July 1st, 1874.

Hon. Member of Lodge 227, Dublin, 1872, and of various foreign bodies 1881–3. Among these he received the "Crown of Kether," admitting to the 5° of the Grand Lamaistique Order of Light.

In 1882–3 he acted as General Giuseppe Garibaldi's Grand Chancellor of the Confederated Rites, which he arranged throughout the world.

Hon. Grand Master of the Sovereign Grand Council of Iberico, October 5, 1889.

Rite of Swedenborg: In 1876 he was appointed Supreme Grand Master for the United Kingdom under the Charter of T. G. Harrington, P. G. Master of Craft Grand Lodge of Canada; Colonel W. Bury M'Leod Moore, Grand Master of Templars, 33°, and Geo. C. Longley. 33°.

Elected Imperial Grand Hierophant, 97°, in Ancient and Primitive Rite, November 11, 1902.

Grand Representative of the Grand Lodge of Germany, 1902–1906.

Hon. Grand Master of the Grand Lodge of Cuba (by patent), January 5, 1907.

Hon. Grand Master *ad vitam* of the United Sup. Grand Council of Italy at Firenze, and of the Society Alchemica, etc., etc., 1910–12.

He also was interested in many of the concordant orders, and held office in several. He was appointed President of Sat Bhai of Prag, and was co-sponsor from 1871 to 1912.

Head of the Rite of Ishmael in England in succession to Dr. Mackenzie and Major F. G. Irwin.

Chief of the Red Branch of Eri in succession to Major F. G. Irwin.

High Priest of the 7th degree of Knight Templar priests, Manchester, revived from 1868 to 1875.

More over from the correspondence of Theodore Reuss, we find that John Yarker was also the Delegate from the *Supreme Conseil Martiniste de France*.

Again we find that this same Theodore Reuss, above mentioned, seems to become eligible in the eyes of Wm. Wynn Westcott and John Yarker to be the founder of the six Swedenborg Lodges in Germany, chiefly on the grounds that he was an English Mason!

Presently, we find that Theodore Reuss, English Mason, is the Delegate of the A. and P. Rite of Memphis from Spain and Bulgaria to Germany, and from Germany to England. Later we find him on intimate terms with Papus, the head of the Martinist order in France.

Turning to the photostat of a patent which we reproduce we find a document which speaks for itself. It is signed Theodore Reuss 33° 90° 96°. John Yarker 33° 90° 96° Franz Hartman 33° 90° 95° and Henry Klein 33° 95°.

In his testimonial as special War-correspondent, Theodore Reuss includes the following letter:—

Kaiserlich Deutsches Konsulat fur Griechenland.

Athenes, le 10/22 Avril 1897.

Le Consulat Imperial d' Allemagne pour la Grèce requiert par la présente toutes les autorités militaires et civiles de laisser passer librement le porteur Monsieur Theodore Reuss, correspondant du Bureau telegraphique des États-Unis, et du Kleines Journal, qui, pourvu d'une letite de recommandation de Son Excellence le Ministre de la Guerre Mr. Metaxas à l'adresse de Son Altesse Royale le Prince Royal, se rendra à la frontière lurco-grecque.

Le Consul General d'Allemagne,

(Signed) LUDERS.

While casually perusing the Masonic Year Book for 1922 (English Grand Lodge), we find on page 522 under the following heading:—

Foreign Grand Lodges. E. Hemisphere

Italy

Grand Orient of Italy

Grand Master—Gustavo Canti

Deputy Grand Master—Carlo de Andreis

Director of the Grand Secretary's office.

Ulisse Bacci.

Then, turning to page 286 of our book, we find that, many years ago, Ulisse Bacci was one of Adriano Lemmi's most efficient assistants!

All this belongs to the realm of history and research, but at least, let us base the future on knowledge of the past and not build the Temple of Solomon on the ruins of the British Empire!

Occult Theocrasy
Part II

Chronological Series

Associations of the 16th Century

CHAPTER XXXIV

THE ILLUMINATI OF SPAIN
(FOUNDED 1520)

THE ILLUMINATI, A Spanish sect called the Alombrados was founded about 1520.

Ignatius Loyola, while a student at Salamanca (1527), was tried by an ecclesiastical commission for alleged sympathy with this sect but was acquitted with an admonition.

See *Enc. Brit*, Ninth Edition, Art. Illuminism.

CHAPTER XXXV

THE ORDER OF THE JESUITS (FOUNDED 1541)

WE GIVE THE following quotations from the *Encyclopaedia Britannica*, in spite of its marked anti-jesuit bias, solely to register certain historical facts, leaving their interpretation to the personal judgment of the reader.[192]

"The Company of the Jesuits was founded by Don Inigo de Loyola (Ignatius Loyola), a Spanish nobleman and soldier, on April 5, 1541, at the church of Saint Paul without the Walls, near Rome, under the sanction of the Pope, Paul III.

"It has six grades. These are novices, scholastics, temporal, coadjutors, professed of the three vows, and professed of the four vows, the latter two grades being the only ones which confer a share in the government and eligibility for the offices of the society. Its head, virtually a commander-in-chief, is known as The General. He wields absolute power over the members who are pledged to blind obedience. The General claims his authority from The Pope.

The "fourth vow" is one of special allegiance to the Pope promising to go in obedience to him for missionary purposes whensoever and whithersoever he may order,—a pledge seriously qualified in practice, however, by the power given to the general of alone sending out or recalling any missionary.

"The question has long been hotly debated whether, in addition to these six avowed grades, there be not a seventh, answering in some degree to the Tertiaries of the Franciscan and Dominican orders, secretly affiliated to the society, and acting as its unsuspected emissaries in various lay positions. This class is styled in France 'Jesuits of the short robe', and some evidence in support of its actual existence was alleged during the lawsuits against the company under Louis XV. The Jesuits themselves deny the existence of any such body, and are able to adduce the negative disproof that no provision for it is to be found in their constitutions. On the other hand, there are clauses therein which make the creation of such a class perfectly feasible if thought expedient. One is the power given to the general to receive candidates secretly, and to conceal their admission, for which there is a remarkable precedent in the case of Francis Borgia, duke of Gandia, afterwards himself general of the society; the other is an even more singular clause, providing for the admission of candidates to the company by persons who are not themselves members of it.... The general, who should by the statutes of the society reside permanently at Rome, holds in his hands the right of appointment, not only to the office of provincial over each of the great districts into which the houses are mapped, but to the offices of each house in particular, no shadow of electoral right or even suggestion being recognized.

"The superiors and rectors of all houses and Colleges in Europe must report weekly to their provincial on all matters concerning the members of the society and all outsiders with whom they may have had dealings of any sort. The provincial, for his part, must report monthly to the general, giving him a summary of all details which have reached himself. But, as a check on him, all superiors of houses in his province are to make separate reports directly to the general once in three months, and further to communicate with him, without delay, every time any matter of importance occurs, irrespective of any information which the provincial may have forwarded. Nor is this all; an elaborate system of espionage and delation forms part of the recognized order of every house, and, in direct contrast to the ancient indictment and confession of faults in open conventual chapter, every inmate of a house is liable to secret accusation to its superior, while the superior himself may be similarly delated to the provincial or the general.

"Nor is the general himself exempt from control on the part of the society, lest by any possible error he be unfaithful to its interests. A consultative council is imposed on him by the general congregation, consisting of six persons, whom he may neither select nor remove,—namely, four assistants, each representing a nation, an admonisher or adviser (resembling the ad latus of a military commander) to warn him of any faults or mistakes, and his confessor. One of these must be in constant attendance on him; and, while he is not at liberty to abdicate his office, nor to accept any dignity or office outside it without the assent of the society, he may yet be suspended or deposed by its authority.

"There would seem at first to be an effectual external check provided, however, in the fact that, while all the officers of the society, except the council aforesaid, hold of the general, he in turn holds of the Pope, and is his liegeman directly, as well as in virtue of the fourth vow, which he has taken in common with the other professed. But such is the extraordinary skill with which the relations of the society to the papacy were originally drafted by Loyola, and subsequently worked by his successors, that it has always remained organically independent, and might very conceivably break with Rome without imperiling its own existence. The general has usually stood towards the Pope much as a powerful grand feudatory of the Middle Ages did towards a weak titular lord paramount, or perhaps as the captain of a splendid host of 'Free Companions' did towards a potentate with whom he chose to take temporary and precarious service; and the shrewd Roman populace have long shown their recognition of this fact [by styling these two great personages severally the 'White Pope' and the 'Black Pope'. In truth the society has never, from the very first, obeyed the Pope, whenever it's will and his happened to run counter to each other.

"The merited odium which has overtaken the Inquisition, usually officered by Dominicans, has induced the Jesuits, whose own controversial methods had been different, to disclaim all connexion with that tribunal, and to represent their society as free from complicity in its acts. But, in truth, it was Ignatius Loyola himself who procured its erection in Portugal in 1545–6, and F. Nithard, one of the very few cardinals of the society, was inquisitor-general of that kingdom in 1655.

"The first successes of the Indian mission were entirely amongst the lowest class; but when Robert de'Nobili, to win the Brahmins, adopted their insignia and mode of life in 1605, a step sanctioned by Gregory XV, in 1623, the fathers who followed his example pushed the new caste-feeling so far as absolutely to refuse the ministrations and sacraments of religion to the pariahs, lest the Brahmin converts should take offence,—an attempt which was reported to Rome by Norbert, a Capuchin, and by the bishop of Rosalia and was vainly censured in the pontifical briefs of Innocent X in 1645, Clement IX in 1669,Clement XI I in 1734 and 1739, and Benedict XIV, in 1745. The 'Chinese rites', assailed with equal unsuccess by 9 popes, were not finally put down until 1744, by a bull of Benedict XIV… By these rites the Jesuit missionaries had virtually assimilated Christianity to heathenism and their practical reply in opposition to a papal decree in 1700 was to obtain an edict from the emperor of China declaring that there was nothing idolatrous or superstitious in the inculpated usages, while in 1710 they flung Cardinal Tournon, legate of Clement XI, into the prison of the Inquisition at Macao, where he perished. Finally, they disobeyed the brief of suppression issued by Clement XIV in 1773, which enjoined them to disperse at once, to send back all novices to their houses, and to receive no more members. It is thus clear that the society has always regarded itself as an independent power, ready indeed to co-operate with the papacy so long as their roads and interests are the same, and to avail itself to the uttermost of the many pontifical decrees in its own favour, but drawing the line far short of practical submission when their interests diverge."

The Jesuit power, much weakened in England by the rise of the Jewish Power with the advent of Cromwell, persisted nevertheless in its efforts to recapture its former status in that land. During the reign of James II, it schemed and intrigued incessantly through its representatives Father St. Germain[193] and his successor Father Columbière.[194] After the enactment of the limitation of the English throne to Protestant succession the Jesuit diplomatists were hard put.

To quote the *Encyclopædia* further:

"After many difficulties they had succeeded in getting a footing in

France, through the help of Duprat, bishop of Clermont, who founded a college for them in 1545 in the town of Billom, besides making over to them his house at Paris, the Hotel de Clermont, which became the nucleus of the afterwards famous college of Louis-leGrand, while a formal legalization was granted to them by the states-general at Poissy in 1561."

From the Jesuit College at Ingolstadt is said to have issued the sect known as "The Illuminati of Bavaria" founded by Adam Weishaupt under the guidance of Nicolai, in 1776. Weishaupt, its nominal founder, however, seems to have played a subordinate though conspicuous role in the organization of this sect.

On July 21, 1773, the Pope had abolished the order of Jesuits but Frederic II of Prussia encouraged and protected them with a view no doubt of using their political knowledge and skill against the Bourbons, the Hapsburgs and the Pope.

The well-known authority on theocratic organizations, Heckethorn, writes the following concerning the Jesuits:

'There is considerable analogy between Masonic and Jesuitic degrees; and the Jesuits also tread down the shoe and bare the knee, because Ignatius Loyola thus presented himself at Rome and asked for the confirmation of the order.

"Not satisfied with confession, preaching, and instruction, whereby they had acquired unexampled influence, they formed in Italy and France, in 1563 several 'Congregations', i. e. clandestine meetings held in subterranean chapels and other secret places. The congregationists had a sectarian organization, with appropriate catechisms and manuals, which had to be given up before death, wherefore very few copies remain."[195]

To show the further similarity of the Jesuit-Judaic-Masonic-Gnostic-Brahmin-Illuminati theology we now quote from a MS. in the library of the Rue Richelieu at Paris entitled *Histoire des congregations et socialites jésuitiques depuis* 1563 *jusqu'au temps présent* (1709).[196]

"Initiation.—From this, as well as other works, we gather some of the ceremonies with which aspirants were initiated into the Order. Having in nearly all Roman Catholic countries succeeded in becoming the educators of the young, they were able to mould the youthful mind according

to their secret aims. If then, after a number of years, they detected in the pupil a blind and fanatic faith, conjoined with exalted pietism and indomitable courage, they proceeded to initiate him; in the opposite case, they excluded him. The proofs lasted twenty-four hours, for which the candidate was prepared by long and severe fasting, which, by prostrating his bodily strength, inflamed his fancy, and, just before the trial, a powerful drink was administered to him. Then the mystic scene began—diabolical apparitions, evocation of the dead, representations of the flames of hell, skeletons, moving skulls, artificial thunder and lightning, in fact, the whole paraphernalia and apparatus of the ancient mysteries. If the neophyte, who was closely watched, showed fear or terror, he remained forever in the inferior degree; but if he bore the proof well, he was advanced to a higher grade.

"At the initiation into the second degree (*Scholastici*) the same proofs, but on a grander scale, had to be undergone. The candidate, again prepared for them by long fastings, was led with his eyes bandaged into a large cavern, resounding with wild howlings and roarings, which he had to traverse, reciting at the same time prayers specially appointed for that occasion. At the end of the cave he had to crawl through a narrow opening, and while doing this, the bandage was taken from his eyes by an unseen hand, and he found himself in & square dungeon, whose floor was covered with a mortuary cloth, on which stood three lamps, shedding a feeble light on the skulls and skeletons ranged around. This was the Cave of Evocation, the Black Chamber, so famous in the annals of the Fathers. Here, giving himself up to prayer, the neophyte passed some time, during which the priests could, without his being aware of it, watch his every movement and gesture. If his behaviour was satisfactory, all at once two brethren, representing archangels, presented themselves before him, without his being able to tell whence they had so suddenly started up,—a good deal can be done with properly fitted and oiled trap-doors,—and, observing perfect silence, bound his forehead with a white band soaked with blood, and covered with hieroglyphics; they then hung a small crucifix round his neck, and a small satchel containing relics, or what did duty for them. Finally, they took off all his clothing, which they cast on a pyre in one corner of the cave, and marked his body with numerous crosses, drawn with blood. At this point, the hierophant with his assistants entered and, having bound a red cloth round the middle of the candidate's body, the brethren, clothed in bloodstained garments, placed themselves beside him, and drawing their daggers, formed the steel arch over his head. A carpet being then spread on the floor, all knelt down and prayed for about an hour, after which the pyre was secretly set on fire; the further wall of the cave opened, the air resounded with strains, now gay, now lugubrious, and a long procession of spectres, phantoms, angels, and demons defiled past the neophyte like the 'supers' in a pantomine. Whilst this farce was going on, the candidate took the following oath:—'In the name of Christ crucified, I swear to burst the bonds that yet unite me to father, mother, brothers, sisters, relations, friends; to the King, magistrates, and any other authority, to which I may ever have sworn fealty, obedience, gratitude, or service. I renounce… the place of my birth, henceforth to exist in another sphere. I swear to reveal to my new superior, whom I desire to know, what I have done, thought, read, learnt, or discovered, and to observe and watch all that comes under my notice. I swear to yield myself up to my superior, as if I were a corpse, deprived of life and will. I finally swear to flee temptation, and to reveal all I succeed in discovering, well aware that lightning is not more rapid and ready than the dagger to reach me wherever I may be'.

"The new member having taken this oath, was then introduced into a neighbouring cell, where he took a bath, and was clothed in garments of new and white linen. He finally repaired with the other brethren to a banquet, where he could with choice food and wine compensate himself for his long abstinence, and the horrors and fatigues he had passed through."

"In 1614, there was published at Cracow what purported to be the Secret Instructions given to members of the Society of Jesus. It is said that Hieronymus Zahorowski, who had recently severed his connection with the society, published the book with the co-operation of Count George Zbaraski and other Polish enemies of the order but the repudiation of the work by the society is no conclusive evidence of its spuriousness as it has been its policy from the beginning to deny all discreditable reports and to take the chance of being proved unveracious."[197]

It will suffice to give the headings of the chapters forming the *Book of Secret Instructions of the Society of Jesus.*[198] "The Preface specially warns superiors not to allow it to fall into the hands of strangers, as it might give them a bad opinion of the Order. The Chapters are headed as follows:—I. How the Society is to proceed in founding a new establishment.—II. How the Brethren of the Society may acquire and preserve the friendship of Princes and other distinguished Personages.—III. How the Society is to conduct itself towards those who possess great influence in a state; and who, though they are not rich, may yet be of service to others.—IX. Hints to Preachers and Confessors of Kings and great personages.—V. What conduct to observe towards the clergy and other religious orders.—VI. How to win over rich widows.—VII. How to hold fast widows and dispose of their property.—VIII. How to induce the children of widows to adopt a life of religious seclusion.—IX. Of the increase of College revenues.—X. Of the private rigour of discipline to be observed by the society.—XI. How 'Ours' shall conduct themselves towards those that have been dismissed from the society.—XII. Whom to keep and make much of in the society.—XIII. How to select young people for admission into the society, and how to keep the m there.—XIV. Of reserved cases, and reasons for dismissing from the society.—XV. How to behave towards nuns and devout women.—XVI. How to pretend contempt for riches.—XVII. General means for advancing the interests of the society.

"The intermeddling of this society in the affairs, political, ecclesiastical and civil, of many countries, is related in numerous works, and repeatedly produced the suppression and expulsion of the order, though it constantly reappeared with new names. In 1716 the French army was infested with Jesuitical and anti-Jesuitical societies. The Parliament of Paris suppressed them in 1762.

"They were abolished by papal bull in 1773 at the demand of France, Spain, Portugal, Parma, Naples and Austria. They are, however, still to be found everywhere, and they hold considerable property in England. A modern writer justly calls them the 'Black International'."

Historically, the Jesuits are given credit for the Gunpowder Plot of 1605, fomenting the Thirty Years war, the encouragement of the aspiration of Mary Stuart which led to her execution, the Revocation of the Edict of Nantes by Louis XIV, 1685, and numerous other great events of history.

The Sanfedesti was founded at the epoch of the suppression of the Jesuits for the defence of religion, the privileges and jurisdiction of Rome and the temporal power of the popes. Their successors were the Calderari, referred to in Chapter LXX.

The Generals of the Jesuits have been as follows:

1.	Inigo de Loyola (Spaniard)	1541–1556
2.	Diego Laynez (Spaniard)	1558–1565
3.	Francisco Borgia (Spaniard)	1565–1572
4.	Eberhard Mercurian (Belgian Jew)	1573–1580
5.	Claudio Acquaviva (Neapolitan)	1581–1615
6.	Mutio Vitelleschi (Roman)	1615–1645
7.	Vincenzio Caraffa (Neapolitan)	1646–1649
8.	Francesco Piccolomini (Florentine).	1649–1651
9.	Alessandro Gottofredi (Roman)	1652
10.	Goswin Nickel (German)	1652–1664
11.	Giovanni Paolo Oliva (Genoese)	
	Vicar-general and Coadjutor, 1661; General	1664–1681
12.	Charles von Noyelle (Belgian)	1682–1686
13.	Tirso Gonzales (Spaniard)	1687–1705
14.	Michael Angelo Tamburini (Modanese)	1706–1730
15.	Franz Retz (Bohemian)	1730–1750
16.	Ignazio Visconti (Milanese)	1751–1755
17.	Alessandro Centurioni (Genoese)	1755–1757
18.	Lorenzo Ricci (Florentine)	1758–1775
	Vicars-general	
a.	Stanislaus Czerniewicz (Pole)	1782–1785
b.	Gabriel Lienkiewicz (Pole)	1785–1798
c.	Franciscus Xavier Kareu (Pole)	
	(General in Russia, 7th Mar. 1801)	1799–1802
d.	Gabriel Gruber (German)	1802–1805

19.	Thaddaeus Brzozowski (Pole)	1805–1820
20.	Aloysio Fortis (Veronese)	1820–1829
21.	Johannes Roothaan (Dutchman)	1829–1853
22.	Peter Johannes Beckx (Belgian)	1853–1887
23.	Antoine Marie Anderledv (Swiss)	1887–1892
24.	Louis Martin (Spanish)	1892–1906
25.	Francis Xavier Warnz (German)	1906–1914
26.	Vladimir Ledochowski (Pole)	1915–

CHAPTER XXXVI

THE DEFENDERS (ROMAN CATHOLIC) (FOUNDED 1562)

THIS IRISH CATHOLIC organization, similar to that of the Spanish Garduña, was founded in 1562 by Roger Moore behind whom were French and Spanish Jesuits.

According to Captain Pollard, author of *The Secret Societies of Ireland*, "The nominal function of the Defenders was the protection of the fugitive priests during the period of proscription and the holding of the passes while Mass was celebrated in some mountain glen. The enemies of the faith being the Protestants, and the Protestants standing for the Constitutional authority of Britain, the Defenders soon became a criminal association of law-breakers and banditti."[199]

In 1641 they rose and massacred many Protestants, but were duly crushed by Cromwell in 1649.

This Irish Catholic element was already opposed by the Roman Catholic Archbishop Plunket, of whom Captain Pollard writes: "Archbishop Oliver Plunket, Roman Catholic Primate of Ireland, who had attempted to put down the criminal association of Defenders in the South of Ireland, was accused by the infamous Oates; and at his trial at Westminster certain of these Irish priests, who had been censured by him, gave false evidence against him. The Archbishop, though innocent, was, through the false evidence of these members of the secret society, sentenced and duly hanged at Tyburn."

Associations of the 17th Century

CHAPTER XXXVII

ANCIENT ORDER OF HIBERNIANS (A. O. H.) (ROMAN CATHOLIC) (FOUNDED 1641)

IN "THE SECRET SOCIETIES OF IRELAND" Captain Pollard writes that, founded in 1641, "Thenotorious modern society known as The Ancient Order of Hibernians is the direct successor of the original society of Defenders; in common with its ancestor it attempts to enable the clerics to exercise control in politics.[200] It claims in its own official history, published in 1910, to be the oldest secret society in Ireland. Independent researches show that the claim is sound and that the present A. 0. H. is the descendant of certain criminal organizations of the past. The open admission of this chain of descent by its own historian is important. American sources trace the A. 0. H. to 1565 but the date 1641 is that more commonly accepted."[201]

"The Jesuit influence in the development of the Defenders was reinforced, and their ceremonies and symbolism slowly changed to an elementary ritual closely modelled on that of the ceremony of initiation to the Society of Jesus of the period. This ritual has descended with many accretions and modernisations to the present time; and the American branch of the Ancient Order of Hibernians, misled by it, traces its origin back, not to 1641 and the Guarduña, but to 1563 and the foundation of the Society of Jesus.[202]

"The A. 0. H. of America is powerfully organized and has over six thousand lodges, and it is said by Heckethorn to be divided into two degrees; in the first no oath is exacted and no real secret communicated. The second or inner degree is confined to officials, who receive their passwords and signs from the Board of Erin in Ireland, who send an emissary every three months."[203]

In 1878, the American order split into two groups. Shortly afterwards the Irish followed suit.

"In America the breach was later healed, but in Ireland it continued until 1902, when a conference was called and both parties agreed to work under a joint board of control representing both sections. This board was termed the A. 0. H. Board of Erin."[204]

Another split, occurring in 1905, lasted two years.

"Ten years ago, the real A. 0. H. of Ireland represented a powerful Nationalist weapon, hostile to the forces of extremism and devoted to the Irish Parliamentary party, but the Board of Erin A. 0. H. was revolutionary."[205]

For root of this movement see Chapter XXXVI.

CHAPTER XXXVIII

JANSENISM
(FOUNDED 1638)

THIS WAS A peculiar form of Calvinism inaugurated by Cornelius Jansenius (1585–1638) from Louvain in the Netherlands.

The doctrine of Jansenism is exposed in a work called *Augustinus*, written by Jansenius, and published after his death in 1640.

According to Jansenius' theory of Predestination, man was either saved or damned according to God's own will, regardless of his merits or demerits.

From the Low Countries, Jansenism penetrated into France and its chief centre was in the Port Royal abbey near Paris. It was Duvergier de Hauranne who had been a great friend of Jansenius during their student days who, as abbot of Saint Cyran, introduced Jansenism into Port Royal.

Antoine Arnauld was the leader of the Jansenists and was followed by Pasquier Quesnel. Many great minds of the seventeenth century were Jansenists, among them Le Maitre de Sacy, Blaise Pascal, Lancelot, Nicole and Fontaine, Secretary of State of Louis XV.

Jansenism, which had undergone severe treatment in France under Louis XIV, revived under the Regency in 1715, and found supporters among the learned and the high clergy against the policy of the Pope.

It is during this period that among the Jansenist sectarians there arose the strange occurrences practised by what is known as the Convulsionaries of St. Médard.

The Jansenist party was very rich thanks to the *boîte à Perrette* (Perrette's box). This was a special fund whence Jansenism took out all the money for its political and other needs. It had taken its name from the servant of Mr. Nicole, a leading Jansenist, who had started the fund and confided the care of it to his servant. In 1778 it amounted already to 1100 livres and in 1865 was still very substantial.

Modern Jansenism, which, since the 18th century, had its chief seat in the Netherlands, principally Utrecht, joined in 1889 the German party of the Old Catholics founded in 1871 which, supported by Bismarck, had been one of the elements leading him to his Kulturkampf policy against the Catholic Church and institutions.

For the root of this movement see Chapter X.

For the development of this movement see Chapter XLII.

CHAPTER XXXIX

CAMISARDS OF THE CEVENNES
(ORIGINATING 1688)

THE CAMISARDS WERE actually a survival of the Waldenses and the Pastoureaux.

Calmeil, an authority on mental aberrations quoted by Madden in *Phantasmata*,[206] thus describes the characteristics of the Camisard movement:—"The prophetic madness (of the Camisards) made its appearance in Dauphiné and Vivarais in 1688; it very soon spread itself over a vast number of places, and continued without any interruption among the Calvinists for nearly twenty years.

"It was especially in the course of the year 1689, that the phenomena of theomania excited the greatest astonishment and rose to the height of its violence. The theomaniacs could then be counted by hundreds; men, women, girls, boys, young children, all of them believed they were inspired and imbued with the breath of the Holy Spirit.

"The punishment of fire, the rack, the torture of the *pendaison*, even the massacres performed by armed troops, whose efforts were directed to the extermination of the pretended prophets, the military executions, all the torments that it was possible to invent, to repress the violence of this religious fanaticism, only augmented the force of the evil which they were employed to abate or suppress.

"When, towards the beginning of the eighteenth century, the Calvinists rose up in good earnest to constitute small bodies of troops, and to dispute inch by inch the soil which had given them birth, with the king's soldiery, by whom they were confronted, this war of extermination was preceded by the apparition of a sort of swarm of pretended prophets and prophetesses. Towards 1701, at one time two hundred of the inspired, who had fallen into the hands of their enemies, were sent to the galleys.

"The madness of the theomaniacs was less talked of during the years 1703 and 1704 than it had been previously; but it is certain that all the armed bands who contended with the royal troops for those two years, never took the field except at the instance of some inspired celebrities. And it is certain that the words of those prophets were listened to as if they had emanated from the mouth of the Holy Spirit; that the inspirations of these monomaniacs habitually decided either the life or death of the Catholics who fell into the power of the Protestants; and there was often at that time to be seen the same person fulfilling among the Camisards the functions of a prophet, and the functions of a commander.

"It was not till the year 1704 that the Marechal de Villars had the charge of the command in Langue¬ doc; this Marechal saw, nevertheless, entire cities infested with theomania."[207]

"It was towards the latter end of 1706 that they (the Camisards) came to England, from the mountains of the Cevennes, where their countrymen had for a considerable time maintained a contest with the troops for the persecuting Louis XIV. As exiles for conscience' sake, they were treated with respect and kindness; but they soon forfeited all claim to respect by the folly or knavery of their conduct. Of this group Elias Marion was the prominent figure; the others acting only subordinate parts. He loudly proclaimed that he was the messenger of Heaven, and was authorised to denounce judgments, and to look into futurity. All kinds of arts were employed by Marion and his associates to excite public attention—sudden droppings down as though death-struck; sighs and groans, and then shrieks and vociferations, on recovering; broken sentences, uttered in unearthly tones; violent contortions; and desperate strugglings with the spirit, followed by submission and repentance; were all brought into play. The number of the believers in their power soon became considerable…

"After a time the sect which they had formed died away, but its ruin was less to be attributed to the punishment of the prophets, or the recovery of reason by their votaries, than by a report which was spread that they were nothing more than the instruments of designing men, who wished to disseminate Socinianism, and destroy orthodoxy."[208]

For root of this movement see Chapter XXIII, Waldenses.

For development of this movement see Chapter XLII.

Associations of the 18th Century

CHAPTER XL

THE RITE OF SWEDENBORG OR ILLUMINATI OF STOCKHOLM (FOUNDED 1721)

EMMANUEL SWEDENBORG WAS born on Jan. 29, 1688, at Stockholm. His father, Jasper Swedberg, was the son of Daniel Isaksson of Fahlun, Sweden. In 1719, Jasper Swedberg's family was ennobled by Queen Ulrika and his name was altered from Swedberg to Swedenborg.[209]

Emmanuel Swedenborg was initiated at Lund in 1706 and progressed to the higher degrees of the Templars as practised in Sweden.

In 1718, Colonel Baltzer Wedmar, in a Stockholm Lodge Lecture, said that Swedenborg was a Mason and that he had seen his signature at the Lodge at Lund. These assertions were confirmed by King Gustavus III.

Founded in 1721,[210] the Rite was first introduced into England by Chastanier, Springer (Swedish Consul), C. F. and August Nordenskjold and others who were members of the first Swedenborgian Society in London known as the Theosophical Society of the New Jerusalem, not to be confused with the Rite of French Theosophists.

The rite was carried from London to the Americas by a Swedenborgian Minister, Brother Samuel Beswick. He lived at Strathroy, Canada, and was the author of a work upon the Swedenborgian Rite. This rite, called the *Illuminati of Stockholm*, was well known until the middle of the 18th century when it amalgamated with that of Zinnendorf.

What is properly known as the rite of Swedenborg was another modification of the order of the Illuminati of Avignon effected by the Marquis de Thome, in 1783, wherein he endeavoured to restore the true meaning of the doctrine of the Swedish mystic.[211]

For root of this movement see Chapter XXII.

For development of this movement see Chapter XCVI.

CHAPTER XLI

SUPREME CONSEIL AND GRAND ORIENT DE FRANCE (FOUNDED 1725)

SOVEREIGN GRAND COMMANDER, SUPRÊME CONSEIL 1929, M. REN E RAYMOND

FREEMASONRY WAS INTRODUCED in France in about 1730, some say 1725.

Its implantation bore a singular character. Due to the time of exile spent in France by Queen Henrietta, widow of Charles I (1649), English ways and customs had become fashionable among the members of the French aristocracy. The exiled English Royal Family and their adherents, warmly welcomed by the Jesuits of France, plotted in secret to regain the throne for Charles II. Later, when the Catholic King James II was also overthrown in 1688, he found refuge in France and his son, The Pretender, and later his grandson, Charles Edward, headed numerous plots fomented to enable them to regain their father's and grandfather's throne from William of Orange.

Meanwhile Masonry had been instituted in England (1717) and introduced in France in 1730. The Jacobites, partisans of the Pretender, secretly plotting as they constantly were, found the newly created Masonic lodges a ground no less well adapted to serve their ends than the Jesuits' colleges whence all their schemes emanated.

Lodges, having thus become fashionable resorts for French aristocrats, presented a double aspect, one which might almost be termed theatrical, inasmuch as the comedy of equality between the lord and his varlet was enacted in the Lodge, and the other far more serious was of a political character. This latter aspect of budding English symbolic Freemasonry in France was anxiously watched by the minister Cardinal de Fleury who ordered its suppression in 1737. Up to that time the French lodges that had been formed considered themselves as depending from the English Grand Lodge, had an English Grand Master and were confining their activities to the practice of the three grades of Blue Masonry.

Then appeared the would-be reformers of Masonry. At their head, in France, was the Chevalier de Ramsay, and with their advent came the innovation of a fourth grade followed by others. This was the beginning of Scotch Masonry whose unavowed aim seems to have been to interpose itself between the existing Lodges and the governing Grand Lodge of France.

De Ramsay, who was one of the foremost exponents of Scotch Rites and already dreamed of the Universal Masonry of Albert Pike, exposed some of his theories in his famous Discourse made in 1740.

By that time, the Grand Lodge of France, known as the Grand English Lodge of France, was no longer headed by an English Grand Master, but by the Duc d'Antin who was succeeded by Louis, Prince de Bourbon, Comte de Clermont, who held the office of Grand Master from 1743 until 1771. During his Grand Mastership, in 1754, the name Chapter of Clermont was given to what might be called an offshoot of the Primitive French Masonry on which, later, the Chevalier de Bonneville grafted some additional degrees. This name "Chapter of Clermont" has been the cause of much confusion arising from the fact that a Jesuit college founded in Paris, in 1550, also bore the name of Clermont College and had been a centre for Jacobite secret plotting against the Protestant rulers of England.[212]

This grafting of higher degrees on those of Symbolic or Blue Masonry gave Scotch Masonry its vitality and strength and a continual superposition and absorption of one rite, to and by another, took place.

The period during the Grandmastership of the Comte de Clermont was eventful for the craft. A masonic writer, William H. Peckham, in his work on Scottish rites, gives a succinct but clear sequence of some of the changes undergone by Masonry in France mentioning Thory, Le Blanc, de Marconnay, Ragon and Clavel as his sources. Thus we learn that the English Grand Lodge of France became the "Grande Loge du Royaume" in 1756, and declared itself independent; further, that an inner body known as the Supreme Council of the Emperors of the East and West had been founded in 1754 by the Chevalier de Bonneville. It had its chamber in the Grand Lodge of France and, likewise, was under the authority of the Grand Master Comte de Clermont whose substitute Chaillon de Joinville was also that of the Council.

The Supreme Council of the Emperors of the East and West practised twenty-five degrees.

As to the disorders in the bosom of Masonry they are attributed to the negligence of the Comte de Clermont who, in 1744, had ceased to take much interest in the Lodges and delegated his authority to two appointees, one a banker named Baure and the other a dancing master by the name of Lacorne who sold charters and degrees. The latter caused a scission in the Grand Lodge whose members rejected him and he formed an independent Grand Lodge. Both these Grand Lodges, as also the Council of the Emperors of the East and West, constituted Lodges and granted charters throughout the kingdom, but in 1772, the Council united again with the primitive Grand Lodge as of yore, and becoming one body they practised the right of perfection of twenty-five degrees. At that time, the Grand Master was the Duc de Chartres, later Philippe Egalité, Duc d'Orleans, who had succeeded the Comte de Clermont in 1771.

But ten years previously, on August 29, 1761, a Jew, Stephen Morin, had obtained a charter from the Council of the Emperors of the East and West and had gone to America as Grand Inspector General. There he founded what is now known as Scottish Bites. Morin held his authority from the Comte de Clermont who, at the request of Lacorne, charged him with establishing Masonry in all parts of the world. His patent was signed by Chaillon de Joinville, Prince de Rohan, Lacorne, Savalette de

Buckolay, Taupin, Brest De La Chaussée, Count de Choiseul, Chevalier de Lenoncourt and D'Aubertin.[213]

The early history of French Freemasonry is a maze of quarrels, but finally, in 1766, under the auspices of a new *Grande Loge Nationale de France*, afterwards called the *Grand-Orient*, a representative system was at last adopted but the quarrels continued, the Orient and the original Grand Lodge being each supported by a separate Rosicrucian organization besides its own proper lodges.[214]

In contradiction to other masonic authorities, Yarker makes the assertion that the primitive Scottish Rite of 33 degrees was established at Namur in 1770 by Marchot and in 1787 united with the Grand Orient.[215]

In *he Culte de la Nature dans la Franc-maçonnerie Universelle* (page 143) D. Margiotta states that Adam Weishaupt and his favorite, Baron von Knigge, introduced the organization of the Holy Vehm as well as certain legends of Illuminism into Masonry in 1783. The only persons exempted from the jurisdiction of this terrible court of "Justice", the Holy Vehm, were the clergy, women and children, Jews and heathens and certain members of the higher nobility.

The Revolution issued from the Masonic Lodges, said Lombard de Langes. France, in 1789, counted over 2,000 lodges affiliated to the Grand Orient: The adepts numbered over 100,000. The first events of 1789 were but Masonry in action. All the Revolutionaries of the Constituent Assembly were 3rd degree initiates.

In the Viennese Freemasonic newspaper of December 1927, the Freemason Arthur Singer of Budapest publishes the following interesting document which he claims to have taken from a book by Comte Vogt d'Hunolstein, which appeared in 1864 under the title *Unpublished letters of Marie-Antoinette*.

It is a letter from the unhappy queen to her sister Marie Christine.

Translation:

"I believe that as far as France is concerned, you worry too much about Freemasonry. Here, it is far from having the significance that it may have elsewhere in Europe; here everything is open and one knows all. Then, where could the danger be?

"One might well be worried if it were a question of a political secret society. But on the contrary the government lets it spread, and it is only that which it seems: an association, the objects of which are union and charity. One dines, one sings, one talks, which has given the king occasion to say that people who drink and sing are not suspect of organizing plots. Nor is it a society of atheists, for, we are told, God is on the lips of all. They are very charitable. They bring up the children of the poor and dead members, they endow their daughters. What harm is there in all that?

"A short time ago the Princess de Lamballe was named Grand Mistress of a Lodge. She told me all the charming things they said to her. Many glasses were emptied, many verses sung. Then two good young maidens were endowed. Admitted. One can do good without all that fuss: but one must let everyone act according to their wishes, the more so when good only results."

The letter sounds as if it had been written yesterday by one of our good English Masons concerning English Freemasonry.

Masonry in France became dormant during the French Revolution, but in 1799, a national union was effected by Roettiers. No sooner, however, was this done, and the statutes, originally based on the English constitutions thoroughly revived, than French masonry again suffered from an invasion of mysticism,—first in the form of the Scottish Philosophic Rite (including such profundities as the luminous ring and the white and black Eagle), and secondly in the American Ancient and Accepted Scottish Rite of 33 degrees, which the charlatan De Grasse-Tilly expounded with great success but which in 1804 was amalgamated with the Grand Orient, the great Marshals Massena and Kellerman being then the leading members of the two bodies. The union did not last, as Napoleon disliked the constitution of the Supreme Council which was largely influenced by the aristocracy. His brother, Joseph, assisted by Murat and Cambacérès, was allowed to take office in the older organization. During the reactionary Catholic policy of the Grand Master Murat the younger

(1852–62), the liberties of the Orient were greatly interfered with and its funds almost exhausted. Since then it has slowly recovered.[216]

Murat was succeeded by General Magnan who ha d been appointed by Napoleon II I to group all Masonic bodies into one. This he succeeded in doing in 1862 with the exception of Scottish Rites, then under Jean Baptist Viennet, which still held aloof.

In 1868, the *Supreme Conseil* (of Scottish Rites) and the *Alliance Israelite Universelle* became merged in the person of the Jew Adolphe Crémieux who was president of both.

We must not omit to mention that Crémieux was also a member of the Rite of Mizraim which in 1862 was absorbed by the Grand Orient of France.

On attaining the 18th degree, a Grand Orient Mason automatically becomes a member of the *Alliance Israelite Universelle.*

The Grand Orient ceased to require belief in a personal God as a test of membership in the year 1877.

From the political movements, the origins of which can be traced to the influence of the *Grand-Orient de France*, one is forced to believe it to be a political organization.[217]

The following quotations from the speech made by Domenico Anghera, Grand Master of the Supreme Council of Scottish Rites when conferring on General Giuseppe Garibaldi the 33rd degree and administering his oath of allegiance, are here of interest in view of the connection of the two masonic powers in France.

> Translation:[218]
>
> "... Our first step, as builders of the new temple to the felicity of human glory, must be destruction. To destroy the present social state, we have suppressed religious teaching and the individual rights of persons. As we have overthrown the temporal power of the Pope, our most terrible and infamous enemy, by means of France and Italy, we must now break France, the strongest prop of the spiritual power. That we must do with the help of our own power and that of Germany." *(This speech was made before the Franco-Prussian War of 1870).*

"Brother, thou hast finished thy instruction as chief of Freemasonry. Pronounce thy supreme oath.

'I swear to recognize no fatherland but that of the world. I swear to work hard, everywhere and always, to destroy frontiers, borders, boundaries of all nations, of all industries, no less than of all families. I swear to dedicate my life to the triumph of progress and universal unity and I declare to profess the negation of God and the negation of the soul'.

"And now, Brother, that for thee, fatherland, religion and family have disappeared for ever in the immensity of the work of Freemasonry, come to us, illustrious, most puissant and very dear Brother and share with us the boundless authority, the infinite power that we hold over humanity.

"The only key of progress and happiness, the only rules of good, are thy appetites and instincts" (Compare with 0. T. 0. Chapter CX).

On the 4th Sept. 1870, the Second Empire fell at the battle of Sedan. The International and Freemasonry seized power, calling their government "The Government of National Defence", and that same day the handpicked ministry of Freemasonry was constituted with Leon Gambetta as Minister of the Interior. Its eleven members, all deputies of Paris had, according to him, been acclaimed by the people. They were:—Emmanuel Arago, Crémieux, Jules Favre, Ferry, Gambetta, Garnier-Pagès, Glais-Bizoin, Pelletan, Picard, Rochefort, Jules Simon.

Nine of them at least were Freemasons, three were Jews—Crémieux, Glais-Bizoin and Gambetta. The Mayor of Paris, Etienne Arago, nominated twenty other mayors to provincial posts, twelve of whom were prominent Freemasons, the others being merely nonentities.

The fourth of September was the nominal proclamation of the Republic, but that date marked the actual seizure of power in France by Freemasonry just as the 20th of September of the same year marked its seizure of power in Italy.

Then came the "Commune", famous through history for its revival of the atrocities of the first French Revolution of 1793.

Slaughter, ruin, torture, all again perpetrated in the name of the people who mutely suffered and died that the Men of Destiny might rule upon the earth!

For root of this movement see Chapter XXVI.

For development of this movement see Chapter LIII.

CHAPTER XLII

THE CONVULSIONARIES OF ST. MÉDARD (FOUNDED 1731)

ST. MÉDARD WAS the name of a cemetery in Paris wherein was the tomb of a famous Jansenist, the deacon François de Paris, and it was said that miracles of all descriptions took place there.

The first recorded case of convulsions in the St. Médard cemetery occurred in August 1731.

On this subject, Madden tells us the following:—"The tomb of the deacon Francois became the scene of wonderful cures, and some very remarkable conversions, which were reputed miraculous. People who came there, especially afflicted with nervous disorders, appear to have been affected in a singular manner, some with cataleptic, others with hysteric and convulsive symptoms.[219]

"The *convulsionnaires* exhibited not only occasionally, but frequently, all the phenomena which are ascribed by mesmerists to animal magnetism, somnambulism, ecstasies, raptures, submission of the will and the senses to the power of the volition of another person, connected in some way with the dominant idea which possessed their minds at the time of falling into the trance. Increased subtlety of thought, quickness of perception, heightened powers of imagination, a vivid energizing influence, fraught with enthusiasm and even eloquence; claims to clairvoyance, to communion with another world, to 'spirit life'; all these phenomena were to be found too, though not all in the same individual, in occasional instances in this epidemic of convulsive theomania...

"Till the month of August, 1731", says Picart, "the wonders wrought at the burying place of the deacon Paris were not accompanied with any considerable difference from those mentioned in Scripture or ecclesiastical history. Those who were afflicted with sickness, and begged the holy deacon's intercession, were laid upon or under his tomb-stone, which was raised from the ground, and were cured. But in August, 1731, God was pleased to work his miracles in a different manner; violent pains, agitations of the body, extraordinary convulsions, were the means by which the sick were healed, not all at once, but gradually. This happened to one Abbe Becheran, to Chevalier Follard, an ancient officer in the army, and to several others. The number of people afflicted with convulsions increased so fast, and consequences of the meetings at the tomb appeared, or were represented to the King, so dangerous, that on the 27th of January, 1732, he issued an order to shut up the little churchyard belonging to St. Medard's parish, where M. de Paris was buried, and to open it only when necessary for burials. Some weeks afterwards, the Abbe Becheran was arrested and confined at St. Lazare, and set again at liberty about three months after in June. But the miracles and convulsions did not cease upon these oppositions; on the contrary, they daily spread further, and gained ground.

"Towards the end of the year 1732, those who were in convulsions began to foretell what was to happen, to discover secrets, to make speeches, pathetic exhortations, sublime prayers; even those who at other times were wholly unable to perform any such things."[220] Montgeron informs us: 'There is nothing which the *convulsionnaires* did not undertake to mortify themselves, to break down and to enfeeble their bodies. The most of those from the time they had convulsions, hardly made use of a bed; they laid down with their clothes on, winter and summer, with only one covering, some lying on planks, and others on the bare ground, others on logs of wood, and some of the m on bars of iron'.

"The fact is, not only the means used for effecting cures were evil in themselves, but many of the leading persons by whom the remedy of the Grand Secours was administered or superintended were persons of ill repute."[221]

"Montgeron reckons that four thousand enthusiasts were employed to kick, and to strike without cessation the infirm, and all those young girls who begged for the violence of their blows. 'They were not ashamed to maintain' says Calmeil 'that it was to be ignorant of pious and charitable duties, not to obey under these circumstances the desires of the *convulsionnaires* whilst the reasonable Jansenists repeated aloud, that it was only a frantic madness which could suggest to these young women to encounter such dangers, and make an excuse for the criminal barbarity of those who had the audacity to boast of the advantages of so scandalous a mode of mortification, or rather martyrdom, and the wickedness to consent to take on them the office of executioners'.

"An observer has recounted that a young girl named Jeanne Mouler, had insisted upon their administering to her as many as a hundred blows with an andiron, on the stomach, and that *a brother*, who had one day given her sixty, had caused a breach in a wall at the twenty-fifth blow, and then went on repeating the same violence on her person which had been previously inflicted upon her. Montgeron, acknowledging that he was the person designated 'the brother', who inflicted the blows, adds: 'The *convulsionnaire* continued to complain that the blows that I was giving her were so slight that they did not bring her any relief, and she forced me again to put the andiron into the hands of a large strong man... This person in no way spared her. Having seen, by the proof that I had already given, that he could not administer too violent blows, he bastinadoed her in so frightful a manner, always in the hollow of the stomach that they shook the wall against which she was leaning.[222]

"The *convulsionnaire* made them immediately give her, with all their force, the hundred lashes that she had already asked for, counting as nothing, those sixty which I had already given her."

"A physician, hearing an account of these things, maintained that they could not be true, as according to him it was physically impossible. He objected, amongst other things, that the flexibility and the softness of the skin and flesh, and all the other fibrous parts of which the skin and the flesh are essentially composed, are incompatible with a force and resistance so extraordinary... They allowed him to make an anatomical demonstration, to set forth all his proofs, and in the end, for reply, they said to him—Come and verify the facts—He hastened to do so, and at the very sight he was struck with astonishment. Scarcely believing his eyes, he begs to administer himself the *secours*... They immediately put into his hands the iron instruments, the strongest and the fittest to beat effectually; He spared nothing, he struck with the greatest violence, he thrust into the flesh the instrument with which he was armed, he made it penetrate beyond the surface... Notwithstanding which, the *convulsionnaire* laughed at all his vain efforts; all the blows which he gave her only served to do her good, without leaving the slightest impression, the least trace, or any vestige whatever, not only in the flesh, but even on the skin itself".

Among other duly attested cases of torture to which the *Convulsionnaires* submitted the most astonishing are those of crucifixion and burning.[223]

Like the Fakirs of India, these people seemed to have achieved invulnerability and the power to defy nature! Science, so far, has still to find a satisfactory explanation of this phase of phenomena.

Hippolyte Blanc, another writer, records the following observations:—

"The girl Sonet, nicknamed 'The Salamander', was seen to rest in the flames for 36 minutes on one occasion without sustaining any burns.[224]

"The mania of the *convulsionnaires* broke out at St. Medard, in the spring of 1731. The royal order, which caused the cemetery of St. Medard to be closed and the pretended miracles to cease, was issued in January, 1732."

In 1733, the Duc d'Anjou, the infant son of Queen Marie Leckzinska and Louis XV, fell a victim to a Jansenist plot which caused his death.

In *Phantasmata*, already quoted, we read further: "From 1732 onward the delirium of theomania began to manifest itself more signally than it had hitherto done, by ecstatic phenomena, and cataleptic symptoms, by predictions, and pretensions to miraculous operations, in the same way as the Calvinist *convulsionnaires* progressed in their fanaticism in the Cevennes, when they were interfered with by the civil authorities; and many of their chiefs were imprisoned, as those of the Jansenists of St. Medard were immured in the Bastille, and the Bicetre. The plea or the pretext of persecution, and the consequent assemblage of the *convulsionnaires* of Paris in secret, concurred greatly and rapidly to augment the evils which it was intended to prevent by those governmental measures. And those evils were not effectually repressed during the following ten years. Nor were they totally then put a stop to. It was of no avail that, in the year 1762, the 'Grand Secours' was forbidden by act of parliament.

"The insanity of the *convulsionnaires*", says Hecker, "lasted without interruption until the year 1790."

The *convulsionnaires* of St. Medard and the Camisards were only manifestations of Gnosticism such as have existed in the esoteric branches of various sects, religious and secret societies ever since the days of Paganism.

Among others can be mentioned:

The Albigenses, The Moravian Brethren,

The Anabaptists, the Baptists, the Quakers,

The Waldenses, the Shakers, the Methodists etc.

Their name is legion!

Sects rise, sects fall or fade away, but God remains.

CHAPTER XLIII

THE ROYAL ORDER OF SCOTLAND (FOUNDED 1750)

THE ROYAL ORDER of Scotland is composed of two degrees—HRDM and RYCS—or those of Heredom and Rosy Cross.

The antiquity and origin of "Mother Kilwinning" is a favourite theme with Masonic authors according to whom the degree of Heredom of Kilwinning was founded in the reign of David I, King of Scotland, and that of Rosy Cross by Robert Bruce in 1314.

Robert Freke Gould, however, places the date of the foundation of the Royal Order of Scotland in "the middle of the last century", and gives us the name of William Mitchell, a Scotsman who obtained his patent as its founder from the Provincial Grand Master of South Britain on July 22, 1750.[225]

CHAPTER XLIV

THE STRICT OBSERVANCE
(FOUNDED 1751–52)

THE FOLLOWING MAIN facts concerning the Strict Observance are mostly gathered from the profusely documented work of R. Le Forestier who, having made a comprehensive study of the subject, took as one of his chief authorities Nettelbladt.

The Templar rite of the Strict Observance was founded in 1751 by Charles Gotthelf, Baron de Hund (born 1722) Chamberlain and Councillor of the Elector of Saxony, King of Poland, as well as Councillor of the Empress Maria Theresa.

In 1764, the Anglo-Jewish adventurer Leucht, variously known as Johnson, de Martin, Robert de Leichten, Becher, Despocher, de Bousch, Somery, Scheel and Koenig, made an attempt to amalgamate the Templar System of Clermont, the control of which he had seized the previous year from Rosa, with that of von Hund, with the view of dominating the latter also. In this he failed.

Rosa had been the Legate for Germany, Holland and the kingdoms of the north while, in Paris, the Comte de Clermont occupied a similar position with regard to France, Spain, Portugal and Italy.

The legend of the Strict Observance is very much involved. Stating that the Stuarts were the unknown superiors of the Order it claimed descent from Pierre d'Aumont, Banneret d'Auvergne, at the time of the death of the Grand Master Jacques de Molay and the successor of Beaujeu, Molay's nephew who, with two Commanders and five Knights had escaped to the Island of Mull where they encountered George Harris, the Grand Commander of Hampton Court, likewise a refugee. They elected d'Aumont Grand Master and adopted the costume and customs of Masons in memory of d'Aumont and his companions who, for two years, had lived thus in disguise while exercising the trade to earn a livelihood. Not daring to recruit openly, the Templars were eventually permitted to marry to perpetuate the order. For over 250 years, admission to the degree of Scotch Master had been restricted to the sons of Templars and only within the last 150 years had the secrets of this order been available to Scotch Masters born of free parents. D'Aumont was succeeded as Grand Master by Harris."[226]

According to Le Forestier, again quoting Nettelbladt, the initiation ceremony of the Strict Observance included the presentation to the postulant of a ribbon to which was appended a small cross which had been in contact with the Baphomet.[227]

At the Convent, sitting from June 4 to 24, 1772, at Kohlo in the Basse Lusace, it was decided to refuse further obedience to the illusive "Invisible Superiors" continually referred to by Hund, and the Duke Ferdinand of Brunswick (Luneburg) (1721–1792) was, with the consent of the Banneret, elected *Magnus Superior Ordinis per Germaniam Inferiorem* and Grand Master of the United Lodges of Scottish Rites, the name of Strict Observance being abandoned as objectionable to Masons of other systems. From that time forward Hund's position in the order was purely an honorary one.[228]

For root of this movement see Chapter XXII.

For development of this movement see Chapter XLVI I.

CHAPTER XLV

THE MARTINIST ORDER
(FOUNDED 1754)

MARTINEZ PASCHALIS FIRST founded in Paris an order called the Elus Cohens or Priests, then in 1754 that of the Martinists. This order was reformed by Louis Claude de Saint Martin in 1775. It had ten degrees.

St. Martin was on intimate terms with the Illumine Jean Willermoz who presided at two of the Great Masonic Conventions—that of Les Gaules in 1768 and that of Wilhelmsbad in 1782 at which was voted the death of the King of France.

The Modern Martinist Order was established with three degrees in Paris in 1887 and was constituted in England in 1902.

Its Grand Master, Marquis Stanislas de Guaita, died in 1897 and was succeeded by T. Ch. Barlet whose successor was Dr. Encausse, generally known as Papus, who became the occult adviser of the ill-fated Czar Nicholas II.

Mr. A. E. Waite tells us that, while Papus was its Grand Master, a Martinist "Supreme Council" was founded with power for the formation of regular lodges, male and female members being admitted on equal terms. This was in 1894. By the year 1899, there were general and special delegations of the Order established in a number 'of European Countries—Great Britain included—in the United States, the Argentine and Guatemala and even in more than one Oriental land.

As regards the Martinist relations with Masonry, Mr. Waite tells us on page 161, Vol. II, of his *New Encyclopaedia of Freemasonry* that Martinism "had of course shut its doors against Masons under authorized obediences." Yet we are able to reproduce (see Appendix IV) a private letter, dated March 26, 1906, written by "Dorec" to Theodore Reuss 33° 90° 96°, English Mason, etc. in which the latter is incidentally informed "that John Yarker is our ('the Martinist') delegate in London."

Another private letter in which Papus refers to himself as the Delegate of John Yarker for the Swedenborg Rite in France is also in existence. Such a correspondence with one of the most noteworthy Masons of their day does not look as if Mr. Waite's information concerning the alleged feud between Masonry and Martinism can have been very reliable!

By 1920, Mr. Waite states that Martinism had abandoned the Rituals of 1887 and appeared to have become a clandestine organization!

For root of this movement see Chapter XXII.

For development of this movement see Chapter LI.

CHAPTER XLVI

THE ILLUMINATI OF AVIGNON (FOUNDED 1760)

THE ILLUMINATI OF Avignon were founded in 1760 by Antoine Joseph Pernety, an unfrocked Benedictine, a Cabalist and alchemist. Modified in 1766 by Chastanier, one of the founders of the English Rite of Swedenborg, this rite was introduced into Paris in the Lodge Socrates of Perfect Union under the name of Theosophical Illumines. In 1770, Pernety, founded *La Grande Loge Ecossaise du Comtat Venaissin*. This Lodge was raided in 1774 and its papers confiscated by order of the Pope. It was revived in 1789.[229]

Among its members were Cagliostro and his friend Baron de Corberon, Mesmer, Marquis de Thome and the Marquis de Puysegur, self-styled Professor of "Mesmerism".

In *Les Illumines d'Avignon* by Joanny Bricaud (page 103) we read that "today, its members having become affiliated to Martinism, the society has ceased to exist". This author also states that the degree of Knight of the Sun, founded by Pernety, which is divided into two degrees, forms now the 27th and 28th grades of Ancient and Accepted Scottish Rites.[230]

CHAPTER XLVII

ANTIENT AND ACCEPTED SCOTTISH RITE (AMERICA)
ANTIENT AND ACCEPTED RITE (ENGLAND)
(FOUNDED 1761)

SUPREME GRAND COMMANDER FOR THE SOUTHERN JURISDICTION OF THE UNITE D STATES, 1929, MR. JOHN H. COWLES

THE READER HAS already been made acquainted with the formation phase of this rite in Chapters XXVIII XX X of this book. We are here therefore mainly concerned with the framework of the order.

This rite, of Jewish origin, has 33 degrees. They are named as follows:—

Symbolic or Blue Masonry:—the Craft Degrees. These are practically the same as in Lodges under the Grand Lodge of England, Scotland and Ireland.

1. Entered Apprentice
2. Fellow Craft
3. Master Mason

Red Masonry or Chapters:—these degrees are conferred in a Lodge of Perfection, the presiding officer must be of the 16th degree at least.

4. Secret Master
5. Perfect Master
6. Intimate Secretary
7. Provost and Judge
8. Intendant of the Buildings
9. Elected Knight of Nine or Elect of Nine
10. Illustrious Master Elect of Fifteen
11. Sublime Knight Elect
12. Grand Master Architect
13. Royal Arch of Enoch or Knight of the 9th Arch or Royal Arch of Solomon.
14. Scottish Knight of Perfection or Grand Scottish Knight of the Sacred Vault or Sublime Mason.

A Council of Princes of Jerusalem confers the next two degrees:—

15. Knight of the East or Knight of the Sword
16. Prince of Jerusalem

A Chapter of Princes of Rose-Croix confers the next two degrees:—

17. Knight of the East and West
18. Knight of the Eagle and Pelican, Sovereign Prince Rose Croix of H. R. D. M.

Black Masonry, or Philosophical Lodges or Areopagi: these degrees are conferred in a Consistory of Princes of the Royal Secret.

19. Grand Pontiff or Sublime Scotch Mason
20. Grand Master of all Symbolic Lodges
21. Patriarch Noachite or Prussian Knight
22. Prince of Libanus or Knight of the Royal Axe
23. Chief of the Tabernacle
24. Prince of the Tabernacle

25. Knight of the Brazen Serpent
26. Prince of Mercy or Scotch Trinitarian
27. Sovereign Commander of the Temple
28. Knight of the Sun or Prince Adept
29. Grand Scottish Knight of St. Andrew
30. Grand Elected Knight Kadosch.

Illustrious Knight of the Temple \
Knight of the White and Black Eagle France
Grand Elected Knight Kadosch /

"White Masonry is Administrative and consists of three degrees conferred by the Supreme Councils:—

31. Grand Inquisitor Commander
32. Sublime Prince of the Royal Secret
33. Sovereign Grand Inspector General[231]

In *A sketch of the Philosophy, Traditions, and records of the Masonic Order of the Red Cross of Constantine* by the Editor, (see *The Rosicrucian and Masonic Record*, page 204) we read:—

"The Premier Conclave of England, which has existed from time immemorial, gave rise, it is said, to the foundation of the Council of 'Emperors of the East and West', a body which was established in Paris about the year 1758 and is considered as the parent of the Antient and Accepted Scottish Rite. (Compare with page 336).

"The Scottish Rite", according to Le Forestier, "issued from the Chapter of Clermont, as a development of the Ramsay Rite. Its foundation dates from 1748 at which period it was introduced into Germany by Count de Schmettau."[232]

The Supreme Council is the arch-stone of this edifice of degrees. It is composed of a minimum of nine and a maximum of thirty-three members, Grand Inspectors General of 33°. Is that a secret 33?[233]

In its present form, the Rite in France dates from 1804."At that date the pecuniary situation of the Grand Central Lodge was however not up to its pretentions. It was already in debt. Brother de Grasse had personal debts and Brother Abraham was a man of venal character. The Grand Orient paid the debts of the Grand Scottish Lodge and of Brother de Grasse, making a life pension of 800 francs to Brother Abraham and proposing the annexation of the Grand Central Lodge to the Antient and Accepted Scottish Rite among those recognized by the Grand Orient."[234]

In 1804, in France, a Supreme Council of Sovereign Grand Inspectors General of the 33rd degree of the Antient and Accepted Scottish Rite was duly constituted. In the construction of this Council, Comte Alexandre F. A. de Grasse-Tilly, (the son of the Admiral) played a leading part. He had been initiated in Paris several years before he went to America where we find him a colonist of San Domingo.

His successor was the Duc Decazes.

As regards the development of Scottish Rites in England, Stillson and Hughan state that:

"After the Antient and Accepted Scottish Rite had been established in England, the Templar body resigned control over the degrees of the 'Rose-Croix' and 'Kadosch,' which then became incorporated with the rite, as the 18th and 30th; it was therefore necessary to suppress the old ceremonies and relegate them to Templar history, but they were still retained in some of the older English encampments.

A revised ritual was issued in 1851 consequent on the omission of the 'Rose-Croix' and 'Kadosch'.[235]

Another authority, Paul Rosen, makes the following comment:—

"The philosophy of the degree of Kadosch (30°), the apotheosis and real aims of Masonic teaching, can be summed up in the following words:—I, I alone, All mine, All for me, by any and every means.

There are seven different ways of carrying out this programme and consequently seven different grades of Knight Kadosch which are:—

- N° 1. The Jewish Kadosch
- N° 2. The Primitive Christian Kadosch
- N° 3. The Kadosch of the Crusades
- N° 4. The Kadosch of the Templars

- N° 5. The Kadosch of the Puritan
- N° 6. The Kadosch of the Jesuit
- N° 7. The Scottish Kadosch (alone true Freemasonry).[236]

Presidents of the United States are honoured by being made 33rd degree Masons, Scottish Rites. King Edward VII and countless other magnates were 33rd degree Masons. What does this prove?—Unfortunately nothing!

This is the great deception. The success of the entire system depends on the solid integrity and political and social prominence of its affiliates whose virtues make them valuable as decoys.

"Antient and Accepted Scottish Rites" runs its own Secret Service which cooperates with the national Secret Services of all countries thus serving the aims and purposes of Internationalism.

Blanchard, himself a high Mason whose masonic studies were induced by a keen desire to fathom the truth and impart the result of his discoveries to those whom he feared might also be duped, thus sums up Scottish Rites:—

"Let the authoritative teaching of Dr. Mackey be continually borne in mind, that:—'the mission and object of Masonry is the worship of the Great Architect of the Universe'. It follows that the lodges must have something for their dupes to do, called worship. And what could wicked men and devils invent craftier or better suited to deceive the simple, than this very scheme of 'the Ancient Scottish Rite', which now rules the rites of the world. It seizes and appropriates all of religion but its holiness and justice; and all of Christ but his truth and his atonement. It mixes things sacred with things profane, till the whole compound is profanity; and quoting the Bible as if it believed it true, which notoriously it does not, it has furnished a dark system, which angels flee from and which devils inhabit.[237] Every Lodge is a Synagogue of Satan and its ritual is Sorcery."[238]

Anyone interested in the rituals etc. of this rite will find much that is interesting in D. Margiotta's *Le Culte de la Nature dans la Franc-Maçonnerie Universelle.*

Masonic philosophy is well summarised in the following exposé made of it by a Jewish mason, Paul Rosen, in Satan et Cie.—

Official ritual of the 33rd and last degree of Antient and Accepted Scottish Rites

"For the Sovereign Grand Inspector General the 33rd is the last degree of the Rite. The Order is the Great Avenger of the assassinated Grand Master and the grand champion of humanity, for the innocent Grand Master is man, man who is Master, King of Nature, man who is born innocent and unconscious." Our innocent Grand Master was born for happiness and for the enjoyment of all rights without exception.

"But he has fallen under the blows of three assassins, three scoundrels have thwarted his happiness and rights and have annihilated him.

"The three infamous assassins are Law, Property and Religion.[239]

"Law, because it is not in harmony with the rights of the individual man and the duties of social man in society, rights which belong to all. Duties are but the immediate consequence of the right inherent in all, for the enjoyment of all rights.

"Property, because the earth belongs to nobody and its fruits belong to all in proportion as they are required by each for the needs of his own well-being.

"Religion, because religions are but philosophies evolved by men of genius and adopted by the people in the belief that they would increase their well-being." Neither law, property nor religion can be imposed on man and as they annihilate him by depriving him of his most precious rights they are assassins on whom we have sworn to wreak vengeance, enemies against whom we have declared war to the death and without quarter.

"Of these three infamous enemies it is on religion that we must concentrate our most deadly attacks, because no people has ever survived its religion. Once Religion is dead, Law and Property will fall to our mercy, and we shall be able to regenerate society by founding on the corpses of the assassins of man, Masonic Religion, Masonic Law, and Masonic Property".[240]

Who will not see therein the dreaded theories of Marxism and Bolshevism and their results, as they are practised in Russia?

For root of this movement see Chapters II, III, IV.

CHAPTER XLVIII

THE ORDER OF THE MOPSE
(FOUNDED 1763)

POPE CLEMENT XIV having excommunicated the Freemasons in 1763, many German Catholics, frightened by the Papal Bull, definitely renounced the society.

They formed however another association which, while restoring their former organization, should not expose them to the censure of the Vatican and, having found a protector in the person of one of the most august German Sovereigns of the day, they secured an influential German nobleman as Grand Master. Many distinguished persons joined the "new" order which, like the Freemasons, had laws, words, signs of recognition, reception ceremonies and appointed officers.

One of the principal lodges was at Frankfort. Adherence to the Roman Catholic faith was declared a requisite of membership, but the rule was not enforced and as a protection from papal excommunication a promise, instead of an oath of secrecy, was exacted from candidates.

Women were eligible to any dignity in the order, excepting that of Grand Master, which position was held for life. There were two Lodge Masters or Grand Mopses in each lodge, one of which was a man and one a woman, while the lodge was governed six months by a man and six months by a woman alternately.[241]

In Italy, the Mopses called themselves Xerophagists.[242]

The following is quoted from an article in *Freemasonry Universal* Vol. 2, part 4, Spring Equinox, 1927:—"Mingled with points clearly stolen from the Masonic ritual, such as the use of the square and compasses, was the veneration of a sort of mascot which was a dog, known as the Mopse, and resembled a rather large pug dog with a curly tail.

"During the ceremony the candidates were admitted blindfolded and were instructed to kiss something. This was nothing more nor less than a life sized model of a mopse, and on the bandage being removed the initiate found that he or she had kissed the tail end of the dog. Whether the ceremonies were merely boisterous fooling, or whether they had any esoteric significance it is difficult to say, as students differ on the point.

"The Order was certainly at one time wide spread and popular, but seems to have entirely died out. Probably its death blow was given by the Revolution, which swept away so many of the aristocrats of France and brought secret societies into disrepute, owing to the supposed share of the Illuminati in starting that tremendous upheaval."

The statement in the last paragraph can hardly be accurate as certain official papers are in existence bearing, as letter head, under the insignia of the double headed masonic eagle, the following words:—

"Antichi cd Ortodossi Sup Cons Dci 33 Federali Italiani de Rit Scoz Anted Acc Delle Valli Sebeto ed Oreto e Delle Sorelle Mopse.

Gr Orienti D' Italia Scdcnti in Napoli c Palermo. Liberta-Uguaglianza-Fratellanza Sup Cons Gen

These papers bear the date 1902.

CHAPTER XLIX

THE RITE OF ZINNENDORF
(FOUNDED 1766)

THIS RITE WAS founded in 1766 by Zinnendorf, the chief surgeon of the general staff of Berlin and a Knight Commander in von Hund's Strict-Observance. Zinnendorf received the rituals and instructions for this order from a Swede named Cklack.

On Dec. 27, 1770, Zinnendorf formed a Grand Lodge in Berlin with the cooperation of twelve lodges which had adopted his opinions. On March 29 of the following year, he demanded a constitution from the Grand Lodge of London. This he finally obtained in 1773 through the influence of Prince Louis George Charles of Hesse-Darmstadt, the Grand Master of the Lodges following his system.[243]

The Rite of Zinnendorf was absorbed at the Convent of Wolfenbuttel in 1778 into the Lodge of the Three Globes of Berlin.

CHAPTER L

THE PHILALETES (CHERCHEURS DE LA VÉRITÉ) (FOUNDED 1773)

THE PHILALETES, AN offshoot of the Martinists, was founded in Paris on April 28, 1773, within the Lodge of *Les Amis Reunis*, by Savalette de Langes, Keeper of the Royal Treasury, M. de St. James, Comte de Gebelin, Condorcet and others.

This order was divided into 9 degrees, which were, Elu, Chevalier Ecossais, Chevalier d'Orient, Chevalier Rose-Croix, Chevalier du Temple, Philosophe Inconnu, Philosophe Sublime, Initie, Philalèthe ou Maitre a tous grades.

Among its members were Frederic-Louis de Hesse Darmstadt, Baron de Gleichen, Willermoz and l'Abbe Siéyès.[244]

For root of this movement see Chapter XLV.

For development of this movement see Chapter LIII.

CHAPTER LI

THE ILLUMINATI OF BAVARIA
(FOUNDED 1776)

THE SECT OF the Illuminati of Bavaria was founded on May 1, 1776 by Adam Weishaupt, a professor at the University of Ingolstadt, educated by the Jesuits.

It was composed of three classes of adepts, each of which was again subdivided into degrees, in the following manner:—

	Preparation	
Nursery	Novice	
	Minerval	
	Illuminatus Minor	
		Apprentice
	Symbolic	Fellow Craft
		Master Mason
Masonry		Illuminatus Major, or Scotch Novice
	Scotch	Illuminatus Dirigens, or Scotch Knight
	Lesser	Epopt, or Priest; Prince, or Regent
Mysteries		Magus, or Philosopher, Rex, King, Homme Roi, or Areopagite
	Greater	

This society seems to have borne a close resemblance to the Order of the Golden Cross which was reorganized in 1767.

According to Le Forestier, Illuminism was just as much Masonry as the system of the Rose Croix, that of the Templars or the crowd of Masonic French degrees, and it is wrongfully accused of having taken in Bavaria the cloak of Masonry.[245]

The intention of the Founder was to constitute a Protestant organization to fight Jesuitism, using Jesuitical methods. He was ably assisted in his efforts by Adolph, Baron von Knigge, Massenhausen, Bode, Anacharsis Clootz, Fischer, Zwack, Merz, Hertal, the Marquis de Constanza, Count Saviola, Bassus, Baron de Montgelas and Nicola'i.

Behind Nicola'i was Moses Mendelssohn, and behind Mendelssohn the Jewish Kahal, the Jewish International World Government.[246]

"Nicola'i had established about the year 1765 at Berlin a literary review with the object of propagating the pernicious doctrines of a shallow Illuminism, and, in that, the infancy of German literature, when this periodical had scarcely a rival to encounter, the influence it exerted was more extensive than can at present be even conceived. Bahardt and Basedow, at the same time, in cheap and popular tracts, scattered among the lower classes the poison of infidelity; and they, as well as Nicola'i, were in close communication with Weishaupt, carrying on with the most reckless violence, and with the weapons of a most shameless ribaldry, the warfare against Christianity.

The great critic Lessing, the founder of the modern German literature, lent his powerful support to the anti-Christian League. While librarian at Wolfenbuttel he edited a work, composed by Reimarus, consisting of various irreligious essays entitled *Fragments of Wolfenbuttel*, and which, from the tone of earnestness and dialectic acuteness wherein they were written, exerted a very prejudicial influence over public opinion."[247]

As the organization of the Illuminati developed, so did its ambitions, which ended in a plot to subvert Freemasonry to its aim of world dominion by any and all means.

Politically speaking, its tendencies were republican; religiously, it was anti-christian. Its members were pledged to blind obedience to their superiors and this was insured by a strict system of secret confessions, and monthly reports checked by mutual espionage. Each individual used a pseudonym instead of his own name to help disguise his identity.

But for the Freemason Baron Adolph von Knigge, a Templar, who succeeded in having it absorbed by Freemasonry, the order would have perished soon after its creation.

After obtaining control of certain Masonic Lodges, Weishaupt and his associates recklessly vaunted their growing power. Their organization then, soon becoming permeated by the agents of their enemies, the Jesuits and Rose Croix Orders, they were denounced to the Elector of Bavaria, Charles Theodore, by the Duchess Marie-Anne of Bavaria (Princess Clementine), his cousin whose secretary, Joseph Utzschneider, had, as an Illuminatus, become acquainted with certain methods of the order.

Constanza had ordered him to hand over certain letters written by Frederic II to the Duchess Marie-Anne and, suspecting blackmail, instead of complying with the request, he denounced the order.

On March 2, 1785, the Elector wrote his second and final edict, suppressing the order of the Illuminati, but it was not until July 10, 1785 that incriminating evidence was obtained on the activities of the sect when one of its members, a priest, Jacob Lang, was struck dead by lightning while walking with Weishaupt at Ratisbon. His body was placed in the chapel of Saint-Emmeran and a Benedictine found some documents and a list of the members of the Illuminati sewn in his clothes. These he handed over to the Councillor of the Government of Upper Bavaria.

More papers were found when the authorities, who were watching Zwack's relations with a certain Jew, Mayer, the superintendent of Bassus' chateau of Sandersdorf, near Ingolstadt, decided to raid the place, and in 1787 the judge charged with the inventory of the succession of the valet of Baron Maendl, the Chamberlain of the Elector, found among his effects an iron box full of papers concerning the Illuminati.

This discovery, Maendl, himself an Illuminatus, was summoned to explain. Among the details of his evidence is the statement that the Lodge

Bader had 97 degrees. The coincidence of this number becomes of interest when compared with the 97 degrees of Memphis sent to England in 1762 by the Grand Orient of France.

When Weishaupt was banished from Bavaria by his sovereign, he was received at the court of the Duke Ernest-Louis de Saxe-Gotha who, besides a pension, gave him the title of Honorary Councillor.

The Marquis of Constanza, his secretary, and Count Saviola, the Keeper of the Archives of the order, two Italian accomplices, were also banished with pensions of 400 and 800 florins respectively, and as Illuminism was already said to have found its way into Italy, there is no reason to suppose that these gentlemen failed in their administration of the subsidy.

In 1788, after the suppression of Illuminism in Bavaria, Bahrdt and Knigge attempted to revive it in the "German Union" but it was not till 1810 that it really reappeared in Germany, this time under the name of *The Tugendbund.*

The introduction of Illuminism into Prance was effected by the Marquis de Mirabeau who, during his residence in Germany, was initiated by Mauvillon, a professor of the Caroline college at Brunswick. He rose high in the order, and, on his return to France in September 1788, initiated the Duc d'Orléans, who was Grand Master of the Freemasons of that country, and also Talleyrand.

Frost, in *Secret Societies of the European Revolution* refers to Barruel as asserting "that the whole of the Masonic lodges comprised in the Grand Orient, 266 in number, were 'illuminated' by the end of March 1789 and there is no doubt that , with the ground so well prepared by the works of Voltaire and Bousseau, d'Alembert and Diderot, and with the example and influence of the Duke of Orleans, and the exertions of men such as Mirabeau, Talleyrand, Sieyès, and Condorcet, the system spread with rapidity."[248]

General La Fayette, Barnave, Brissot, La Bochefoucauld, Payne and Fauhet were also members of the sect for France.[249]

The following curious piece of information is furnished by *Le Grand Dictionnaire Universel du XIXe Siecle* by Larousse in the article on "Illuminisme":—"The Illuminati did not disappear after the last century.

They are still to be found in Germany, England and Russia where they have formed a queer sect in which castration is one of the features of initiation. The taste for the supernatural, the passion of the marvellous constantly urge these mentally unbalanced men in whom the imagination is fanaticised, to throw themselves into the fantastic visions which constitute Illuminism."

For root of this movement see Chapter XXII.

For development of this movement see Chapters LI I, LV, LXXXVII, CVI, CX.

CHAPTER LII

THE TUGENDBUND
(FOUNDED 1786)

THE NAME OF *Tugendbund* or Union of Virtue was first given to the association of men and women who met at the house of the Jewess Henrietta Herz whose husband, Marcus Herz, a Jewish Illuminatus, was the disciple, friend and successor of Moses Mendelssohn. Noted Illuminati were frequenters of this abode of licentiousness about which Graetz, the Jewish historian, wrote:

"The salon of the beautiful Henrietta Herz became a sort of Midianite tent. Here a number of young Jewish women assembled whose husbands were kept away by their business. The most prominent male member of this circle was Frederick von Gentz, the embodiment of selfishness, licentiousness, vice and depravity whose chief occupation was the betrayal of women.[250]

"A so-called Band of Virtue (Tugendbund) was formed of which Henrietta Herz, two daughters of Moses Mendelssohn[251] and other Jewesses together with Christian profligates were members."

He also adds that "Mirabeau, in whose mind the storm-charged clouds of the Revolution were already forming, and to whom the Jews owed so much during his secret diplomatic embassy (1786) to Berlin, was more in the society of Henrietta Herz than in that of her husband."

Other frequenters of this salon were William von Humboldt, Jean Paul Richter, Schleiermacher, a foremost Moravian brother, and his friend Frederick Schlegel.

Later, in 1807, a second Tugendbund or Union of Virtue was formed, a purely political league of which Thomas Frost wrote:—

"The nucleus of the Association devised by von Stein which received the name of the Tugendbund, or League of Virtue, was formed during the latter months of 1807. His colleagues, Hardenberg and Scharnhorst; Generals Wittgenstein and Blucher; Jahn, a Professor of the Berlin Gymnasium, and Arndt, the popular author, were amongst the earliest members. The initiations multiplied rapidly, and the League soon numbered in its ranks most of the Councillors of State, many officers of the army, and a considerable number of the professors of literature and science. By the active and zealous exertions of Stein, Hardenberg and Jahn, its ramifications spread quickly from the Baltic to the Elbe, and all classes were drawn within its influence. A central directorate at Berlin, presided over by Stein, had the supreme control of the movement, and exercised, through provincial committees, an authority all the more potent from emanating from an unknown source, and which was obeyed as implicitly as the decrees of Emperor or King."[252]

With Heckethorn, we follow the Tugendbund further, for he tells us that after its suppression by the police of Napoleon I, the Tugendbund continued "concealing itself however more strictly than before in the masonic brotherhood."[253]

One of its first acts "was to send auxiliary corps to assist the Russians in the campaign of 1813. Prussia having, by the course of events, been compelled to abandon its temporizing policy, Gneisenau, Scharnhorst and Grollmann embraced the military plan of the Tugendbund. A levy *en masse* was ordered. The conduct of these patriots is matter of history. But, like other nations, they fought against Napoleon to impose on their country a more tyrannical government than that of the foreigner had ever been. They fought as men only fight for a great cause, and those who died fancied they saw the dawn of German freedom. But those who survived saw how much they were deceived. The Tugendbund, betrayed in its expectations, was dissolved; but its members increased the ranks of other societies already existing, or about to be formed" such as the 'Black Knights' under Jahn,

'The Knights of the Queen of Prussia', 'The Concordists' under Dr. Lang and the Deutscher Bund, founded in 1810."

The Tugendbund was revived in the Burschenschaft, or associations of students of the universities, where they introduced gymnastics and martial exercises, but the organization was broken up and its objects frustrated, after the stabbing of Kotzebue by a student. It revived between 1830–33. It is said to have failed again.

For root of this movement see Chapter LI.

CHAPTER LIII

THE JACOBINS
(THE CLUBS OR LODGES OF THE FRENCH REVOLUTION)
(FOUNDED 1786)

THE BISHOP OF Autun (Talleyrand), Mirabeau, and the Duc d'Orléans, Grand Master of the *Grand-Orient de France* founded a Lodge in Paris in 1786 which was duly "illuminated" by Bode and Guillaume Baron de Busche. This was the *Club Breton* which afterwards became known as the Jacobin Club, a name of Templar origin, recalling that of Jacques de Molay.

Le Forestier in *Les Illumines de Baviere et la FrancMaçonnerie Allemande* gives the substance of a book written by Girtaner, quoting the latter as to the funds available at that date for revolution.

"In his *Nouvelles Historiques et considerations politiques sur la Revolution Française* (1793) the Swiss Girtaner, an ex-freemason who had joined the ranks of the enemies of the sect, states that, from 1786, there had existed in Paris a Propaganda Club whose chiefs were then the Duc de la Rochefoucauld, Grand Master of the Lodge in the rue Coq-Heron, Condorcet and Sieyes and that the aim of the organization was to further the triumph of dogmatic Atheism and create a great social upheaval.

"The members charged with spreading the proganda of the subversive principles of the club numbered 50,000. In 1790, it had twenty thousand livres at its disposal, but by the end of 1791, these had increased to thirty millions."[254]

The conspiracy formed by Philippe of Orleans (Duc de Chartres, Masonic name, "Egalite") to overthrow Louis XVI, was directed by Sillery and Mirabeau and, of the 605 elected members of the Tiers Etat, 477 deputies were Freemasons.[255]

Revolutions cost money. "L'Or de Pitt" (Pitt's gold) had to go through some channel that would not compromise the English government and, in dealing with such a delicate matter as the fostering of revolution in a foreign country, it was good policy to organize a similar movement at home which however should remain abortive, being led by Lord Stanhope, Pitt's brother-in-law.

In this connection, the history and failure of Wolfe Tone's Bantry Bay expedition is interesting.

The history of the Terror in the French Revolution of 1793 is the history of lodges such as that of the Philaletes, among whose members the following Jacobin leaders are known to us chiefly for their uncompromising bestiality.

Among the members of the "Club de la Propagande" Condorcet, Duc de la Rochefoucauld, Sièyès, de Beauharnais, Charles Theodore Lameth.

Among the members of the Lodge "Les Amis Beunis" Babeuf, Ceruty, Marat, Hébert, Dupont.

Among the members of the Lodge "Les Neuf Saurs"[256] Condorcet, Jean Sylvain Bailly, Emmanuel Joseph Siéyès, Dom Gerle, Claude Fauchet, Jean Pierre Brissot, Beniot Camille Desmoulins, Cerutti, Danton, Nicolas de Bonneville, Rabaud Saint Etienne, Lalands, Duc de la Rouchefoucauld.

Among the members of the "Amis des Noirs" (Founded 1787) Brissot, Siéyès, Condorcet, Mirabeau (the elder) Due de la Rochefoucauld, Pelletier de St. Fargeau, Lafayette, Gorsas, Valadi, Carra.

Other prominent Jacobin Freemasons of the Revolution of 1793 were: Guillotin. Dupui, Fouche, Robespierre, Collot-d'Herbois,

According to Barruel (*Histoire du Jacobinisme*, vol. II, page 446 *et seq.*) the last mentioned lodge of the "Amis des Noirs" appears to have been only the cover name behind which operated the Comité Regulateuf or Central Committee of the combined lodges and clubs. An international organization with foreign branches in America and Europe, the deliberations of this group of conspirators were sent to the Central Committee of the Grand Orient from where they were relayed to the provinces, addressed to the various Worshipful Masters or Presidents of the Lodges. This group according to Barruel, was the central guiding committee of the Revolution. The "Club Regulateur" is said to have numbered at least 500,000 brothers.

Lafayette (Loge de la Candeur), when he marched on Versailles at the head of 15,000 national guardsmen and brought the King back to Paris, was already, presumably, fully informed of Dupont's plan of revolution which he himself and Mirabeau had approved at a session of the "Amis Reunis" early in June.

While remarking that the vote for the death of the King of France, Louis XVI, was carried by a majority of one, Pignatel[257] further states that, in consequence of certain irregularities in the balloting, some five votes for death were cast by unqualified persons while four others voted twice.

After the storm of revolution had subsided, the power in France seems to have been vested in the *Comite de Salut Public*, but the 300 who controlled France and of whose power we read in Memoirs of the time[258] were the 300 masonic leaders. That they in turn were controlled by a small clique is obvious. Even the 300 masonic leaders of the French Revolution of 1793 seem to have had their successors in modern history—Rathenau mentioned them in his works.

One of the most interesting episodes of the French Revolution was that known as the Conspiracy of Babeuf. Babeuf formed the Society of the Pantheon which, according to Professor Laski,[259] was operated by "a secret committee of direction. Among them were some extraordinary men, Darthe, Sylvain Marechal, Germain and Buonarroti, who was to survive them all and be their historian."

The particular brand of communism favoured by the conspirators was based on the theory that the poor could not help themselves or improve their position, that the rich must be suppressed and that the ideal state could only be reached by class war, and a dictatorship of the proletariat led by the Babouvists. Prof. Lasky remarks that anyone who reads the voluminous literature of this period "with attention and compares the habits it postulates with the operations of Bolshevism, cannot help being impressed by the resemblance."

The Babouvist movement though suppressed by the Directory in 1796 survives today having successfully penetrated an English Literary Society called the Fabians where its predatory principles pass for Socialism.

For root of this movement see Chapter LI.

For development of this movement see Chapters LXV, LXXI, LXXXV, XCIII, CVI and CXXV.

CHAPTER LIV

THE KNIGHTS TEMPLAR AMERICA
(FOUNDED PRIOR TO 1790)

IN AN ADDRESS by Col. W. J. B. Macleod Moore, of the Grand Cross of the Temple Royal Arch, Grand Prior of the Dominion of Canada, published in *The Rosicrucian and Masonic Record,* page 167, we find that, in America, Templarism is founded on the craft degrees of Masonry and that one is inseparable from the other.

The earliest records in the United States of a Templar Lodge meeting are dated 1790.

NOTES

1. Bataille, Le Diable au XIXe Siècle, vol. I, p. 28.
2. Ibid. p. 29.
3. Bataille, Le Diable au XIXe Siècle, vol. I, p. 35.
4. P. 143.
5. Bataille, op. cit., p. 35.
6. Ibid. p. 36.
7. Bataille, op. cit., p. 36.
8. Bataille, op. cit., p. 36.
9. "The G which the Freemasons place in the middle of the flamboyant star signifies Gnosticism and Generation, the most sacred words of the ancient Cabala." See Eliphas Levi, Dogme et Rituel de la Haute Magie, vol. II, p. 97.
10. In reference to the Pagans "who (as we read in divers authors) consecrated most kinds of Distempers of the Body, and Affections of the Mind; erected Temples and Altars to Fevers. Paleness. Madness, and Death; to Laughter, Lust, Contumely, Impudence, and Calumny. Every strange Disorder, as well as Epilepsy, is the Sacred Disease. Sua cuique Deus sit dira Cupido (Each bold Fancy grows into a God). "But it must be remembered this Distemper was called also Morbus Comitialis; because if any one fell into it, during the Assembly, it was a fatal Omen, and they immediately broke up". Bishop Lavington, The Enthusiasm of Methodists and Papists compared, p. 123.
11. This refers to Gnostic Secret Societies described in this book.
12. "Inquire Within" op. cit., pp. 116–117.
13. Hudson, The Law of Psychic Phenomena, p. 236.

14. Freemasonry Universal vol. V, Part 2, Autumn Equinox, 1929, p. 58.
15. Ibid. vol. V, Part 3, Winter Solstice, p. 108.
16. In Hinduism it is known as Kala Yoga.
17. Stillson and Hughan, The History of Freemasonry and Concordant Orders, see the chapter entitled "Hindoostan", p. 74 et seq.
18. Mafia (Sanscrit) = grand.
19. Louis Jacolliot, Occult Science in India, pp. 92–93.
20. Bataille, op. cit., for a fanciful description of such rites.
21. Louis Jacolliot, op. cit., p. 72. and Bataille, op. cit.
22. Louis Jacolliot, op. cit., pp. 73 to 101.
23. Article on Brahminism: Enc. Brit. 9th Edition.
24. Jacolliot, op. cit.
25. Ibid.
26. E. Levi, Dogme et Rituel de la Haute Magie, p. 70. et seq.
27. Edward Sellon, Annotations on the Sacred Writings of the Hindus, p. 8.
28. Ibid. p. 8.
29. Ibid. p. 10.
30. Ibid. p. 12.
31. Ibid. p. 20.
32. Ibid. p. 21.
33. ibid. p. 23.
34. Ibid. p. 40.
35. Bataille, Le Diable au XIXe siècle, for fanciful description of such rites.
36. Sellon, op. cit., p. 53 et seq.
37. Author's note: Sex power = Kundalini, electro-magnetic force, astral light, fire.
38. See Lotus-Padma, explanation in chapter on Symbolism.
39. Heckethorn, Secret Societies of all Ages and Countries, vol. II, p. 307.
40. Heckethorn, op. cit., p. 318, vol. II.
41. Heckethorn, op. cit, vol. II, p. 318 and, for recent corroboration, see Katherine Mayo, Mother India.
42. Heckethorn, op. cit., vol. II, p. 323.
43. Passim.
44. Lt. Gen. A. Netchvolodow, Nicolas II et les Juifs, p. 139.
45. Ibid. p. 139 et seq.
46. Carlile, Manual of Freemasonry, p. 88.
47. Ibid. p. viii.
48. Ibid. p. xi.

49. Ibid. p. v of Introduction.
50. Pythagore, Les Vers Dorés.
51. Bishop Lavington, The Enthusiasm of Methodists and Papists compared, p. 313 et seq.
52. Lavington.
53. The Chevalier de Ramsay, A Discourse upon the Theology and Mythology of the Antients in The Travels of Cyrus, vol. II, P. 76 et seq. (published 1728).
54. The Daily Telegraph, Sept. 24, 1928.
55. Pastos—The altar upon which the ritual desecration of virginity obligatory for initiation into the phallic cult took place.
56. C. W. Olliver, An Analysis of Magic and Witchcraft, p. 102.
57. C. W. Olliver, op. cit., p. 103.
58. M. Summers, History of Witchcraft and Demonology, p. 17.
59. C. W. Olliver, op. cit., p. 106.
60. "Epiphanius gives an account of a sect of Heretics called Satanians. 'Satan, say they, is a very great and potent Person, and author of much Mischief. Why, therefore, should we not chiefly fly to him, and adore him, honour, and praise trim, that for our flattering worship he may do us no harm, but Pardon us as being his own servants?' Hence they call themselves Satanians." Bishop Lavington, The Moravians Corn Pared and Detected, p. 170.
61. Margaret Alice Murray, The Witch-cult in Western Europe, p.186.
62. La Satire en France au Moyen-Age, p. 422.
63. Eliphas Levi, La Clef des Grands Mystères, p. 308.
64. David-Neel, Parmi les Mystiques et les Magiciens du Tibet, pp. 110–111.
65. David-Neel, op. cit., p. 115.
66. Ibid. p. 111.
67. Ibid. p. 118.
68. David-Neel , op. cit., p. 110.
69. Ibid. p. 259.
70. David-Neel, op. cit., p. 260.
71. David-Neel, Initiations Lamaiques, p. 59.
72. David-Neel, op. cit., p. 103.
73. Ibid. p. 104.
74. Ibid. p. 208.
75. Ibid. p. 262.
76. David-Neel, Initiations Lamaiques, p. 116.

77. Seabrook, Adventures in Arabia, pp. 310 and 325.
78. Heckethorn, Secret Societies of All Ages and Countries, vol. I, p. 162.
79. Jewish Encyclopaedia, Art. Abdallah Ibn Saba.
80. Ibid., Art. Caliphs.
81. Mahdi-Messiah.
82. Heckethorn op. cit., p. 165.
83. Compare with Lamaism.
84. Von Hammer, History of the Assassins.
85. Heckethorn, Secret Societies of all Ages and Countries, p. 168 et seq.
86. Blanchard, Knight Templarism Illustrated.
87. Morris' Dic. Art. Templar Knight.
88. Mackey's Lexicon, Art. Knights of Malta.
89. Followers of Theophrastus Bombastus von Hohenheim (1493–1541).
90. Whereas the article mentions only two kinds of demons tne Rose Croix are credited with recognizing four different species accredited to each of the four elements: Earth spirits 77 Gnomes, Fire spirits—Salamanders, Water spirits—Undines, Air spirits—Sylphs.
91. Charlotte Fell Smith, John Dee.
92. Fire, alias Kundalini, alias sex-force.
93. Hastings, Encyclopaedia of Religions and Ethics. Art. Hussites.
94. Wittemans, Histoire des Rose Croix, p. 71.
95. Charlotte Fell Smith, op. cit., p. 182.
96. This is still customary. Many of the English Guilds of today such as the Goldsmiths have honorary members who, for attending their dinners receive a box of chocolates and £3 in cash.
97. A. E. Waite, The Works of Thomas Vaughan, Biographical Preface, p. xii.
98. Henry Blount, 1602–1680, Father of Charles Blount, the Rosicrucian.
99. Heckethorn, Secret Societies of All Ages & Countries, vol. I, p. 342.
100. Afterwards James II.
101. According to Sedir (see Histoire des Rose-Croix, p. 112) the last master of Rose Croix died in 1750. His name was Brun.
102. Grand Lodge of England.
103. Said to have been head of the Rose Croix, succeeding Theophilus Desaguliers; he was Spener's godchild.
104. Diaspora = The Jews of the Dispersion.
105. For the foregoing refer Enc. Brit, Art. "Moravian Brethren", 9th Edition, p. 812.

106. Bishop Lavington, The Moravians Compared and Detected, p. 157.
107. Madden, Phantasmata, vol. II, p. 457.
108. Ibid. vol. II, p. 450.
109. Madden, op. cit., vol. II, p. 456.
110. Bayles Dictionary, vol. 2, Art. "Comenius", p. 1011, year
111. Said to have all been members of the English Rose Croix.
112. Heckethorn, op. cit., p. 266, vol. I.
113. Freemasonry Universal, The Official organ of the British Federation of the Co-Masonic Order, vol. 2, part 2, Autumnal Equinox, 1926, p. 79.
114. Paul Rosen, Satan et Cie, published 1888.
115. J. M. Ragon, Orthodoxie Maçonnique, p. 368, Paris.
116. Henri Cauchois, Grand orateur du Grand Orient de France, Cours oral de Franc-Maçonnerie symbolique, p. 140. Paris, 1863.
117. Clavel, Histoire pittoresque de la Franc-Maçonnerie, p. 43. Paris, 1844.
118. Mackey, Lexicon of Freemasonry, pp. 59 and 241. London, 1873.
119. George Oliver, Grand Commander of the Supreme Council of England, The Book of the Lodge, p. 45. London, 1867.
120. Mackey, op cit., p. 241. London, 1873.
121. Richard Carlile, The Mysteries of Freemasonry, p. 64. London.
122. Comte de Grasse-Tilly, Tableau des grades écossais suivant l'ordre général décrete par le Suprême Conseil du 33e degré, daté du 22 décembre 1804.
123. George Olivier, History of Initiation, p. 128. London, 1841.
124. Albert Thomas, George Pearson, Grand Master of the Templars of the United States, The Tradition of Freemasonry, New York, 1850.
125. Moise Reghellini de Scio, La Maçonnerie considérée comme le résultat des Religions Egyptienne, Juive et chrétienne. Paris, 1833, n° l, p. 364.
126. John Yarker, Grand Master of Ancient and Primitive Rite, Speculative Freemasonry, p. 27. London, 1872.
127. Clavel, Histoire Pittoresque de la Franc-Maçonnerie, p. 49. Paris.
128. Gargano, Irish Freemasons and Their Foreign Brothers, p. 55.
129. The means for the attainment of Crémieux's ambition are set forth in a book entitled Paris: Capitate des Religions, by Jean Izoulet.
130. Gargano, Op. cit.
131. John Yarker, The Arcane Schools, p. 480. "He (Morin) probably—ignorant charlatan as he was—mistook Frederick II , Grandson of Barbarossa, an actual King of Jerusalem, for his contemporary Frederick II of Prussia."

132. The Comte de Clermont was Grand Master of the Grande Loge Nationale de France.
133. H. L. Stillson &W. J. Hughan, op. cit., p. 243. See also Morris's Masonic Dictionary, Article, "Sovereign Grand Inspector General".
134. Peckham, Ancient and Accepted Scottish Rites, p. 6.
135. H. L. Stillson & W. J. Hughan, op. cit., p. 649.
136. Ibid. p. 801.
137. Ibid. p. 247.
138. Margiotta, op. cit., p. 86 et seq. Isaac Long was the son of Isaac Long, a Dutch writer, one of the foremost Moravian brethren, and closely connected with Count Zinzendorf.
139. The 9th, 10th, 11th and 21st degrees.
140. Margiotta, op. cit., p. 88 et seq.
141. Michael di Gargano, Irish and English Freemasons, p. 66.
142. See Larousse: Grand Dictionnaire Universel du XIXe siècle. Mazzini. 1808–1872. He had become the chief of a particular sect much given to mysticism. Without being a catholic he was profoundly religious... In Oct. 1871, he organized in Rome a congress of workmen which attracted little attention. "I am not a christian." he wrote to Daniel Stern.
143. Michael di Gargano, op. cit.
144. Carlile, Manual of Freemasonry, p. 94.
145. Thomas Frost, Secret Societies of the European Revolution, vol. II, p. 1 et seq.
146. André Jacques Manuel (1791–1857).
147. Marc-René de Voyer, Marquis d'Argenson, harboured Buonarotti, one of the group of conspirators led by Babeuf.
148. Thomas Frost, op. cit., vol. II, p. 174.
149. Margiotta, Adriano Lemmi, p. 93 et seq.
150. Gerard de Nerval, Les Illumines, p. 172. Translation: "Several philosophers of this period followed Quintus Aucler in this revival of the ideas of the school of Alexandria. It is towards the same period that Dupont (de Nemours) published his Philosophy of the Universe, founded on the same elements of adoration of planetary intelligences. Likewise, he established, between man and God, a chain of immortal spirits which he called "Optimates" and through whom any illuminé can have communication. It is always the doctrine of the "ammoneans" gods, the "eons" or "eloims" of antiquity.

151. In his Cyclopædia of Fraternities Stevens writes that the 'Order of the Palladium' was founded in 1730 and soon afterwards introduced in Charleston where it remained inactive until 1886, It blossomed anew under the name of 'Reformed Palladium' and gave a new impulse to the traditions of High Masonry. Stevens adds that the Palladium is little known as the number of its members is strictly limited and the deepest secrecy surrounds all its deliberations.
152. Margiotta, op. cit., p. 97 et seq.
153. Margiotta, op. cit., p. 100.
154. Rosen, Maçonnerie pratique, vol. I, p. 434.
155. Bataille, Le Diable au XIXe siècle, p. 360 et seq.
156. Ibid. p. 391.
157. Bailey, Initiation Human and Solar, p. 106.
158. Bailey, op. cit., p. 133.
159. Ibid. p. 174.
160. Ibid. p. 204.
161. Bailey, op. cit., p. 68.
162. Gargano, Irish and English Freemasons, p. 73.
163. Blanchard, Scottish Rite Masonry Illustrated, p. 33. "In his address before his Council in 1878, Albert Pike said: 'I am often asked why we do not publish our old transactions, to which I am compelled to reply, that we have none to publish. We have no records of the transactions at Charleston from 1801 to 1860. What records we had were destroyed... during the war. (American Civil War.)'"
164. Bataille, op. cit., pp. 475, 478.
165. Bataille, op. cit., vol. I, p. 346 et seq.
166. Chacornac, Eliphas Levi, p. 191. "Importuned by his friends Ch. Fauvety and Caubet, who both belonged to the Grand Orient, Eliphas Levi became a Mason on March 14, 1861, being initiated in the Lodge Rose du Parfait Silence of which Caubet was the Venerable. The ceremony was performed in the presence of many brothers." In his reception speech, Eliphas Levi, to the great astonishment of his auditors, little inclined to paradoxes, made the following statement. 'I come to bring you your lost traditions, the exact knowledge of your signs and emblems, and in consequence to show you the aim for the attainment of which your association has been constituted'. He then tried to demonstrate to his coreligionists that Masonic symbolism is borrowed from the Cabala. It was time wasted. No one believed him."

167. Such a system, owing to its apparently democratic character would admirably serve the purposes of an autocracy. After five months it is obvious that none of the original members who proposed a resolution would be present and five months gives plenty of time for manipulation of nominees pledged to vote according to the dictates of invisible masters.
168. Thomas Palamenghi-Crispi, The Memoirs of Francesco Crispi, vol. I, p. 75.
169. Much of the above is recorded in: Le 33° Crispi, by D. Vaughan.
170. Giolitti, Memoirs of my Life, p. 99 et seq.
171. Margiotta, Francesco Crispi, Son Œuvre Néfaste.
172. Thomas Frost, The Secret Societies of The European Revolution (1776–1876), vol. 2, p. 147.
173. Melegari, Lettres Intimes de Joseph Mazzini, p. 182.
174. Thomas Palamenghi-Crispi, The Memoirs of Francesco Crispi, vol. 1, p. 80–81.
175. It is a curious fact that the book from which the above is translated was written in 1894 and that these points were actually achieved in 1919 at the Treaty of Versailles. The machinery which the German monarchical power thought it was using for its own ends, was already, in reality, being guided by the unseen Jewish power controlling Freemasonry.
176. Margiotta, Adriano Lemmi, p. 18.
177. Jewish Encyclopaedia, Art. "Italy".
178. E. T. Raymond, The Alien Patriot, p. 214.
179. Count Corti, The Reign of the House of Rothschild.
180. The name of Diana Vaughan has been mentioned as that of the person who obtained the paper.
181. P. B. Gheusi, Gambetta, Life and Letters, pp. 11 and 302.
182. Rosen, L'ennemi social, for oath taken by Edward VII.
183. E. T. Raymond, The Alien Patriot.
184. Margiotta, Adriano Lemmi, op. cit., pp. 104–105.
185. Margiotta, op. cit., pp. 105 et seq.
186. The reader must remember that at the date when the above was written by Margiotta, Lemmi was still alive.
187. At that date the franc was at 5 to the dollar.
188. De la Rive, Les Juifs dans la Franc-Maçonnerie. Re treaty between the B'nai Br'ith and the supreme authority at Charleston.

Translation."... Albert Pike and the Jew Armand Levy affixed their Palladian signatures to this document. Armand Levy styled himself—33 Lieutenant grand assistant and sovereign delegate of the Grand Central

Directory of Naples, honorary member ad vitam of the Sublime Federal Consistory of the B'nai B'rith of Germany, acting as general agent for this Consistory as well as those of America and England, the various federations of the B'nai B'rith having given him full powers..."

189. Onslow Yorke, Secret History of The International, pp. 52 and 55–56.
190. According to "The Royal Blue Book" for January 1895, p. 1065, Mr. Hugh David Sandeman's London address was 33, Golden Square. In Devil Worship in France, Mr. Waite refers to 33, Golden Square as the address of the Supreme Council of Ancient and Accepted Scottish Rite. Until two years ago, this address was that of the Faculty of Arts, where lectures and concerts were given in a Masonic Temple.
191. Domenico Margiotta, Le Palladisme, p. 32. Quotation from La Croix du Dauphiné. May 18th 1895.

...''Doctor Domenico Margiotta has given us the following details which complete the telegram which, thanks to him, we published two days ago, on the discovery of the Temple of Satan at Rome:—

"Naturally the agents of the Borghese family were admitted without hindrance to all the halls and rooms of the palace, with the exception of one which was closed, and which the satanic keepers refused obstinately to open. Then the agents of the proprietor of the premises, (Prince Borghese) insisted on being allowed entrance to that room and threatened finally to have the door forced.

"In the face of such a threat, the guards of Lemmi were compelled to give in and the representatives of the lessor entered the palladian temple. "Its lateral walls were hung with magnificent red and black damask draperies. At the further end was a great piece of tapestry upon which was the figure of Satan at whose feet" was an altar. Here and there were arranged triangles, squares and other symbolic signs of the sect as well as books and masonic rituals. All around stood gilt chairs. Each of these, in the moulding which capped its back, had a glass eye, the interior of which was lighted by electricity, while in the middle of the temple stood a curious throne, that of the Great Satanic Pontiff.

Owing to the state of terror into which this unexpected sight plunged them, the visitors beat a hasty retreat without further examination of the premises."

192. Enc. Brit., Ninth Edition, Art. Jesuits.
193. Once regent of the Jesuit College of Clermont.
194. D. Jones, The Secret History of White-Hall, 1697, p. 41.

195. Heckethorn, Secret Societies of all Ages and Countries, vol. II, p. 296.
196. Schaff-Herzog, The Encyclopaedia of Religious Knowledge. Art. Jesuits.
197. Schaff-Herzog, op. cit., Art. Jesuits.
198. Heckethorn, op. cit., vol. II, p. 302.
199. Pollard, The Secret Societies of Ireland, p. 2. et seq.
200. Pollard, op. tit., p. 3.
201. Ibid. p. no.
202. Pollard, op. cit., p. 8.
203. Ibid. p. 115.
204. Ibid. p. 113.
205. Ibid. p. 115.
206. Madden, Phantasmata, vol. II, p. 530; quoting De la Folie, by L. F. Calmeil (1845), vol. II, p. 304.
207. Madden, op. cit., vol. II, p. 532 et seq.
208. Ibid. quoting Sketches of Imposture, Deception and Credulity, Lond. 1836, p. 42.
209. U. S. E., Emmanuel Swedenborg, the Spiritual Columbus.
210. Sedir, Histoire des Rose-Croix, p. 112.
211. Mackey, Lexicon of Freemasonry, p. 301.
212. Rev. E. Cahill, S. J. , Freemasonry and the Anti-Christian Movement, p. 213, definitely refutes the story of certain Masonic authorities by whom it has been alleged that The Chapter of Clermont was founded in the Jesuit College of that name. He states that it was "founded in 1754 and was named the Chapter of Clermont' manifestly borrowing its name from the title of the Masonic Grand Master who in fact became its head."
213. Wm. Peckham, Ancient and Accepted Scottish Rite.
214. Encyclopaedia Britannica, Art. Freemasonry.
215. John Yarker, The Arcane Schools, p. 479.
216. Enc. Brit., op. cit.
217. Gould, Hist. of Freemasonry, vol. III, p. 179.
218. Domenico Margiotta, Le Culte de la Nature dans la Francmaçonnerie Universelle, p. 45 et seq.
219. Madden, Phantasmata, vol. II, p. 541.
220. Madden, op. cit., vol. II, p. 544.
221. Ibid. p. 573.
222. Madden, op. cit., vol. II, p. 579.
223. Hippolyte Blanc, Le Merveilleux, p. 118.

224. Ibid. p. 114.
225. Robert Freke Gould, The History of Freemasonry, Pub. 1887, p. 75.
226. R. Le Forestier, Les Illumines de Baviere et la Francmaconnerie Allemande, p. 162.
227. Ibid. p. 172.
228. R. Le Forestier, op. cit., p. 175.
229. Marc de Vissac, Dom Pernety et les Illumines d'Avignon, 1906.
230. Joanny Bricaud, Les Illumines d'Avignon, p. 103.
231. Encyclopaedia of Freemasonry, The Speculative Mason, vol. 19, Jan. 1927.
232. R. Le Forestier, Les Illumines de Baviere et la Francmaçonnerie Allemande, p. 145.
233. Blanchard, Scottish Rite Masonry Illustrated, 33°, vol. II, p. 451. "But the one 'mission and object' (Mackey) of Masonry is kept steadily in view; which is the worship of the god of this world, who is Satan, as the 'Grand Architect of the Universe;' and to accomplish this by inventing 'a religion in which all mankind agree;' and this, by putting all earth's religions upon a level, and uniting them together in Masonic worship, which is boldly avowed in rituals, lexicons, and philosophical degrees. This is (in Revelation, XIII, 14) called the image of the beast, made by 'them, that dwell on the earth' that is, everybody; every creed, and no creed; all who join the secret lodges. But this world-religion must have some form, and shape, to hold together; and be taxed; hence, it takes the form, or image, of the beast. Lodge despotism is as absolute as Romish despotism and is the image of it...

    "Note now the profound craft, by which this is to be accomplished, viz., Masonry promises men salvation by ceremonies invented by men, administered by priests, and inhabited by devils. This is the sum and substance of all the false religions on earth, and will ultimately unite them against Christ. But the only opponent Masonry dreads is Christ, who refused to worship Satan, and his followers."
234. Histoire du Grand Orient, p. 305, Rennes, 1865.
235. Stillson and Hughan, History of Freemasonry and Concordant Orders, p. 774.
236. Paul Rosen, Satan et Cie, p. 142.
237. Blanchard, 33° op. cit., p. 162.
238. Ibid. p. 462.
239. Esoteric explanation of the legend of Hiram.

240. Paul Rosen, op. cit., p. 335. (Documents justificatifs). Also compare with The Theosophical Society Programme.
241. L'Ordre des Franc-Macons Trahi et le Secret des Mopses revélé. Author unknown, Published Amsterdam, 1763.
242. The Rosicrucian and Masonic Record, p. 87.
243. Revue Internationale des Sociétés Secrètes, Nov. 19, May 6, 1928. p. 397.
244. Revue Internationale des Societes Secretes, Nov. 19, May 6 1928, p. 400.
245. Le Forestier, Les Illumines de Baviere et la Franc-Maconnerie Allemande, p. 486.
246. Samuels, Memoirs of Moses Mendelssohn, p. 159, appendix, Published by Longman & Co.
247. J. A. Moehlen D. D., Symbolism, translate d by James Robertson, pp. 34–36, introduction.
248. Thomas Frost, Secret Societies of the European Revolution, vol. I, p. 53.
249. Le Foreslier, op. cit., p. 654.
250. H. Graetz, History of the Jews, vol. V, p. 422.
251. Dorothe a and Rebecc a Mendelssohn.
252. Thomas Frost, Secret Societies of the European Revolution, vol. I. p. 183.
253. Heckethorn, op. cit, vol. II, p. 187 et seq.
254. Le Forestier, Les Illumines de Bavière et la Franc-Maçon-nerie Allemande, p. 635.
255. Louis Aimable, Les Neuf Saurs. La R I,
256. Louis Aimable, op. cit.
257. Fernan d Pignatel, Batailles Maçonniques, p. 143.
258. Autobiography of Wolfe Tone.
259. Harold J. Laski, The Socialist Tradition in the French Revolution.